Reclaiming Diasporic Identity

STUDIES OF WORLD MIGRATIONS

Marcelo J. Borges and Madeline Y. Hsu, editors

For a list of books in the series, please see our website at www.press.uillinois.edu.

Reclaiming Diasporic Identity

Transnational Continuity and
National Fragmentation
in the Hmong Diaspora

SANGMI LEE

UNIVERSITY OF
ILLINOIS PRESS
Urbana, Chicago, and Springfield

© 2024 by the Board of Trustees
of the University of Illinois
All rights reserved
1 2 3 4 5 C P 5 4 3 2 1
♾ This book is printed on acid-free paper.

Library of Congress Cataloging-in-Publication Data
Names: Lee, Sangmi, 1982– author.
Title: Reclaiming diasporic identity : transnational
  continuity and national fragmentation in the
  Hmong diaspora / Sangmi Lee.
Description: Urbana : University of Illinois Press,
  [2024] | Series: Studies of world migrations |
  Includes bibliographical references and Index.
Identifiers: LCCN 2023032333 (print) | LCCN
  2023032334 (ebook) | ISBN 9780252045769
  (cloth) | ISBN 9780252087868 (paperback) | ISBN
  9780252056628 (ebook)
Subjects: LCSH: Hmong (Asian people)—Foreign
  countries. | Hmong (Asian people)—Ethnic
  identity. | Hmong (Asian people)—Foreign
  influences. | Transnationalism. | Hmong (Asian
  people)—Social life and customs.
Classification: LCC DS509.5.H66 L455 2024 (print) |
  LCC DS509.5.H66 (ebook) | DDC 305.8959/72—
  dc23/eng/20230815
LC record available at https://lccn.loc.gov/2023032333
LC ebook record available at https://lccn.loc.gov/2023032334

For the Hmong people who allowed me
to be part of their story

Contents

Introduction   1

PART I. THE MAKING OF THE HMONG DIASPORA:
HISTORY, MULTIPLE HOMELANDS, AND AMBIVALENT
BELONGING

1   Hmong Diasporic History and Multiple
Homeland Narratives   39

2   Locating the Hmong Diaspora in Ambivalent
Local Belongings   71

PART II. TRANSNATIONAL ETHNIC AND
CULTURAL CONTINUITY

3   An "Imagined" Community of Transnational Kin:
Hmong Kinship Continuities in the Diaspora   103

4   Compassionate Money: Monetized Longing
and Emotional Remittances in the Transnational
Familial Economy   129

5   From Local to Transnational: Hmong Shamanism
and Spiritual Rituals across Borders   148

PART III. CULTURAL DIFFERENCE
AND DISCURSIVE FRAGMENTATION

6 Cultural Differences in the Diaspora:
Hmong Funerals and the Nation-State   181

7 Diaspora's National Affiliations: Relative
Belonging to the Nation-State and Discursive
Fragmentation   206

Conclusion   233

Notes   241

Bibliography   251

Index   273

Introduction

On a sweltering day during the dry season in Dao Tha, a village in Vang Vieng, Laos,[1] a small group of Hmong men from the Lee clan gathered outside one of their houses for a spirit-calling ritual called *nyuj dab* to be conducted by an elderly shaman. They were placing plates of food on mats on the ground in order to feed the returning souls of the ancestors that were to be summoned. The other clan members in the backyard of the house were busy cooking as they prepared for a feast after the ritual was over.

Yang Lee, a middle-aged Hmong man from the US state of Michigan, stood at the corner of the front yard with his brand-new camcorder and started video recording the proceedings. He and his wife, Shoua, had flown to Thailand and then taken a long road trip to Dao Tha to participate in the spirit-calling ritual for his parents, who had passed away more than a decade ago. Yang was dressed in a bright, clean, custom-ordered white shirt on which was printed the faces of his father and three uncles of his family, all of whom were deceased. Not only did he wish to record this important ritual; he also planned to share it with his relatives back in the States.

According to Hmong villagers, nyuj dab is a memorial ritual conducted more than a decade after the death of one's parents to commemorate and care for their souls and to indicate that they have not been forgotten. Despite the very localized nature of this ritual in Dao Tha village, it had been transnationally arranged through months of communication on the phone between Yang in the United States and his elderly cousin Teng in Laos, who negotiated and planned the logistics for the event.

Yang Lee from the United States video recording the spirit-calling ritual conducted locally in Laos.

Once Yang finalized his travel itinerary to Laos, the entire Lee clan in the village participated in preparations, especially by purchasing cows and pigs to sacrifice during the ritual.

Although this was the first time I met Yang and his wife, I was delighted to finally see them in person, since I had heard about the extensive transnational coordination across national borders that was necessary to make this occasion possible, and I was eager to witness the ultimate outcome. Yang said he was quite emotional about finally realizing his dream of conducting nyuj dab for his deceased parents by returning to his natal homeland. He stood very still with his camcorder, holding his breath in anticipation as he made sure every moment of the entire ritual was fully and thoroughly recorded.

* * *

The nyuj dab ritual in Dao Tha is a good example of how local Hmong communities are embedded in dense transnational connections and relations with other Hmong in the diaspora, who are scattered across numerous countries around the world. Ever since I first became acquainted with Hmong villagers in Dao Tha, it has been clear to me that their local lives cannot be fully understood without locating them in a broader diasporic context. Although the Hmong diaspora is not anchored by a definitive ancestral homeland, it has been maintained by transnational socioeconomic relations across national borders and shared cultural practices and ethnic traditions.

This book explores the contemporary diasporic experiences of Hmong people living primarily in Vang Vieng, in central Laos, and Sacramento, California, in the United States. While many parts of their ethnic history remain uncertain, the Hmong have a long history of diasporic dispersal. According to scholars, Hmong migrated from southwest China and scattered to various countries in mainland Southeast Asia (Vietnam, Laos, Cambodia, Thailand, and Burma) in the late seventeenth century in response to ethnic conflicts and persecution by the ruling Han Chinese (Entenmann 2005; Hillmer 2010; Jenks 1994; G. Lee 2007; Lemoine 2005).[2] During the Vietnam War, which spilled over to and heavily affected Laos, many Hmong in the country were involved on both sides of the local military insurgency. While there were some Hmong who fought to support the establishment of the Pathet Lao Communist government, those recruited by the US Central Intelligence Agency for an anti-Communist alliance to support the Royal Lao Government (RLG) fled the country and were placed in temporary refugee camps in Thailand. They migrated to and resettled in the United States, France, Germany, Canada, Australia, New Zealand, French Guiana, and Argentina or eventually returned to Laos in the late 1990s.

The total population of the Hmong diaspora is not well documented due to insufficient demographic data, which makes it difficult to provide a reliable estimate. According to some of the available data (collected at different times and often not updated), large populations of Hmong reside in Vietnam (1,068,189),[3] Laos (595,028),[4] Thailand (118,000–150,000),[5] the United States (299,000),[6] and France (15,000).[7] In addition, the ethnic Miao minority group in China are believed to share a common ancestry with diasporic Hmong in their supposed ancestral homeland (see chapter 1) as part of the global Hmong population. The total number of Miao is estimated at over nine million, based on 2010 Chinese census data (e.g., Shi et al. 2019),[8] technically making them by far the largest Miao/Hmong community in the world. However, many Hmong informally noted that they believe there are many more Miao/Hmong than indicated by official records.

This extensive geographical dispersal is the basis of the Hmong diasporic condition, with co-ethnics scattered in other countries as part of their diaspora. However, the only appropriate way to characterize the Hmong diaspora would be through diversities that are based on different historical experiences and varying local contexts. For instance, unlike Hmong in Laos, those in other Southeast Asian countries were not forced to scatter as refugees after the Vietnam War; thus, they may have a quite different diasporic consciousness and transnational relations than Hmong who live in or trace their migratory dispersal to Laos. Moreover, Hmong diasporic communities can be differentiated by both the nation-states where they are situated and internal differences.

There have been efforts by scholars to document Hmong lives in different parts of the diaspora, such as in Australia, Vietnam, and Thailand.[9] However, there is also a significant gap in terms of how much scholarly attention various Hmong communities have received. Even among the two Hmong diasporic communities I studied in Laos and the United States, there is a serious imbalance in terms of available resources and research (i.e., scholarship about Hmong American communities is much more abundant and prominent than it is for Hmong communities in other countries). Hmong historian Chia Vang has attempted to fill this gap through her research with Hmong diasporic communities in the "Global South" (French Guiana and Argentina) and has made an important contribution to the geography of the Hmong diaspora by illustrating how Hmong in this region have historically had more confined and isolated lives compared to their co-ethnics elsewhere (see C. Vang 2018).

The term "Hmong diaspora" seems to involve the juxtaposition of two words that initially appear incompatible. In the mass media, as well as public and some earlier scholarly accounts, Hmong have previously been represented as isolated and localized "hill tribes" or "guerillas" with a distinctive and static traditional culture at the margins of the nation-state in Southeast Asia and China (e.g., Barney 1967; Bernatzik 1970).[10] In 2003 the Hmong appeared in a black-and-white photo on the cover of *Time* magazine and were described as guerilla fighters who were left behind and forgotten in the jungles of Laos. In the photo, they were kneeling in the dirt, looking distressed and in despair.

On the other hand, Hmong are also frequently referred to in the literature as a "diaspora" (e.g., S. Lee 2020, 2021[11]; Pfeifer et al. 2013; Tapp and Lee 2004; C. Vang 2010), an ethnic peoples who disperse from an ancestral homeland to multiple nation-states around the globe because of ethnopolitical and religious persecution as well as economic reasons and colonial displacement (Safran 1991; Tölölyan 1996). This concept invokes transnational mobility and cultural fluidity, defying stereotypes of Hmong as geographically bounded people.

How are these two seemingly contradictory representations of the Hmong people to be reconciled? Are the Hmong a village or tribal people localized in specific communities on the fringes of the nation-state, or are they diasporic and deterritorialized people who transcend nations and reside in transnational communities? Or do their lives simultaneously encompass both of these localized and diasporic dimensions? If so, what does life situated in both the local and the transnational look like?

Diasporic Identity: Simultaneous Belonging *Within* and *Beyond* Nation-States

This book ethnographically illustrates Hmong people's simultaneous transnational and national engagements and explores their diasporic consciousness. It employs the concept of *diasporic identity* to demonstrate that the sense of belonging among diasporic peoples consists of both the transnational continuity of their cultures and social relations across national borders and cultural and discursive differences stemming from their simultaneous affiliation with the localized nation-states where they reside. Diasporic identity not only is based on deterritorialized, transnational processes but also incorporates the impact of nation-states on diasporized subjects; therefore, it is a *trans/national* phenomenon. Despite its frequent use, diasporic identity as a concept is still undertheorized and not always clearly defined in the literature. Earlier studies initially considered the ethnic homeland of ancestral origin as the source of diasporic people's belonging and identification (Safran 1991; Tölölyan 1996; see also Butler 2001). Based on this, diasporic identity has sometimes been associated with homelands and the sense of nostalgic longing for and memories about them.

As a critique of this focus on territorialized homelands, some scholars have moved away from the notion of diasporic "origins" (or "roots") and instead have examined diaspora as a denationalized community that challenges nation-states and their power (e.g., Axel 2000; Brah 1996; Clifford 1994; Gilroy 1993; Malkki 1992). They often refer to the cultural productions and practices of diasporic peoples as a unique phenomenon that is independent from specific national contexts. However, others have not always adopted such an emphasis but recognized the continued importance of the homeland for the cultures of highly mobile, diasporic people (see Abdelhady 2011; Lai 2011; McConnell 2015; Vertovec 2001, 2011; Werbner 2000). Such a perspective enables us to examine transnational connections of diasporic peoples with the homeland as well as other scattered co-ethnic communities as the source of their cultural and ethnic identities (Paerregaard 2010; Tsuda 2016; see also Shukla 2003; Waldinger 2013).

The concept of diasporic identity captures the complexity of diasporic identifications at the trans/national levels by examining both cross-border (transnational) cultural continuities and national discontinuities. Therefore, I propose that a comprehensive understanding of diaspora needs to take into account the importance and influence of nation-states where diasporic people actually reside as ethnic minorities. The two Hmong communities I studied in Laos and the United States have exhibited simultaneous affiliations with each other across national borders and with the specific countries in which they live. Their diasporic cultures have been maintained and promoted through transnational social relationships while also being differentiated along national lines, producing different practices and diverging perceptions toward each other. In order to understand diasporic identity, this book uses transnational continuity and national differentiation/fragmentation as an analytical framework.

Beyond Hybridity and Fluidity in the Conceptualization of Diasporic Identity

The scholarship about diaspora is an interdisciplinary field that has generated both theoretical and empirical research across disciplines. Among them, Stuart Hall's notion of hybridized cultural identities is perhaps the most relevant to diasporic identities and has often been understood as interchangeable with the concept. The recognition of hybridized cultural identities shifts the focus from a de facto territorial ethnic homeland to the recreation and transformation of "cultures" and historical memories of dispersal in newly resettled places by diasporic peoples. Hall (1990) developed this perspective in the context of the black diaspora in the Caribbean, which is the product of the "New World" experiences embedded in Afro-Caribbean pop culture. According to him, hybridized features are "precisely the mixes of colour, pigmentation, physiognomic type" as well as the "'blends' of tastes that is Caribbean cuisine and the aesthetics of the 'cross-overs' and 'cut-and-mix' features found in black music" (Hall 1990, 235–36). This cultural hybridity in the diaspora results from and constantly evokes the longing and desire for lost ethnic origins among African descendants in the Caribbean.

Hall further describes the cultural identity of displaced people outside their homelands as a process of both "being" (based on shared and collective sentiments) and "becoming" (represented by others' discourses or through power/knowledge holders in a Foucauldian sense) (Hall 1990, 225). As he notes, identities become meaningful because of the way individuals are positioned, and position themselves, in various contexts. In this sense, hybridity is positively regarded because it celebrates how cultural identities among diasporized people are not based on fixed and static meanings but are fluid and flexible as they are negotiated under conditions of transnational mobility that are detached from specific national or territorial entities.

I find that this fluid, relational, and contextual nature of identity does not fully explain what is specifically "diasporic" about diasporic identities. In fact, for a long time, anthropological theories, such as those of Fredrik Barth (1969) and Henrietta Moore (2007, 28–30), have demonstrated how identities are constituted through self-recognition of constantly changing external factors manifested through relations with others. Moreover, anthropologists and other theorists have also attempted to problematize the conventional distinction between "self" and "other" itself by demonstrating that various individual identities are constructed through power relations that exclude and create hierarchies based on multiple positionings among different actors (Kondo 1990; see also Apiah 2006; Bilgrami 2006; Dhamoon 2010; Foucault 1995) in an inherently fluid and flexible manner. Indeed, hybridized identities are not only the property of dispersed and displaced peoples and migrants per se. Because of current cultural and economic globalization, ordinary residents who never migrate or cross borders can certainly experience hybridization in their daily lives, because the localization of global cultures means they are combined with local cultures (the "glocal"; Robertson 1995), which peoples can appropriate to produce hybrid identifications.[12]

If this is the case, what is really diasporic about the identities of geographically dispersed and displaced people? In this book I clarify and refine what it means when already hybrid and fluid identities become diasporic. One important factor that influences diasporic identity is the presence of the nation-state and its relation to diasporic people. The numerous examples of how they engage with different nation-states are the source of diversities in the diaspora. Going back to Hall's idea of the "New World," which he defines as the source of hybridized cultures, it is not quite clear whether the term can refer to nation-states or national differences. Clearly, he does not mean a mythical, homogeneous homeland that unites diasporic members; instead he believes that there are "several interlocking histories and cultures" that belong at "one and the same time to several homes" (Hall 1995, 629). In some sense, Hall does not seem to deny that there are uniting forces for diasporic people, but he avoids territorializing them.

However, African/Black diaspora researchers recognize the diversities and differences within a diasporic community that have been ambiguously subdued under pan-diasporic representations. For example, while Paul Gilroy (1993) does consider diversity within the Black diaspora, scholars like Floya Anthias (1998) critically note that his "Black Atlantic" does not sufficiently look at national and gendered differences that exist within many diasporic communities. Edmund T. Gordon and Mark Anderson (1999, 288) also point out that such widely accepted terms as "African diaspora" are still limited to a binary conception of mystical and essentialized Afrocentric origins and celebratory notions of hybridity. They further argue that the emphasis on hybridity does not fully consider the political, cultural, and racialized experiences and subordination of specific African diasporic communities in different localities and the diversity of their cultural affiliations and identifications.

While these critiques address the shortcomings of hybridity approaches to diasporic identity, the specificity and substantial impact of "local" nation-states is still largely missing. For example, Aihwa Ong's (1999) analysis of "flexible citizenship" among elites residing in various countries in the Chinese diaspora portrays them as subject to global capitalism but does not specifically compare their localized differences and generally de-emphasizes their national loyalties. However, diasporic people often reside as minority groups in "strong" states with clear nationalist agendas, which can involve different assimilationist or multicultural nation-building projects and policies toward immigrant minorities (e.g., see Brubaker 1992; Glick Schiller et al. 1995; Joppke 1998; Kymlicka 1995). In this sense, diasporic identity cannot simply be equated with cultural hybridity and transnational affiliations with co-ethnics scattered in other countries without examining the specific presence and impact of the nation-states where all diasporic peoples actually reside.

The case of the two diasporic Hmong communities I studied allows us to examine how the identities of diasporic peoples are based on a sense of belonging to transnational ethnic communities (socioeconomic relations across national borders that sustain continuities in shared ethnic cultures) and partial affiliations to the nation-states in which they reside (which produce cultural differences and fragmentation in the diaspora). In this sense, diasporic identities are simultaneously positioned between the diaspora and the nation-state and situated trans/nationally, or what

Anastasia Christou and Elizabeth Mavroudi (2015, 5) describe as "living in and beyond states." By examining such diasporic belonging, developed through both transnationally expansive and nationally differentiated co-ethnic Hmong communities, this book ultimately "reclaims" diasporic identities. "Reclaiming diasporic identity" does not mean that such identities were lost in the past and must be recovered anew. Rather, diasporic identities are continuously transformed and reconstituted in response to changing conditions within and beyond national boundaries. Thus, their coherence and relevance must be retained and constantly "(re)claimed" by diasporic peoples through modifications in sociocultural practices and discourses.

Transnational Continuity as Part of Diasporic Identity

The transnational continuities examined in this book broadly refer to cultures practiced in diasporic communities that are shared by dispersed co-ethnic communities. They are enabled by cross-border social and economic connections and constantly evoke a sense of transnational ethnic belonging and mutual identification. Both transnational cultural continuities and socioeconomic relations are especially meaningful for diasporic Hmong because they lack a definitive ethnic homeland that can provide them with a shared sense of identity and cultural continuity. Because of their long history of migratory dispersal and displacement, Hmong I studied have long since lost their connections to their original ancestral homeland. As will be shown in the first part of this book, many of them remain uncertain about its actual location and have developed multiple and contested theories about their ancestral origins.

In the second part of this book, I analyze transnational social connections between diasporic Hmong living in Vang Vieng and California by providing ethnographic accounts of their adherence to kinship principles that have led to the development of extensive economic relationships across national borders based on remittances. Such transnational kinship networks and economies allow cultural traditions such as Hmong shamanism (as well as funerals and New Year festivals) to successfully spread across the diaspora to multiple countries, producing cultural commonalities among geographically dispersed Hmong communities.

While the primary transnational social relationships examined in this book are kinship and socioeconomic exchanges (chapters 3 and 4), which help produce continuities in cultural beliefs and practices across national borders, there are other types of cross-border engagements and migrations among diasporic Hmong across multiple countries, including China, Thailand, Laos, and the United States, some of which will be briefly discussed in this book. Two prominent examples include transnational romances and marriage migration (which usually consist predominantly of Hmong women in Laos moving to the United States to live with Hmong American men) (see Schein 2005) and the missionary activities of Hmong Christians from the States who travel to Hmong/Miao communities in China or Thailand (and to a lesser degree, Laos) (see chapters 4, 5).

Some Hmong rituals involve transnational coordination among kin (chapters 3, 5), and events like the Hmong New Year festivals in California draw Hmong from across the global diaspora (as visitors, vendors, businesspeople, and performers) (see chapter 6). Hmong films, DVDs, and videos are also actively shared and sold among diasporic communities (see chapters 1 and 6; see also Leepreecha 2008; Schein 2004b). Likewise, trade in Hmong clothing and other types of ethnic goods is active across borders and includes Hmong/Miao peddlers from China who visit Laos and the United States to sell their products (see chapters 1 and 6). Not all of these activities are transnational, involving mutual participation across national borders, but they can enhance transnational connections and further interactions across the Hmong diaspora.

Although first-generation diasporic migrants generally have shown stronger transnational affinities compared to those of the later generations, my research found that second-generation US-born Hmong in California have also engaged transnationally to varying degrees while becoming more integrated in the nation-state (e.g., see chapters 4, 5). This was also the case with young Hmong I studied in Laos, whose transnational engagements remained quite prominent through economic and cultural exchanges (see chapters 2, 4, 5). Despite generational and religious differences in transnational and national affiliations, these young Hmong have simultaneously engaged in diasporic cultures at both levels, thus sustaining diasporic identities while remaining firmly embedded in the nation-states where they reside (see chapters 6, 7).

When Diasporic Cultures Continue Transnationally: Essentialized versus Collective Diasporic Identities

Since the diasporic dimensions of Hmong identities are partly based on transnational cultural continuities and social relations that have persisted and endured across borders, despite migratory displacement, geographical separation, and national differences, we may face the potential prob-

10   Introduction

lem of homogenizing or essentializing diasporic cultures and identities. In fact, most scholars of diaspora studies are highly cautious and critical about portraying the cultures of diasporas as "unitary" or collective (Amelina and Barglowski 2019, 37; Mavroudi 2010, 246; Vertovec 2011; Wimmer and Glick Schiller 2002, 324) even if they are deterritorialized and detached from specific places and nation-states.

Nonetheless, as Pnina Werbner notes, even if cultural hybridity has been an "empowering, dangerous or transformative force," essentialisms are still somewhat "difficult to transcend" (Werbner 2015b, 4). Examining the collective aspects of diasporic identities and claiming transnational "continuity" is *not* a type of cultural essentialization. If certain social and cultural practices are collectively shared and some of them even become hegemonic within a diaspora, it is not because they have some fixed and natural essence that allows them to structurally reproduce and persist unchanged, despite migratory displacement and other historical contingencies.

More importantly, we need to remember that diasporic peoples themselves also voluntarily (and often selectively) essentialize and naturalize their own diasporic cultures as if they were timeless traditions for various reasons. During numerous interviews and conversations, Hmong participants in my research often made generalizations about the Hmong people and culture when discussing similarities and differences among co-ethnics in different local and national contexts. In addition, as part of their ongoing diasporic consciousness, many Hmong in my study continued to represent and refer to themselves as a "people without a country" (see also Chan 1994) and an ethnic minority at the margins of the nation-state. They would point out that because they are a dispersed, diasporic peoples who lack a unifying homeland, their shared cultural traditions, beliefs, or kinship practices are what makes them "Hmong" and that those who do not practice them properly are forgetting the essence of "Hmongness."

Such voluntary self-essentializing about unitary Hmong diasporic culture may not reflect the fluid and constantly changing nature of cultural practices nor national and localized differences. However, it should be emphasized that homogenizing cultural discourses have enabled and promoted transnational continuities among diasporic Hmong across borders and led to efforts to sustain and reconstruct them in the face of national differences and fragmentation (see chapters 5 and 6). Therefore, instead of simply assuming the fluid and hybrid nature of diasporic cultures, it is also necessary to examine what makes geographically dispersed diasporic communities maintain and promote common cultural practices and traditions that anchor their collective ethnic identities and develop a sense of transnational belonging beyond national borders. For example, within the Muslim diaspora, the concept of *ummah*, a pan-Muslim community connected through its common religion, indicates that Pakistani communities residing in the UK have developed a shared identity with other dispersed co-ethnics across national borders and generations as a diasporic peoples (Werbner 2002). Likewise, political agendas and the claiming of rights in the face of state-led oppression and violence have caused part of the Kurdish diaspora to insist on a unified discourse, despite diverging and multivocal communities within the diaspora (Eliassi 2015).

The continuity of diasporic cultures in the face of migratory dispersal and separation is therefore possible not because they are static, unitary, or homogeneous, but precisely because they are modified and reconfigured in response to different national socioeconomic and political contexts as they travel across borders through the diaspora while retaining the authority of tradition. In fact, the transnationally fluid nature of cultural traditions and their adaptability to varying local circumstances is what enables diasporas to develop continuities and commonalities across national borders. Therefore, collective diasporic identity has the potential to overcome the binaries of essentialism and hybridity (see McConnell 2015, 108), for it consists of a constant process of negotiating and changing shared cultures.

National Differences and Discursive Fragmentation: Another Component of Diasporic Identity

Despite the importance of transnational continuities that sustain cohesive Hmong diasporic communities and create a sense of ethnic belonging across borders, it is equally important to realize that diasporic cultures and experiences are refracted through the nation-states in which they are situated. Although diasporic peoples' sense of belonging is partly constituted by transnational and deterritorialized processes, it is undeniable that they are physically residing in specific national territories and not completely free from the presence of the nation-state. This is the other integral part of diasporic identity.

The third part of this book examines how the cultural practices and ethnic perceptions of diasporic Hmong I studied in Laos and the United States are influenced by the national socioeconomic and political differences in each country. As noted above, significant national differences have emerged in their diasporic cultural traditions and the way they are practiced. In addition, the partial affiliation of diasporic Hmong in these two communities to their separate and respective nation-states also produces discursive fragmentation because of the contrasting and critical perceptions they have developed about each other. Ultimately, diasporic people and their identities are positioned trans/nationally because they simultaneously develop a partial sense of national belonging within the nation-state's territorial boundaries while also maintaining transnational connections and shared cultural practices beyond national borders.

While Stuart Hall recognizes the "strong links to and identifications with the traditions and places for [diaspora's] 'origin'" as part of hybridized cultural identity (Hall 1993, 362), its ability to transcend particular places and undermine the power of the nation-state has been noted favorably by many scholars across disciplines (Appadurai 1996; Axel 2000; Brah 1996; Braziel and Mannur 2003, 234; Kearney 1995; Lavie and Swedenburg 1996, 8; Malkki 1992). Some of them point out that identity formation among diasporic people challenges not only hegemonic national power (Bhabha 1994; Clifford 1994; Gilroy 1993) but also the "essentialist" idea of origins, homelands, and fixed national identities (see Falzon 2003; Koinova 2018; Lai 2011, 567).[13]

However, other scholars have expressed concerns about the overemphasis on the "borderless" status of refugees, immigrants, and diasporic peoples (Hindess 2004; Portes and Rumbaut 1996; Sparke 2004, 278; Wahlbeck 2002, 233). They point to the problems of celebrating the supposedly empowering ability of such peoples to transgress nation-states and their borders (see also Gerson 2001; Sheffer 2003), which risks condemning them to a permanent, liminal, and even "stateless" condition. It is important to recognize the continuing impact of nation-states on diasporic peoples that lead to a multifaceted sense of belonging and to consider how their identities are hybridized as they are negotiated in the different political and cultural contexts of nation-states (Blumer 2011; see also Dwyer 2000, 476; Kleist 2008; Turner 2019).

It is indeed difficult to determine the extent to which the nation-state matters for diasporas (and what can be considered as a national impact). Concerned about treating diasporas as an "entity," Rogers Brubaker (2005, 12) suggests examining them as "a stance, an idiom, a claim," a useful concept that enables us to analyze what people actually say and why. However, the making of national affiliations and frequent references to countries of residence among diasporic people like the Hmong are too important to be overlooked. Similar to Pnina Werbner (2015a), who recognizes the creation and coexistence of diasporic peoples' multiple boundaries, I emphasize that diasporic Hmong's discourses about and

Introduction   13

affiliations with the nation-state are one such important boundary, even if they are temporary or conditional connections.

Therefore, we should be attentive to the cultural diversities that inevitably emerge in all diasporas in relation to specific national conditions. As is the case with all diasporic peoples, Hmong are influenced by local material and socioeconomic conditions, political ideologies, and mainstream culture and public opinion in their respective countries of residence. In response to such pressures, their shared cultural practices, such as funeral rituals and New Year celebrations, have inevitably become modified and reconfigured in national contexts, producing notable cultural differences and differentiation in the diaspora (chapter 6). In this sense, diasporas do not simply transcend or decentralize the power of nation-states. Diasporic identities are not only based on a sense of belonging to transnational and deterritorialized communities constituted by collectively shared cultures, but they are also simultaneously impacted by the continuing presence of the different nation-states within which diasporic peoples are embedded.

In addition, since diasporic peoples are located and partly incorporated into nation-states, they eventually develop a sense of belonging to different countries. The nation-states where they reside may eventually be accepted as an "adopted homeland" (see Parreñas and Siu 2007) or become part of their multiple "homes" over time (Lindholm Schulz 2003, 186–87; Pattie 1999), especially among diasporic descendants. Such national affiliations of diasporic communities caused Hmong I met and interviewed in both Laos and the United States to develop critical attitudes toward their co-ethnics elsewhere, leading to considerable discursive fragmentation in the diaspora as they compared and hierarchically positioned themselves in relation to one another (chapter 7). In fact, Hmong in the two communities where I conducted research spoke about "Lao Hmong" versus "US Hmong" as generalized entities and compared their national differences in the diaspora in a homogenized manner, which makes their voluntary essentializing both transnational/ diasporic and national in scope.

From Territory to Condition: Diasporic Consciousness in the Hmong Diaspora

As an important source of diasporic identity, I further argue in this book that the diasporic *condition* also evokes a consciousness of dispersal and displacement among scattered ethnic groups. This includes collective

14　Introduction

historical experiences and memories of dislocation and exile, multiple affiliations with different countries, or an ambivalent, partial sense of belonging to nation-states caused by their marginalized ethnic minority status in different local contexts. As discussed earlier, diasporas are not always centered on or unified by territorialized ethnic homelands, and the scholarly focus has moved away from an emphasis on a territorialized place of origin as the source of collective identity among diasporic peoples. In fact, some diasporas develop antagonistic relations with countries of their ethnic origin (e.g., Skrbiš 1997; Winland 2002). Over time, diasporic peoples can also experience significant changes and internal generational differences in the way they perceive their homelands (see Berg 2011; Tsuda 2016; Vertovec 1997). Likewise, the hybridized cultural and ethnic identities of diasporized peoples are not always spatially bounded to territorial homelands (Appadurai 1996; Clifford 1994; Hall 1990; see also Koinova 2018; Siu 2005).

Unlike most diasporas, which are located within a specific ethnic homeland, Hmong who participated in my research expressed considerable uncertainty about their place of ethnic and ancestral origin, despite the dominant theory that places the Hmong ethnic homeland somewhere in southwest China. The simple fact that there is no country named "Hmong" in the world makes it difficult for them to territorialize their sense of ancestry. Some studies of Hmong have examined the development of messianic (religious) or "millenarian" movements in parts of the diaspora that seek "liberation" from hegemonic national (and colonial) powers or establish an independent "Hmongland" or Hmong "state" (see Baird 2015; Hickman 2021; M. Lee 2015; T. Ngo 2016; Rumsby 2021). However, none of the Hmong who took part in my study in Vang Vieng or California (including elderly former veterans) engaged in these collective efforts, although some of them were aware of such political mobilization. For example, a few Hmong individuals in both countries introduced me to a symbol that resembles a Hmong flag that circulated among their acquaintances in the diaspora.

During the Hmong Cultural Festival in Chico, California, I attended a ceremony to commemorate a statue of General Vang Pao, a former Hmong leader who fought on the side of the anti-Communist alliance during the Vietnam War. Those Hmong community members in the audience from the Sacramento area expressed criticism and skepticism toward some members of politically organized groups (dressed in veterans' uniforms) who were also present at the ceremony. The divisions and disagreements between ordinary Hmong and these political groups indicate that certain members of the Hmong diaspora have not unified around one political leader, nor do they have a shared vision to establish a coherent Hmong ethnic homeland (see S. Lee 2019). In other words, members of the Hmong transnational community in the two localities and their sense of diasporic belonging are not necessarily based on an emotional attachment to territorialized places of ancestral origin or dominant ethnic leaders. Hmong may have developed a "homing desire" (Brah 1996, 180), as shown by their continued search for the location of their ethnic homeland, but they do not always have a "desire for the homeland" itself (that is, a desire to return to or regain a specific homeland).

In this sense, the diasporic consciousness of Hmong in my study is not always rooted in, nor does it revolve around, territorialized origins. Instead, it is based on the diasporic *condition*—that is, historicized memories and narratives of migratory displacement and dispersal (see Clifford 1994, 311–12; Cohen 1997, 23; Falola 2013; Safran 1991), which constantly evoke a sense of ethnic commonality among certain members of the Hmong diaspora. Their diasporic consciousness can therefore emerge from historical dislocations and shared sentiments that Hmong are a "people without a country," a common expression used by many of those in my study.

In contrast to other diasporas, which are mainly a product of one migratory dispersal from a singular homeland over a period of time, the Hmong diaspora was constituted by multiple geographical dispersals during different historical periods. As mentioned earlier, an initial migratory displacement of Hmong supposedly occurred from China to various Southeast Asian countries around the late seventeenth century, followed by a second, contemporary dispersal from Laos to various Western countries after the Vietnam War. Because of the multiple historical dispersals and displacements that diasporic Hmong have endured over their history, those in my research expressed an ambivalent sense of belonging to various countries based on their ongoing ethnic minority status, which is another fundamental aspect of diasporic consciousness.

Ironically, despite the shift from territory to condition in diaspora studies, the problem of territory seems to remain important for the Hmong diaspora. Because of the lack of a unified homeland and multiple migratory dispersals, diasporic Hmong participants in my research have developed ambivalent, partial affiliations with different nation-states that have been involved in their history of diasporization, such as China, Laos, Thailand, and the United States. This indicates that territory still matters not because diasporas focus on homelands with the possibility of return but because the absence of such a territorialized place of ancestral origin produces diffuse and ambivalent identifications with other countries as possible homelands.

For example, Hmong in my study who believe that their distant ancestors are from China felt an emotional disconnection from their supposed ethnic homeland partly based on narratives of persecution and oppression by the Chinese embedded in their oral history, folklore, and ritual practices. However, they do feel a sense of affiliation with their co-ethnics (Miao) living in the country based on cultural identification and presumed ethnic commonalities. Since Hmong dispersed from Laos to various Western countries after the Vietnam War, Laos serves as an ethnic homeland of sorts for the contemporary Hmong diaspora while also being one of the countries in the diaspora to which Hmong previously scattered after their displacement from the possible homeland of China (see chapter 1).

Chapter Summaries

Part I of this book explores the historical formation of the Hmong diaspora and examines the contemporary experience of Hmong as ethnic minorities in the local contexts of Laos and the United States. Chapter 1 discusses the history of Hmong migratory dispersal by incorporating narrative accounts from interviews and cultural practices, which trace Hmong ethnic ancestry to China, while revealing considerable uncertainty and multiple theories about ethnic homeland and ancestral origins. It also examines how Hmong interviewees in Laos and the United States have developed an ambivalent and complex relationship with multiple nation-states as possible homelands and retain a diasporic consciousness as a "people without a country" because of their long diasporic history of multiple dispersals and the absence of a concrete ancestral homeland.

Chapter 2 examines how the experiences of socioeconomic marginalization and ethnic exclusion of Hmong I studied in the two countries have constantly made them conscious of their status as an ethnic minority that does not fully belong to the nation-states where they reside. As a result, Hmong in both locations continue to have ambivalent perceptions of and relations with their own countries of residence. In order to illustrate this process, the chapter provides the specific local contexts of diasporic Hmong communities in Dao Tha, Vang Vieng, and Sacramento, California by focusing on their overall ethnic and economic status along with living conditions for both younger and older generations of Hmong.

Because the contemporary Hmong diaspora is also the product of a more recent dispersal from Laos after the Vietnam War, the chapter also highlights how the country may also function as an ethnic homeland.

Part II focuses on the transnational cultural continuities in the two Hmong diasporic communities I studied and the way they are constituted by extensive kinship networks across national borders. Chapter 3 analyzes how three fundamental kinship principles (clan hospitality, clan exogamy, and ethnic endogamy) initially became entrenched and hegemonic among diasporic Hmong as a pervasive cultural system that transcends national boundaries. Since these kinship rules were inculcated and naturalized through parental education from an early age and are seen as essential for maintaining the cohesion of the dispersed diasporic community in the absence of a territorial ancestral homeland, they became culturally ingrained and taken for granted by Hmong participants in my research through their voluntary consent and did not have to be enforced by overt power and coercive means. However, like all hegemonies, the Hmong kinship system has confronted increasing challenges and contestation as it is enacted in the different nation-states where Hmong reside. The chapter therefore examines how kinship hegemony is transitioning to an ideology that needs to be actively enforced and imposed by the direct use of power, especially in the United States.

Extensive diasporic kinship networks are the important basis for active transnational economic relations between the two Hmong communities under study. By analyzing transnational economic relations among family and extended kin members across national borders, chapter 4 argues that remittances from Hmong in the United States to their kin in Laos are not simply an economic means of sustenance but are imbued with social meanings and emotional values. However, there is a discrepancy in the meaning of money between senders and receivers of remittances. Although Lao Hmong interviewees perceived the financial contribution from their co-ethnics residing in the United States as an important symbol of familial "love," the remittance senders did not clearly make such connections and were less enthusiastic about the emotions or feelings of love expressed through money. Nonetheless, such "emotional remittances" promote transnational social continuity and solidarity between Hmong in both countries that are critical to their diasporic belonging and identity.

Both extensive transnational kinship networks and economic relationships between these two diasporic Hmong communities enable various cultural traditions to persist and thrive in the diaspora. One of these important transnational cultural continuities is Hmong shamanism. Al-

18 Introduction

though shamanistic rituals tend to be seen as locally embedded and territorially bound, chapter 5 illustrates how their power and efficacy can be transnationally projected across specific communities in the Hmong diaspora through extensive kinship and economic networks as well as cultural beliefs about shamanistic births and the mobile nature of souls. More importantly, Hmong shamanism has been transformed as it has traveled across national borders through the diaspora from a socially rich, localized community event to an individualized and commodified practice while retaining its "traditional" authority. The transnational nature of shamanism allows geographically separated Hmong to reaffirm their shared ethnic and cultural identities across national borders. Additionally, the chapter examines the relationship between shamanism and Christian Hmong in the local US context.

Because Hmong diasporic belonging and identity are not simply a product of transnational cultural commonalities and connections, part III of the book examines cultural differences and discursive fragmentation in the Hmong diaspora by focusing on specific cultural practices and the perceptions of Hmong I studied in Laos and the United States. Chapter 6 makes clear that diasporic cultures are also subject to the shifting power of the nation-state, which produces significant differences between these two Hmong communities in terms of ethnic traditions as well as discourses about cultural authenticity. Through the examples of funeral rituals and New Year festivities, the chapter examines how diasporic Hmong in each country have modified their cultural practices in response to varying national economic systems, policies and regulations, and mainstream social pressures.

It is important to recognize that the level of national intervention in the cultural affairs of diasporic peoples varies. In the case of funerals, Hmong in Sacramento changed their funeral ceremonies to a greater extent than Hmong in Vang Vieng in response to government restrictions and public pressure. In contrast, for New Year festivals, the Lao nation-state appears to be more interventionist than their US counterparts. Such national differences have become a source of debate among diasporic Hmong about cultural authenticity. Hmong interviewees in Laos felt that Hmong Americans have modified their funeral rituals to such an extent that they have strayed from tradition. However, in the case of New Year festivals, since both Lao and US Hmong in my study have changed this tradition to a considerable extent, neither of them claimed to practice the original, "authentic" New Year celebration.

Chapter 7 analyzes how diasporic peoples' partial belonging and affiliations to the nation-states in which they reside can produce contrasting discourses and discursive fragmentation along national lines. Because of national economic and political differences, Hmong communities in Laos and the United States have come to develop contrasting perceptions and have adopted critical attitudes about their co-ethnic counterparts. Each diasporic Hmong community positions itself hierarchically by claiming that their own country is "better" in terms of social and political status, which does not always reflect the geopolitical positioning of Laos as "lower" on the global hierarchy. This chapter specifically examines the concept of "freedom" and illustrates how each Hmong community adopts contested interpretations about its meaning because of differences in economic systems and development between the two countries. Although such disagreements occur mainly at the level of discourse and do not necessarily affect their continuing transnational social relations, diasporic identities and communities are not homogenous deterritorialized entities removed from specific national contexts.

The book's objective is to dialogue with the theories and scholarship about diaspora and transnationalism through the lens of two Hmong communities based on in-depth comparative ethnographic detail. It does not claim to provide a generalized portrayal of the entire Hmong diaspora or represent its lived experience as a whole. As illustrated in various chapters, even within the same Hmong national community, there are internal differences based on generation and religious affiliation as well as class and regional location.

Reflections on Fieldwork and Methodology

This book is based on fourteen months of multi-sited, ethnographic fieldwork between 2011 and 2013 with Hmong residing in Dao Tha in Vang Vieng, central Laos, and Sacramento, California, as well as surrounding villages and cities in both locations. During this period, I conducted a total of 111 interviews and extensive participant observation, along with two focus groups in both countries and surveys in the United States.[14] My research about the Hmong diaspora was enabled by my long-term relationships with these Hmong communities.

Previous Experiences with Diasporic Hmong Communities in Dao Tha, Vang Vieng, and Sacramento, California

Prior to my fieldwork, I had the opportunity to live in Dao Tha for seven months as an undergraduate student foreign volunteer from South Korea.

During this initial stay, I learned about the lives of local villagers from three different ethnic groups while helping them promote and manage various community development projects. At that time, my main responsibilities included assessing the financial needs of villagers and mediating between them and the nonprofit organization. However, as soon as I arrived in the village, one of the very first things I was asked to do was teach English to the children and youths from the village. My host father, who is a member of the majority Lao Loum ethnic group, told me that a small group of the Hmong and Lao Loum students had briefly studied some English with an American tourist who stayed long term before my arrival and that they were eager to continue learning the language in order to improve their future job prospects. He wanted my English classes to include Dao Tha youth from all three ethnic groups (Lao Loum, Hmong, and Khmu) in order to promote ethnic "equity" in the village.

"But you know that I am not a native English speaker," I initially responded unenthusiastically to his request. I was reluctant to teach English not only because it is a foreign language to me but also because I did not wish to perpetuate the global hierarchies embedded in this world language. Since I had just arrived, my ability in the Lao language was also too rudimentary to communicate with students and teach classes. However, I soon discarded this somewhat naïve idea during one of my earlier trips to the capital city of Vientiane. While the bus I was in was waiting at an intersection, I saw a group of young, urban students in their clean, white school uniforms on new motorbikes rushing out of a private English institute after their class.

As the bus started to move, my reluctance to teach English suddenly dissipated. I thought to myself, "If only wealthier students who live in the city can afford private English lessons, will Dao Tha village youth ever have such an opportunity? If a foreign volunteer like me does not teach the language for free, will they be able to learn it?" In fact, because of the burgeoning global tourism in Laos, English had already become equated with power and prestige as well as promising job opportunities. Even a rural village like Dao Tha, which is located on the outskirts of the town of Vang Vieng, was no exception, since the entire town had become dependent on foreign tourists as well as increasing investment by multinational corporations.

Upon my return to Dao Tha, I started teaching English class right away in the large dining area at my host family's farm guesthouse in the evening. At that time, my skill with the Lao language was still very limited. Because I had no books or resources to learn the local language before coming to Laos, I could only say "hello" (*sa bai dee*) and did not even know how to say "thank you" (*kop jai*). My host father, who studied abroad and was fluent in English, was my primary contact and communication channel.

Since I was desperate to communicate with my students on my own, I taught myself the Lao language every night for two hours in my room by reviewing all grammar, words, and phrases I learned and wrote down during the day in my native language of Korean. On the first night, I studied the language under a dim florescent light; I realized the next morning that I had used up all the available electricity allocated to the farm that day! It was a disaster, as all the electric devices at the guesthouse farm ran out of power. After that initial embarrassing incident, I studied at night with candles and a flashlight. A few months later, I had made progress fast enough to engage in daily conversations (and also to speak in the Vang Vieng dialect).

Eventually, teaching English classes became one of the most important and meaningful parts of my life in Dao Tha. Hmong students were the largest group in my classes, followed by Khmu and Lao Loum students. I was still occasionally skeptical about whether learning English would really help impoverished village youth, especially those of Hmong and Khmu ethnic minority backgrounds, because I observed how they were inserted in a structural system of ethnic marginalization and class stratification and would not be granted equal opportunities even if they spoke some English. I did not imagine that my efforts would eventually lead to very positive relationships, not only with my students but also with their families and ultimately with the entire village. I never expected that I would be glorified as the "teacher" who generously offered free classes in English, which was seen as the key to success by many parents and the only way to escape from grinding rural poverty.

After finishing my college education in South Korea, I returned to Dao Tha for another eight months to continue volunteer work. During my second stay, my English class was relocated from the farm guesthouse to the new community center on the hill inside the Hmong residential area of the village. By that time, I had come to know almost all the Hmong villagers, including those who usually sat outside their homes and greeted me every day on my way to English class at the center. The numerous daily conversations and interactions I had with them became a critical foundation for my future ethnographic fieldwork.

As a result, I learned not only about the local lives and cultural practices of the Hmong but also about their extensive family relationships with their co-ethnics residing in the United States. As I came to fully realize the importance of such transnational connections between the two countries, I became interested in visiting the US Hmong community. After three Hmong students from my English class became involved in arranged marriages with Hmong in the United States and two of them eventually moved to Sacramento, I went to visit them there three times between 2008 and 2010. During these visits, I stayed with one of them for over two months, which enabled me to develop a relationship with the Sacramento Hmong community, conduct pilot studies, and establish connections for future research.

Fieldwork in the Globalized Ethnic Village of Dao Tha

Before I returned to Laos a third time to conduct fieldwork, whenever I talked to my former Lao host family on the phone, I was told that if I arrived in Vang Vieng, I would not be able to recognize anything from the past, because "everything has changed" with the increasing flood of global tourists. Despite the warning, I did not take it that seriously. I had already witnessed how global tourism had become entrenched in Vang Vieng for a decade since the mid-2000s. The town initially gained its tourist reputation because of its dynamic and beautiful natural environment, especially the mountain caves along the Song River.[15] In fact, the first and largest tour company in the country had developed an eco-tourism program, specializing in kayaking and mountain cave climbing in the area. Dao Tha, which was about two and a half miles north of the Vang Vieng town center, had already become a popular starting point for foreign tourists to launch rubber inner tubes into the river and a stopover for kayakers.

However, when I went back to conduct fieldwork, I soon realized that I had underestimated the extent to which global tourism had changed the village and town. The banks of the Song River were completely lined with countless tourist bars built with bamboo and shabby wood panels, which continued endlessly into the center of Vang Vieng. Western tourists who ostensibly came to Dao Tha for tubing in the morning ended up drinking, dancing, and getting drunk as they moved from one bar to another until sunset.[16] The bars, owned by majority Lao Loum residents from the village, would play deafening rock music all day.

Because of the location of the farm guesthouse right across the river, we lived with the constant noise and loud music blaring all day from the bars along the riverbank. I was never able to catch a nap in my room or

Part of a Hmong village in Vang Vieng where I conducted research.

even take a short break during the hottest time of day. It was strange to become acquainted with new American pop songs, such as Adele's "Set Fire to the Rain" and Jay-Z's "Empire State of New York," both of which eventually became my favorites, while living in a remote Lao farming village. The highlight of my day was definitely when Oasis's "Don't Look Back in Anger" was played after sunset, because it unofficially signaled that the river bars were closing for the day, finally allowing us to have a tranquil night (for further discussion about global tourism in Vang Vieng, see chapter 2; S. Lee, 2023).

In 2011–2012 the estimated population of Dao Tha was about 250–300, which included Hmong, Lao Loum, and Khmu villagers, who live in adjacent but separate communities. The majority of Hmong residents in the village were previous returnees who had lived in Thai refugee camps for decades after fleeing Laos because of the Vietnam War. Because they could not (or did not want to) be resettled to Western countries as refugees, Hmong whom I interviewed told me that they felt they had

A scene during the height of the dry season with many foreign tourists engaging in activities (e.g., drinking and dancing) at the bars owned by Lao Loum villagers.

been forcibly returned to Laos in the late 1990s and relocated to Dao Tha, which was strategically formed by the government as an ethnically diverse village.[17] This multiethnic village was an atypical living environment for Hmong, compared to other areas in Vang Vieng, where they live in predominantly homogeneous ethnic enclaves (as is mostly the case in the northern provinces as well).

Once I started my "official" fieldwork in Laos, I was able to freely visit and speak with Hmong villagers in Dao Tha because of my prior familiarity with them. I continued to participate in their everyday activities and community events as I had done during my previous stays. However, it was important for me to explain to everyone why I had returned and how different my position as a "researcher" would be from before, when I was an individual volunteer. I soon realized that my new status ironically and unexpectedly made some Hmong villagers nervous and

Introduction 25

initially hesitant to participate in my research, even if they were willing to be interviewed. Before each interview, I usually started by reading a lengthy informed consent form as part of the required research process. However, most of the time, people cut me off and said, "Okay, okay, no problem. I trust you. I am uneducated so I don't know how much I can help. But if my interview can help you to write a book, go ahead." I was also told, "You first came to us when you were only 21. Why are you still studying? Gather all the information you need, write it up, and come back here."

Despite my former relationships and experience with the Hmong, I was constantly reminded of the inevitable and unbridgeable gap between my own educational, class, and national backgrounds and those of Hmong research participants. They often assumed that I must be well off, since I could "afford international flight tickets." Although they did not explicitly expect or pressure me to make a financial contribution to improve their lives, I often felt the need to give back to the community because I sometimes felt that I was taking their time without contributing sufficiently to their lives. As a result, I ended up teaching English to village youth again as an indirect way to give back to the community for its participation in my research. Needless to say, regardless of how much I engaged in their daily lives and contributed to the village, my status as a foreign outsider remained and was often reaffirmed in different ways (see below).

During my seven months of fieldwork in Laos, I conducted a total of forty-eight semi-structured interviews with Hmong individuals (fifteen female and thirty-three male). A majority of these interviews were conducted in Dao Tha, but I also did interviews with Hmong in surrounding villages in Vang Vieng as well as with three diasporic Hmong from abroad (one man from France and two men from the United States) who were visiting Laos. Individual interviews typically lasted from one and a half to three hours and were audio-recorded with interviewee permission. While the primary language used during interviews was Lao, for interviews with some elderly Hmong who preferred to speak only in Hmong, I received help from their children or grandchildren during the interview.

Almost all interviews were arranged based on my personal contacts and former relationships with Hmong residents in Dao Tha. Crucially, my previous students from the English class who were now parents with children also helped me to connect with people outside of Dao Tha and enabled me to participate in various cultural events and activities. They sometimes accompanied me to the interviews and eagerly introduced me to new people, allowing me to engage in snowball sampling. As a result,

The anthropologist conducting participant observation in Laos: harvesting rice with Hmong villagers in a field (top) and hand-pounding it in one of their homes (bottom).

I was able to conduct one focus group interview in a different village in Vang Vieng. Although there was no monetary compensation for interviewees, I brought food (mainly eggs and snacks) and drinks (bottles of Pepsi soda or instant coffee, which were popular but purchased only occasionally for special events) with me as an expression of my gratitude for their participation.

While the ages of interview participants were quite diverse, my interview sample in Laos has a gender imbalance because of the reluctance of women to be interviewed. Hmong women were extremely helpful and always talked to me casually on numerous occasions, but when I asked for a formal interview, they often told me that they were too "shy" and "uneducated" to help with my research. Some of those who were married even referred me to their husbands. In general, it was difficult for me to engage in purposive sampling by recruiting more female interviewees. Nonetheless, because women were aware that I was in the village to conduct research, I was able to have extensive conversations and do participant observation with them; as a result, their voices and perspectives are also integrated in this book.

The majority of Hmong villagers in my study were predominantly subsistence farmers, while a small number of them had other occupations, such as *tuk tuk* (motorized rickshaw, common public transportation in Laos) drivers, tourism workers, and government employees. Out of my entire sample of forty-eight interviewees, only four men had college educations, and three of these individuals were living in the capital city of Vientiane. The rest (including all the women) had some primary or secondary education. I conducted participant observation throughout my fieldwork by attending many village activities on a daily basis as well as special events. Some of my daily activities include working in rice fields and vegetable gardens with different Hmong families, visiting local markets with them, preparing and eating meals together, helping with community projects, and attending family meetings and gatherings.

From "Global" Vang Vieng to Hmong "Villages" in Sacramento, California

By the time I conducted fieldwork in Laos, two of my former Hmong students whom I initially met through English classes in Dao Tha had already migrated to Sacramento through arranged marriages. When they were still living in the village, I had helped one of these students, Chia, when she needed to open an email account after she first started to exchange photos and phone calls with a Hmong American man introduced by her uncle and aunt in Sacramento. The marriage proceeded very quickly, and a couple months later, I met her soon-to-be husband, Steve Thao, who came to Laos in order to "officialize" and complete the marriage process with Chia's family.

I stayed in touch with Chia after she migrated to the United States to live with Steve. When I later visited the Hmong community in Sacramento multiple times for preliminary research, they generously offered me their sons' room to stay in. I was able to quickly join their family's everyday lives and extensively participate in numerous events and activities with their extended family and clan community, as well as with the broader Sacramento Hmong community. Upon my return to Sacramento for fieldwork, I stayed with Chia and Steve again for three weeks before renting my own room in a house in their neighborhood.

California is the state with the largest Hmong population in the United States, followed by Minnesota and Wisconsin.[18] Upon their arrival to the country as refugees, Hmong were initially dispersed and resettled to different cities (such as Chicago, Denver, and Spokane) as refugees depending on the location of their American sponsors, charity groups, or previously resettled relatives, but they gradually moved from these cities to the West Coast and Midwest with larger Hmong communities in order to live with family members and relatives in the same area. As a result, subsequent internal migration further consolidated the Hmong refugee communities in specific cities and states. In Sacramento, Hmong in my study resided in certain neighborhoods or streets, leading some of them to refer to these sections of the city as urban "Hmong villages" (see chapter 2).

Compared to Dao Tha, Laos, I initially knew far fewer people in person in urban Sacramento, since there was no rural "village" environment where I could freely visit and interact with people on a daily basis. In addition, my preliminary research visits to Sacramento had been relatively short, in contrast to my long stays in Laos. However, through participant observation, I became acquainted with the local Hmong community and met new people who not only were willing to be interviewed but who also connected me with other potential interviewees. In particular, a senior Hmong scholar and a college student, both of whom I initially met as interviewees, made significant contributions to my research. Not only did they help me to expand my contacts for fieldwork, but their support has had a crucial and positive impact on my work to this day. Because of the abundance of published materials publicly available in the local community, I was also able to individually contact interviewees outside my personal network by using community resources, such as business cards and directories, community newspapers and magazines, and advertisements posted at Hmong markets. This enabled me to better diversify my interview sample in terms of gender, age, religious affiliation, and socioeconomic and educational backgrounds.

I conducted semi-structured interviews that lasted from one and a half to three hours with sixty-three individuals (twenty-four female and thirty-nine male participants), all of which were audio-recorded with permission. While most of these were in Sacramento, I also did interviews in other cities of California (see below), as well as with two Hmong (Miao) visitors from China. Hmong in California were more familiar with researchers and their activities than those in Laos and did not necessarily find their participation in my research to be intimidating or logistically difficult. Most interviewees were first- and "1.5-generation" immigrants (1.5 meaning those who were born in Thai refugee camps but migrated to the United States as teenagers or younger children), but I also interviewed ten US-born, second-generation Hmong Americans in their twenties. As former refugees, all first-generation Hmong adults were either permanent residents or naturalized American citizens. There was also no monetary compensation for interviewees except cooked food and fruits that I brought for interviews taking place at their homes. For some interviews with Hmong women, small gifts like cosmetics were included. Additionally, when I conducted interviews at restaurants or cafes, I paid for the check as a small token of my appreciation.

During my research, I conducted interviews primarily in the Lao language with elderly first-generation and some older 1.5-generation Hmong, but English was also used for younger-generation interviewees and others depending on their preferences. For elderly Hmong who wished to speak mainly in the Hmong language, I obtained assistance from their children or grandchildren. The original words quoted in this book include both Lao and Hmong languages as well as English, depending on which the interviewees and speakers were using during my fieldwork. Foreign words in the Hmong language are noted as such in the text.

Many of the elderly first-generation Hmong interviewees had no substantial educational background. The rest of the interviewees (more than half of my sample) had some sort of education in the United States, which ranged from English as a Second Language (ESL) certificates to high school diplomas and college or higher degrees. Interviewees in the

United States were in a more diverse range of occupations than those in Laos. Some had professional jobs, including public school teachers, real estate and insurance sales agents, nurses/health-care assistants, and social workers. However, half of the interviewees of working age who were not students were in less-skilled jobs or unemployed (often laid off from previous factory assembly line jobs). The majority of elderly first-generation Hmong had never held stable jobs and were supported by monthly governmental welfare assistance, such as Supplemental Security Income (SSI) or food stamps. In addition to individual interviews, I conducted one focus group interview with thirteen elderly Hmong at a local organization and collected in-person surveys (self-administered questionnaires) with a total of eighty-three Hmong students from three different colleges in the Sacramento area (forty from California State University, Sacramento; nineteen from Sacramento City College; and twenty-four from the University of California, Davis).

I was also able to conduct participant observation on numerous occasions at various places and events in California. Part of my fieldwork in California involved traveling to other locations within and outside Sacramento County to attend various community events, such as New Year festivals in different cities, sports games, and community ceremonies and rituals, as well as to conduct interviews. These include the cities of Galt (the location of a well-known Hmong flea market), Stockton, Marysville, Chico, and Fresno, where the weeklong International Hmong New Year's Festival is held annually in late December to January 1. In addition to daily activities such as family and clan gatherings, housework, and grocery shopping, I also accompanied people to their workplaces and social organizations. Although my research did not necessarily focus on Hmong Christianity, I regularly attended a Hmong Christian church in Sacramento on Sundays, which helped me broaden my understanding of the Hmong people's lives in the US national context. As a result, I was able to interview male and female church members of different ages, who constitute roughly 20 percent of my total US Hmong interviewees.

A Transnational Messenger: Multi-Sited Fieldwork as a Racialized and Gendered Partial Insider/Outsider

During my fieldwork, I constantly observed the impact and presence of borderless transnational influences that were entrenched across the localities in Laos and the United States, which indicates the inseparable and simultaneous coexistence of both the local and the transnational in

Hmong people's everyday lives. Although multi-sited fieldwork is locally embedded and does not occur in simultaneous, transnational spaces per se, I unexpectedly became a transnational messenger, or an "occasional postman" in Paolo Boccagni's words (2016, 9), who connected two geographically separated Hmong diasporic communities by delivering news, information, and photos to family members living in different parts of the world.

Because many Hmong of my research in both Laos and the United States longed for family members living abroad, some of whom they have never been able to visit, they often felt geographically confined and had to endure a forced separation. My mobility as a foreign outsider and researcher was privileged in this sense and, ironically, allowed me to freely travel, visit Hmong people's families and relatives in each country, and participate in their numerous events. As a transnational messenger, I may not have fully bridged the geographical distance between diasporic Hmong and alleviated their separation and emotional longing for each other, but through this process I felt that I was sometimes a "partial" insider who transnationally mediated between separated families.

Nonetheless, my positionality in the field remained ambiguous as I crossed the boundaries between the insider and outsider, which were complicated further by the intersection of my racialized, ethnic, national, and gendered status. In fact, intersectionality is crucial for ethnographers, not just for the people they study, since their multiple and overlapping positions and identities interplay in the field in various ways, often unexpectedly. In Laos I was frequently racialized as "Hmong" in mainstream Lao society because of my East Asian racial appearance, which was apparently seen as similar to that of the Hmong and phenotypically distinct from other ethnic groups (see chapter 2). I was constantly mistaken as Hmong (or asked if I am Hmong) in public, even when I was not with them. However, in the United States I was immediately racialized as "Asian" in public (without being identified specifically as Hmong).

Despite our shared racialization in mainstream society, I was always othered by both Lao and US Hmong communities because of my Korean ethnicity/nationality. Regardless of how often I wore the same skirts as Hmong women (in Laos) and cooked with them and participated in their community and family events in both countries, I was ethnically identified as a non-Hmong person who was not one of them. I sometimes asked people how they were able to single me out as an ethnic outsider among them, apparently with no hesitation. Not surprisingly, people did not have a concrete answer but told me, "We just know." Nonetheless,

32   Introduction

our shared, racialized position (as "Hmong" in Laos and "Asian" in the United States) undoubtably made me feel like a partial racial insider to the Hmong community in both countries and may have facilitated rapport and acceptance during fieldwork.

However, my ethnic/national status as an outsider from Korea also unexpectedly drew a lot of attention and interest from part of the Hmong community in both countries, especially Hmong youth who were interested in K-pop music and Korean popular culture and beauty products. In reality, I hardly watched any Korean dramas and was never a fan of any Korean pop stars. In Laos I was frequently asked to further elaborate and explain some of the scenes in popular Korean dramas by people when they watched Hmong- or Thai-dubbed DVDs at home. One time I even received a request to teach them an original song from a popular Korean drama I had never seen. I also conducted fieldwork in California when the Korean pop singer Psy's "Gangnam Style" was a massive global hit. Because of my relative ignorance about Korean pop culture, I ended up studying my own culture as part of my fieldwork so that I could meet Hmong people's ethnic expectations and become more culturally conversant with them.

My racial and ethnic positionality as someone who was both an outsider and insider to the Hmong community was also related to my initially ambiguous gendered status during my fieldwork. Because my gender intersected with my ethnicity as a non-Hmong, Korean foreigner, I was initially free from gendered expectations imposed on Hmong women. Earlier in my fieldwork in both countries, I was allowed to sit with men and eat with them during community/family events while Hmong women were working in the kitchen. I was ambiguously positioned somewhere between woman and man, which allowed me to cross gender boundaries and conduct participant observation in purely male-dominated settings.

However, as I became more of a partial insider familiar with the Hmong community, I started to feel that it was more appropriate and natural for me to join the Hmong women in the kitchen or backyard to cook and serve food to the men, which also meant I had to wait and eat later with the women. During community events, when I walked straight into the kitchen or backyard to help cook or clean with the women, I realized they had also become comfortable with my gendered behavior. By gaining a more partial insider status, I became subject to traditional female gender expectations. However, this meant I could now do intensive participant observation in exclusively female spaces and thus feel better culturally situated in the field. Ultimately, this ambiguous status was not simply a (dis)advantage for research, but rather it allowed me to negotiate my positionality in multiple and productive ways during my fieldwork that may not have been possible if I had been a complete insider or outsider.

Multi-Sited Fieldwork and Transnational Ethnographies

As described above, my research with diasporic Hmong led me to conduct multi-sited fieldwork, which enabled me to write a transnational ethnography. When anthropologists do research about diasporic communities that span national borders, they are positioned across and between local and national territorial boundaries, which are considerably blurred by people's transnational engagements. My fieldwork experience therefore led me to further reflect on theoretical issues related to transnational ethnographies and multi-sited fieldwork.

While transnational ethnographies and multi-sited fieldwork are closely related, they are also fundamentally different. Researchers writing transnational ethnographies do not necessarily have to conduct multi-sited fieldwork (see Tsuda et al. 2014). Even if they conduct single-sited research in one community, they can still write about its transnational engagements across national borders by observing people in specific locales who live transnational lives through their social and cultural connections with those in other countries. Conversely, researchers can conduct fieldwork in multiple geographical and national locales as independent case studies without studying the transnational relations between them across national borders. In this case, ethnographies can be multi-sited but not necessarily transnational (see also Carney 2017).

I consider this book as *both* a multi-sited and transnational ethnography since it is based on fieldwork in two diasporic communities and examines their transnational connections. As scholars have noted, multi-sited fieldwork enables ethnographers to grapple with the highly mobile lives of people (especially those who are migratory and diasporic) while articulating the ongoing presence and power of the nation-state (Marcus 1995; Wimmer and Glick Schiller 2002). In fact, in order to understand the influence of nation-states on transnational communities and diasporic peoples, it is necessary to compare how different local communities are affected by the countries in which they are situated through multi-sited research.

Generally, many studies of contemporary diasporas tend to focus on a diasporic community in one geographical location instead of in multiple countries (e.g., Aiyar 2015; Collins 2002; Pfeifer et al. 2013; Tapp and Lee 2004). However, it is difficult to fully grasp the complexity of diasporic identity if studies mainly examine diasporas in only one locale without looking at their transnational connections and commonalities and analyze national differences among co-ethnic diasporic communities in multiple countries. There are some diaspora researchers who have conducted multi-sited fieldwork and substantially examine actual transnational socioeconomic and political linkages between two or more diasporic communities (e.g., Abdelhady 2011; Göksel 2022; Nibbs 2014; Parreñas 2001; Tsuda 2003), although they do not necessarily comparatively analyze their diasporic cultures and discourses within specific national contexts.

In this sense, this book will be one of the few multi-sited ethnographic studies that substantially examine actual transnational socioeconomic and cultural linkages between two diasporic communities while also comparing how their cultural practices and discourses are refracted through different nation-states. It is true that multi-sited ethnographic fieldwork can be more time-consuming and costly compared to fieldwork in one place (Falzon 2009; Hannerz 2003). Though this may be a valid concern, many ethnographers are able to maintain long-term relationships with multiple communities over the years through repeat visits and multiple sojourns. I therefore emphasize that transnational ethnographies can still be based on traditional, in-depth fieldwork embedded in multiple local societies, because the transnational lives of people are locally situated while their local practices are transnationally connected.

Thus, the local and the transnational are not always mutually exclusive for researchers and for those they study. Just as localized (and even immobilized) peoples can engage actively in transnational practices, researchers conducting in-depth, long-term fieldwork in local communities can illuminate how these localities are engaged in and constituted by transnational relations with those living far away. The local and the transnational, as well as the national and the diasporic, are often in dialogical and dialectical relations with each other, sometimes unknowingly.

PART I

The Making of the Hmong Diaspora

History, Multiple Homelands, and Ambivalent Belonging

1

Hmong Diasporic History and Multiple Homeland Narratives

This chapter provides introductory historical background about the Hmong diaspora. By highlighting the voices of the Hmong I interviewed and spoke with during my fieldwork, I will trace the basis of their diasporic consciousness and present their histories and memories of displacement. This involves multiple migratory dispersals to various locations over the centuries in response to wars and conflicts, ethnic persecution, and other dislocations connected to both ancient China and the aftermath of the Vietnam War.

Much of Hmong diasporic history remains unclear and uncertain, partly due to the lack of reliable historical documents and sources. Scholars who have studied Hmong history generally note the difficulty of establishing a concrete and authoritative historical account (Michaud 1997a; Tapp 1988, 1998; Tapp et al. 2004), including the exact origins of the Hmong people. Ma Vang (2021) refers to the history of the Hmong diaspora as a "fugitive history" that was not only recorded in a variety of forms but also has parts that are missing because people were constantly on the "move" and "on the run."

In this chapter I demonstrate that this historical uncertainty is not necessarily negative but can be productive, for it enables multiple (contested) discourses and perspectives to emerge and be considered instead of silenced under a single and supposedly authoritative historical account of the Hmong diaspora. Rather than simply adopting one dominant scholarly theory about Hmong's ethnic origins, many Hmong in my study subscribed to multiple theories about possible ethnic homelands, thus expanding the scope of their diasporic consciousness to encompass exploratory and even speculative imaginings. While my analysis of historical accounts of Hmong in this chapter recognizes scholarly work, I also shift the focus from the search for definitive diasporic histories and facts (such as the "true" location of the Hmong homeland) to the Hmong people's own subjective historical understandings and diasporic consciousness as narrated by different individuals in multiple ways.

This chapter indicates that the consciousness of diasporic history for Hmong I studied is rather distinctive in two ways. As noted in the introduction, diasporic Hmong lost their ties to their country of ancestral origin a long time ago during centuries of dispersal and migratory displacement. Unlike most diasporas, which have identifiable ethnic homelands (even if they are not always independent nation-states), Hmong in my research had considerable uncertainty about the territorial location of their ancestral homeland. In this context, their diasporic consciousness includes not only dominant, widely accepted narratives about ethnic origins in China and emotional connections to Miao in the country but also multiple discourses and stories about various other homelands.

In addition, histories about the Hmong diaspora indicate that it was constituted by multiple dispersals through time. In general, the initial dispersal of Hmong was from southwest China to various countries in Southeast Asia; the subsequent dispersal occurred after the Vietnam War (see Hein 2013), when Hmong from Laos were resettled as refugees to various predominantly Western countries, including the United States, after residing in Thai refugee camps. However, the multiple and incongruous discourses from Hmong interviewees discussed in this chapter open the important possibility that their consciousness of diasporic history is much more complex and expansive and cannot be simply encompassed by such dominant historical narratives. Indeed, the historical uncertainties in the narratives of origin, ethnic homeland, and migration among Hmong in my study were based on diasporic memories as well as current lived experiences that include multiple dispersals to (and also within) various countries, such as China, Thailand, Laos, and the United States. Such dissonances have resulted in a diasporic subjectivity based on simultaneous affiliations to multiple nation-states where they or their ancestors migrated through and lived as marginalized ethnic peoples.

Therefore, the diasporic consciousness of Hmong is decentered and grounded in discordances and dissonances caused by the relative absence of a single, coherent homeland and diasporic history. Instead of revolving around a strong affiliation to one territorialized country of ancestral origin, it invokes multiple ruptures and dis/connections to different nation-states. In turn, such historical dissonances have configured their transnational diasporic connections in specific ways. Because of the absence of centripetal ties to a singular ethnic homeland at the *center* of the diaspora (such as China), the transnational circuits of capital and culture in the Hmong diaspora are *decentered* and predominantly flow laterally across the diaspora between geographically dispersed co-ethnic communities (such as those in Laos and the United States).

As will be discussed in chapters 3, 4, and 5, these lateral transnational social and cultural continuities between specific local communities in Laos and the United States include kinship systems, cross-border familial economic exchanges, and shared rituals (e.g., shamanism, funerals, New Year celebrations). The diasporic identities of Hmong in my research are therefore the product of both transnational and national affiliations with multiple countries at different historical moments in the process of diasporization, not with a definitive ancestral homeland. The diverse and diverging stories I collected are valuable not because they replace any "official" or "correct" version of Hmong's history but because they are people's actual diasporic, historical consciousness, which often contrasts with official and unified narratives.

Historical Dis/Connections to China and Miao

Predominant theories of Hmong ancestry indicate that they originated in China and are related to an ethnic minority group officially known as the Miao in that country (Cheung 2004; Michaud 1997a; Tapp 1998; Tapp and Lee 2004). In fact, Hmong in my research were generally aware that China is defined as perhaps the most plausible ancestral homeland and identified with the Miao somewhat as part of their historical consciousness of ethnic origins and subsequent dispersal, even if they did not affiliate with China itself.

Scholars have traced Hmong history in China back to as early as the Qin dynasty (221–206 BC), when Hmong were living as various individual groups with no specific name and dispersed in the central area of the country (Barney 1967; Jenks 1994). It is suggested that among those various small groups, the "Miao" (who are supposedly the ancestors of contemporary Hmong) were considered a "pivotal threat" by Chinese rulers because of their "incorrigible and inassimilable nature" (Bernatzik 1970; Mottin 1980). An overview of early Hmong ethnic history in relation to China is particularly challenging, as it consists of disparities in how the relationship between the Miao in China and the contemporary diasporic Hmong abroad is defined and understood by Chinese officials, academic scholars, and the Hmong themselves.

The official Chinese recognition of the people called Miao allegedly began in the mid-sixteenth-century Ming dynasty and continued into the seventeenth-century Qing dynasty (Hostetler 2000, 626; G. Lee 2007). During these periods, the Miao were referred as *miaoman*, literally meaning "southern barbarians," which included all non-Han minorities who had been forcibly dislocated and resettled in the southwestern areas of what are the Yunnan, Sichuan, Hunan, and Guizhou provinces today. Therefore, there was considerable internal migratory dispersal of Miao, who were initially scattered across these southern parts of China during this period. This raises the possibility that the diasporic history of Miao/Hmong can also be traced to this earlier internal dispersal, which predates their gradual southward migratory flow across fluid borders out of China and eventual dispersal to the various Southeast Asian countries of today.

Such internal migratory dispersals across a wide geographical area in China likely fragmented Miao into multiple subgroups and resulted in their living with different, mutually unintelligible dialects. In fact, the *Miao Album*, one of the few available earlier official documents about Miao produced by the Qing dynasty, lists about ninety ethnic groups residing in Guizhou (see Deal and Hostetler 2005), indicating how ethnically heterogeneous this group already was at that point. During this time, sub-Miao categories were created under the umbrella ethnic term "Miao," such as *hua* (flower), Black, White, Green Miao, and so forth, based on the color of women's skirts (Deal and Hostetler 2005). Miao were also often negatively portrayed in Chinese history through different categories, such as cooked (*shu*) versus raw (*sheng*) Miao. From the perspective of ruling elites, the former refers to more "civilized" Miao and the latter to those who are "unassimilated" (see also Michaud 1997a). Because the origin of this highly diverse Miao group is uncertain and subject to debate even in China (Schein 2000), singular histories about Hmong origins in the country are problematic.

Although the Miao are supposedly the ancestors of diasporic Hmong currently residing outside China, scholars of the Miao in China have critically examined how contemporary Chinese official ethnic categories used today do not correspond to the way ethnic minorities actually identify and perceive themselves. It is therefore questionable whether Miao in China should be employed as a broad category that represents and encompasses all the diverse groups of ethnic minorities classified as

Miao by government officials (see also Schein 2000; Tapp 2002). Based on language and geographic residence, the contemporary Miao category is divided further into four subgroups: Hmong, Mhu, Quo Xiong, and A Hmao (Enwall 1992; Lemoine 2008; Tapp 2002, 79), which indicates that equating entire Miao with Hmong can also potentially be problematic.[1] This is further complicated by the fact that there is no officially recognized ethnic group called "Hmong" in China.

Some scholars deal with this problem by differentiating the "real" Hmong from other "Miao" ethnic minority groups who "falsely" claim to be Hmong, as if doing so provides them with certain advantages (see Tapp 2002). From a linguistic perspective, Nicholas Tapp argues that the Hmong in China are "a particularly clearly identifiable group who do refer to themselves customarily as Hmong, and who speak dialects of the Western or Chuanqiandian branch of the Miao language in the Miao-Yao language family" (Tapp 2002, 78),[2] and he confirms that the "Ch'uan Miao" in the southwestern part of China call themselves Hmong. Louisa Schein notes that "only a portion of those identified as Miao—the ones distributed over western Guizhou and parts of Yunnan, particularly the border areas—call themselves 'Hmong' in their own language" (2004, 275). In sum, it is difficult to accurately identify the "true" Hmong among the various different Miao groups.

In 1949 the People's Republic of China (PRC) identified fifty-six official minorities and declared them to be ethnic nationalities (*minzu*) (Cheung 2004; Schein 2000, 68), in contrast to the majority Han ethnic group. Miao was recognized as one of those minzu and the fifth-largest ethnic minority in the nation, and it is reported that more than nine million Miao currently reside in China, according to the 2010 Chinese census. However, since the ethnic name "Hmong" simply does not officially exist in China, such estimates likely include other subethnic minorities in southern China broadly classified as Miao and may not be an accurate estimate of the entire Hmong population.[3] Apparently, there is an inherent disparity in how the Chinese state defines Miao and how these people perceive themselves. As scholars note, some of them may not accept their homogeneous categorization as "Miao" (Harrell 1995; Schein 2000, 2004a; Tapp 1998, 2002; Z. Yang 2009).

In sum, scholars recognize that contemporary Hmong living in the diaspora are the descendants of a subset of Miao in China (in the supposed ethnic homeland), and some of them argue that Hmong there are a distinct ethnic group who have their own self-designations. However, there is not much ethnographic information about the extent to which

Hmong currently residing in the diaspora consider China to be their country of ancestral origin as well as possible ethnic relations and identifications between Hmong abroad and the people referred to as Miao in China. There are considerable disparities and gaps in the discourses of ethnic origins among Hmong I interviewed, and such discrepant claims make it difficult to construct a coherent and chronological narrative of Hmong diasporic history.

Tracing Ancestral Histories to China

Despite uncertainty about their ancestral ethnic history, many Hmong in my study generally recognized China as a supposed ethnic homeland to varying degrees based on their knowledge of scholarly history, Hmong folklore and community rituals, and even DNA studies (see G. Lee 2007). Some Hmong in California consulted and read books about their ancient history, which, for instance, were sold at the Hmong New Year festivals. However, such books and published materials were not accessible or available for most Hmong in Laos and other parts of Southeast Asia. Therefore, those who believe their ethnic homeland is China based their claims more on Hmong folklore, oral history, and ritual narratives and cultural practices, as will be shown below.

Hmong oral traditions about their ethnic history do reference their presence in ancient China. For example, the chants and songs during the funeral rituals were of great importance to Hmong communities in tracing their ethnic history. In Hmong funerals the "soul" of the deceased person is considered mobile and borderless, asked to leave the body, and is sent back to its "original" place to reunite with the ancestors (see chapter 6). The chanter, who conducts the ritual, narrates the entire journey of the soul before it reaches its "final" destination. In particular, the chanting becomes lengthy and dramatic when it describes conflicts and fights against the "Chinese enemy" in distant times. Once the soul overcomes the crisis caused by the war with the Chinese army, it is finally sent to its "ultimate" destination.

In addition to scholarly and folklore references to Hmong ancestral origins, genetic research has also been conducted through a DNA project by researchers in China and the United States, which is based on over five hundred individual blood samples of residents in the southwestern and southeastern part of China. This research concludes that Hmong in Southeast Asia have close "relatedness" to current Miao in the Hunan province of China (in the southwest region) as well as some genetic similarities with the ethnic Han people in northeast China (see G. Lee 2007). The result of this DNA research was mentioned by about one-fourth of interviewees during my fieldwork in both Laos and the United States. However, among those who believed that their ancestors originated in China, only one person called it "scientific" evidence for his claim. In other words, such genetic research did not necessarily convince Hmong in my study to accept China as their de facto country of ancestral origin.

Overall, about half of the interviewees in both Laos and the United States answered that China is their possible ethnic homeland. Nonetheless, they expressed uncertainty, since they believed there may have been a more ancient place of origin before China about which they have no concrete evidence. For example, Cheng Her, a Sacramento resident in his forties, remarked, "Before the Hmong settled in Laos and Vietnam, they were from China. But that's the farthest that we may have physical evidence for, so we are not sure before that. Maybe some still have relatives over there, but that's like the earliest that we can remember."

Likewise, Sheng Her, a clan representative in his forties, who often conducts funeral rituals for the local Hmong community in Sacramento, commented:

> Absolutely [Hmong are] from China. Beyond that, I don't know. If you do your anthropological work, people might have different theories. Maybe we were from Mongolia before China. We have folklore stories that kind of indicate that we were from Mongolia. But when you compare those people [Mongolians] to us, Hmong are different. So the actual, original homeland of Hmong? We don't know.

While Hmong interviewees remained uncertain about China as their country of ancestral origin and had lost substantial connections to it, it did not prevent them from developing a sense of ethnic affinity and affiliation to the Miao living in China. In numerous interviews and conversations, Hmong in both Laos and the United States frequently made references to the Miao as the descendants of their possible ancestors.[4] In addition, Hmong in Vang Vieng have encountered Miao peddlers from China, and some Hmong in California have traveled to China for various reasons and visited Miao villages. Such encounters and interactions with their supposed co-ethnics have become a type of "forged transnationality" (Schein 1998a) that produces cross-border identifications between previously separated people of shared ancestry.

Perceptions of Lao Hmong toward Miao in China

Hmong I studied in Laos generally viewed Miao in China as "ethnic brethren" (Schein 1998b) with shared Hmong cultures and had positive perceptions of them. Some of them had irregular personal interactions with Miao peddlers from southwest China, who occasionally traveled to different Hmong villages on their motorbikes, carrying bundles of herbal medicines and various products like traditional Hmong clothes, jewelry, and other miscellaneous articles.[5] Calling Miao peddlers from China "the same people" or "brothers and sisters," my interviewees believed that they share a common ancestry with the Miao. Based on observed similarities in dress, language, cultural traditions, as well as shared last names (which indicates membership in the same clan), they claimed that Miao in China still carry on the same cultural traditions, such as funeral rituals and the New Year ceremony, although some details may have changed due to their geographic separation.

Some of the Hmong villagers had positive perceptions of the Miao based on their apparent ethnic affinity and connections as co-ethnic peoples. They also believed that Miao in China might have preserved their traditional culture better than they have in Laos, given that they apparently brought "real and authentic Hmong stuff" from China, especially traditional clothes made of old fabrics and designs. As a result, they felt "proud" of the Hmong (Miao) in China and praised them for being "smarter" and more capable of producing "really beautiful hand-made traditional clothes for the Hmong New Year," which they no longer make in Laos.[6] Their shared ethnic affinity with Miao in China is illustrated in the comments from Toua Her, one of the villagers in Dao Tha:

> When Hmong [Miao] peddlers came from China, I also asked them many questions. Hmong in China know how to publish books and they are very good and smart. But their government is the Chinese government and there are of course many more Chinese than Hmong there. So even if Hmong are smart enough to publish something, they have to publish in Chinese. For people who don't know the details, they would believe that those books are written by some Chinese. But in reality, *we* Hmong made them. With that cleverness, if Hmong from all over the world come together and live in one place, then you wouldn't have to yearn for other countries at all. [emphasis mine]

In addition, some of the villagers characterized Miao in general as an ethnic minority group that has confronted "constant hardship" and perceived this as a "shared and universal" destiny of the Hmong at the margins of the state. As a result, they sympathized with the hardships endured by Miao in rural China, which is perceived as similar to their own situation in Laos, and believed that their impoverished co-ethnics are living in a "sterile land" that is inhospitable for farming.

In fact, when I asked Chong Lee, an older farmer in Dao Tha, about possible differences between the Miao in China and Hmong in Laos, he stressed the common ethnic identity that they share, regardless of their national differences based on the countries in which they live. "You know, the life of Hmong consists of waking up really early in the morning; going to the hill; carrying corn, rice, and pumpkins back home; pounding those crops; and then finally being able to eat them. This is the life of Hmong, regardless of where they live," Chong remarked. He seemed to believe that Hmong as a people share such a lifestyle, "regardless of time and space." This kind of generalized narrative of the Hmong way of life has enabled my interviewees to imagine a shared ethnic experience and sense of affiliation with Miao in China.

Miao from China were also regarded as their kin by Hmong in Laos based on a system of clan kinship that consists of shared last names, revealing a type of indiscriminate ethnic affinity with them. This also applies to other diasporic Hmong who consider co-ethnics of the same clan dispersed around the world as family members and relatives, despite the lack of known biological relatedness (see chapter 3). In fact, when Miao peddlers visited Laos for business, they first inquired about Hmong families in Dao Tha village with the same last name. Despite being total strangers and foreigners, they were welcomed and allowed to stay with these Hmong families as if they were close relatives.

During my research in Laos, Hmong repeatedly told me about the immediate inclusion of the Miao from China in their kinship system. A good example is the following discussion I had with Nou Thao, an elderly man in a Hmong village outside Dao Tha:

> NOU: They [the Miao peddlers] can speak Hmong. Those from China are also Hmong Thao [same last name as Nou's], so they are our relatives since we are from the same family. When they came to do business here, they stayed with us.
>
> AUTHOR: Really? So I assume they contacted you before they came here?
>
> NOU: No, they never contacted us in advance, because they did not know about us until they arrived here. They initially came to do business in Lak 52.[7] One time, there was a Hmong guy from China,

and he was like our brother-in-law. His last name was Yang, but his wife was from the Thao clan, so we are relatives.

AUTHOR: Do you know where in China he was from?

NOU: He said that he lives in *paj tawj lag*.[8]

AUTHOR: How did you feel when you first met him?

NOU: He said, "Oh, I am Hmong Yang [last name] but my wife is a Hmong Thao. I am your brother-in-law." I was of course very happy to see him. We shared food. He ate whatever we had and stayed with us.

It is important to note that interviewees' interest in and ethnic affiliations with the Miao are not a *national* attachment to China as the country from which the Hmong may have originated. Instead, their sentiments represent a diasporic ethnicity that embraces their *co-ethnics* living in the supposed ethnic homeland with a similar, shared culture and ethnic history as well as memories of persecution and impoverishment as marginalized minorities.

Making Dis/Connections between Miao "People" and the Chinese "Nation-State" among US Hmong

Similar to Hmong interviewees in Laos, those in the United States also expressed ethnic affinity and extensive kin affiliations with the Miao in China. While they encountered Miao peddlers to a limited extent during their New Year festivals, some individuals have traveled to China for sightseeing, missionary activities, dating and marriage, or academic exchanges, and had opportunities to interact with various Miao ethnic minority villagers in the southern part of the country with whom they felt ethnic commonalities.[9] Among the fifteen Hmong I met or interviewed who had been to China, the majority went there mainly for tourism or Christian missionary activities. Only three individuals had visited the country for other reasons, such as being a visiting scholar and an exchange student, while another went to pursue a marriage. Although these interviewees did visit Miao villages and felt ethnic affinity with Miao individuals they encountered, they also made it clear that the purpose of their trips was not necessarily to reconnect with their ancestral homeland and explore their ethnic roots. There was very little indication that they had developed a strong sense of ethnic attachment to the Chinese nation-state itself.

Hmong American Christian missionary trips to China have become an important component of Hmong transnational activities in the diaspora that connect them across national borders. However, they also commonly noted that their goal was not simply to "proselytize" Miao in rural areas. Because of the strict regulations on Christianity by the Chinese government, it was not easy for them to conduct missionary activities freely. As a result, they pursued their religious mission rather carefully and also actively engaged with community development projects.

Hmong who had the opportunity to encounter Miao in China shared with me joyful experiences upon discovering cultural activities and ethnic dress and artifacts in southwestern Miao communities that they found to be similar to diasporic Hmong outside China. After returning to the United States, some of them turned their personal recordings into DVDs, circulated them around the community, or sold them at Hmong supermarkets and community events (see also Schein 2004b). During my visits to different households, Hmong families would show me their large Hmong DVD collections and play them in the background. In some of these videos, the co-ethnics are portrayed as evoking a sense of longing for peaceful and idealized past lives in remote rural villages, or what anthropologist Louisa Schein (2016, 255) calls "émigré nostalgia." Schein critically examines how the visual images in these videos produce gendered and sexualized subjects through the "male gaze" of urbanized Hmong.

Hmong from California who visited China also spoke about their ethnic connection with the Miao based on observed cultural similarities. For instance, Chong Her, a Christian member at a local Hmong church, recalled his two visits to rural China and his encounters with Miao there:

> One thing that amazed me was that I really felt connected to the Hmong in China because of their customs and culture there. Wherever you go from one [Miao] village to another, you really feel that the same culture and same Hmong values are still there. If they realize that you are also part of *Miao-zu* ["Miao people," in Chinese official terms] like them, they will come to talk to you. Also, think about Hmong traditional clothes. If you see their fabrics and dress at the supermarket or other places in China, you can tell "oh, they are Hmong people" and you are able to connect to them.

Leng Thao, who also visited China and traveled around the country for a total of three weeks, had a similar view. When I asked him whether he felt the Miao in China he met were of the same ethnicity, even if it was difficult for him to communicate, he responded:

> I believe that they are still the same Hmong because of their culture. The traditional musical instruments like *qeej* [mouth organ pipe made of small bamboos] or *raj* [flute] are the same. Dress is the same, too.

You can tell they are Hmong and wear Hmong dress. It's just that they don't speak the exact same language, but it is not really that difficult to understand or different, either. For example, we say "*noj mov*" [eat food, have a meal] while they say, "*noj-wav*." "Noj-wav" is more like baby talk.

Even those who have never been to China or seen any Miao people in person still expressed feelings of affinity toward the Miao partly based on their knowledge of cultural similarities. For example, a Sacramento resident, Sheng Her, who believed that China is the Hmong's original homeland, explained:

> The reason I am certain about China [as the ethnic homeland] is because we have the same last name with the Hmong there. Another simple thing is the bamboo pipe. They [Miao] blow the bamboo pipe, not exactly the way we blow, but you hear the sound and understand what they are blowing about. That's one of the things that really tells us that we are related. The Hmong in China, I don't know where they originally migrated from, but they have been living there for many long years.

In addition to these cultural continuities, US Hmong interviewees were also struck by what they perceived to be the low standard of living of the Miao in China. A middle-aged Christian woman in Sacramento, Mai Xiong, who visited China twice with a group of people from her Hmong Christian church, compared the situation between Hmong in Laos and China from her "American" perspective in terms of their socioeconomic condition. "In Laos, even if you don't have education, you at least have the land," Mai noted. "You can at least become a farmer and can survive there. But in China, oh my God, it's much more difficult! No land, no water, no place to live."

"The Hmong in China don't live in the city," Lao Vue, a 1.5-generation Hmong in his late twenties, remarked when he described his travel experiences. "They don't have much education or a piece of land. The land is very limited. From my observation, I think Hmong in China are much poorer than Hmong in Thailand or Laos." Similar to Lao Hmong in my study, their co-ethnics in the United States sympathized with co-ethnic Miao in rural southwest China, who were apparently enduring continued poverty and lack of means to improve their living condition. However, these interviewees did not affiliate with the Chinese nation-state as their "ancestral homeland," nor did they homogeneously see themselves as returning to their country of ethnic origin when they traveled to China.

In fact, many of them noted that they wanted to see "life in China" and observe Chinese society and local living conditions from an "American" perspective. They said they were more interested in exploring famous cities like Beijing and Shanghai rather than visiting rural Miao villages.

In sum, US Hmong interviewees who regarded China as a possible country from which their ancestors came (and where their co-ethnics still reside) did not feel national affinity to the Chinese country itself as an ethnic homeland of the Hmong diaspora. Nonetheless, the ethnic encounters they had with Miao during their visits to China for tourism, education, marriage, or missionary reasons have enabled them to develop an ethnic affinity with the Miao. Such a sense of ethnic attachment remains a diasporic identification with an ancestral ethnic minority rather than a broader national affiliation with the general country of China.

The Search for Ethnic Origins: Beyond China

Although about half of the Hmong interviewees in both Laos and the United States defined China as their country of ancestral origin to some degree, others expressed considerable uncertainty about the location of their ethnic homeland and did not believe that China is where they originated. Because of centuries of dispersal and displacement across numerous countries and the absence of concrete historical records, there was a remarkable lack of consensus about possible ancestral homelands among interviewees. Instead, as they continue to search for their ethnic origins, they made multiple claims in their discourses about their ancestral origins in ways that defy simple characterization.

The varying discourses about ethnic origins reflect a diasporic consciousness based on memories of dispersal and dislocation rather than a clear territorial homeland, making the Hmong constantly feel like they are a "people without a country [or homeland]." As many of them pointed out, there is no country called "Hmong" in the world. In this context, uncertainty about their homeland was always at the center of my conversations with Hmong. For example, during an interview, Chong Her in Sacramento told me that he is interested in reading books about the ethnic origins and history of Hmong. He took out a thick book titled *Operation China: Introducing All the People of China* from his bookshelf and put it on the table in front of me. Based on his own research, Chong did not subscribe to the scholarly theory that Hmong are one of the original peoples of China. Instead, he felt that in the distant past, Hmong were from an even older homeland:

I personally believe that Hmong people came from Mesopotamia before they went to China. We have someone who has a theory that Hmong lived in Mesopotamia, which is the area of Iraq and Iran nowadays. Thousands of years ago, they moved to Russia, and then to the west to Mongolia, and they finally settled down in southern China for thousands of years. I truly believe that the Hmong originally come from Mesopotamia, and we are the same family and same clan.

Similarly, Hmong I spoke to in Laos who expressed considerable doubt about their ethnic origins in China also had multiple theories of origin. According to a short report written by a Hmong college student in Laos in 1972, "Mostly they [Hmong] did not remember their history well and sometimes told you a mythical history if you asked them a question 'where did Hmoob [Hmong] come from?'" (T. Thao 1972, 9). Despite the dominant theory (and oral histories and cultural practices) about the Hmong presence in ancient China, this Hmong student notes that the Hmong he spoke with mainly had memories about a mythical history, which indicates that they have been unsure about their territorial origins for some time.

While collecting multiple individual theories and discourses of ethnic origin, I particularly remember the comments of Moua Cha, a Hmong man in his fifties who migrated to France in 1979, whom I met in Laos while he was traveling there. According to him, "It is very difficult to be certain about where our original homeland is, because there are no documents or written historical records. According to Hmong oral history, Hmong originated from Mongolia, and the name of the country sounds so similar to Hmong.[10] But we can only guess."

In fact, Hmong I met in Laos frequently claimed in their discourses that Mongolia is a possible location of their ethnic homeland, a theory that was also shared by those in California. This theory about Mongolia was well developed among some interviewees and competed with the discourse that Hmong originated in China. For example, Teng Xiong, a man in his late thirties in Dao Tha, explained the logic of this theory based on mythical history:

> In the distant past, when Mongolia was the most powerful country, there was a general in charge of the whole Asian region. He sent an army to China to ask the people to cooperate with Mongolia. When Mongolia became weaker, the general tried to take the army back to his country, but many soldiers did not want to go back. I think maybe Hmong were a part of that group who did not want to return

to Mongolia. So it is possible that those Mongolian soldiers were the ancestors of Hmong in China.

While speculating on the ancient history of Hmong ancestors as warriors, Teng further elaborated upon his reasoning:

> I heard old people saying that in the past, Hmong were much stronger and better than Chinese during wars. Indeed, Hmong were very good at shooting [arrows]. This was how they had been warriors for many thousands of years, just like the Mongolians today. Otherwise, Hmong would not have been able to survive through all the wars. Based on these facts, I believe Hmong were once the warriors of Mongolia.

Other notable discourses about ethnic origins I frequently encountered include one from Mor Thao, an elderly villager outside Dao Tha, who suggested a new theory during our conversation:

> MOR: Initially, Hmong lived in the USA a long time ago and then they migrated to China after many wars. I don't know the details and who first took our ancestors to China, but after many days of darkness during the journey, Hmong finally reached the land of light. That was how Hmong ended up being in China after escaping from America, and no one knows the exact timeline of that. We suspect that our original place was Alaska in America. Once we left Alaska, everywhere was dark. In Alaska, about half of the year is dark and another half is bright, right?
>
> AUTHOR: Ah . . . I guess. . . . Have you seen people in Alaska? Do you think that they are the same ethnic people as Hmong?
>
> MOR: I am not sure. But I would say Alaska was the original Hmong country once upon a time.

Indeed, Alaska struck me as one of the last places on earth that could be considered a possible ethnic homeland of the Hmong. However, ten months later I came across the same theory during my fieldwork in California and found that several Hmong in Sacramento subscribed to it. For example, Tou Vang, a retired man in his late fifties, gave me a series of migratory destinations in Hmong diasporic history:

> According to older Hmong people, the Hmong originated in Alaska here in America, then they migrated to Mongolia, and then to China. Some old people like my father believed that by coming to America and living here now, we have returned to our original homeland. When we look at Alaskan Eskimo cultures, there are some similarities to Hmong culture. Some people believe this because of lifestyle and traditions,

such as bows and arrows and millstones when making tofu. The Eskimos also do that kind of grinding, just like Hmong.

In this sense, Hmong interviewees had multiple discursive claims about their ethnic homeland also because of temporal differences in how they conceived of their ancestral origins. Even those who believe Hmong lived in China at a certain point in their ethnic history wish to go even further back in time to search for their ultimate ethnic origins, leading to divergent theories and speculation.

The more I talked with people, the clearer it became that Hmong's discourses about their ethnic homeland are not as simple or unified as indicated by official reports or some scholarly writings (see also S. Lee 2016). Other places of ethnic origin suggested by Hmong for various reasons ranged widely from the northern border of India to Siberia, the Iranian plateau, Australia, or even Korea. Others, like Lena Thao, a representative of one of the Hmong community organizations in Sacramento, did not identify a specific country or territory as the Hmong ethnic homeland but suggested a mythical place of ancestral origin:

> In Hmong funerals, special songs are sung based on the oral history about traditional homelands that refer to the "land of snow" without naming a country of origin. The soul of the dead is asked to go back to that place with warm shoes and clothes, since it will be cold and snowy. If we think about this, China does not have many days of snow, so it must be somewhere else different from China, a place that has a lot of snow.

Neng Her, another young 1.5-generation Hmong in Sacramento who is quite knowledgeable about traditional rituals, also subscribed to a theory based on similar Hmong folklore, which refers to an abstract place as the possible homeland of ethnic origin. He said, "Based on storytelling and songs from *txiv xaiv* [pronounced *tzisai*] and *zaj tshoob* [pronounced *jachong*],[11] they say the Hmong's ancestral homeland is where the 'sun never shows up,' which some people suspect is Siberia. If you look at the pictures of Siberian people, they really look like Hmong, too." Such abstract places as "land of snow" or "where the sun never shows up" not only expand the possible geographic locations of the ethnic homeland but also leave room for varying interpretations and imaginings.

Therefore, instead of relying on official or scholarly accounts of their ethnic origins, Hmong in my study used oral traditions from funerals, religious rituals, and wedding ceremonies to speculate about their ethnic ancestry in an attempt to trace their ancient and ultimately unknown ethnic history. The distinctive nature of diasporic consciousness is based on such decentered discourses among geographically scattered ethnic groups, like Hmong, who cannot locate a definitive place of ancestral origin. In fact, I argue that such "homelandless-ness" is more emblematic of the diasporic condition than those centered on clearly territorialized homelands.

Diasporic Dispersal from China

In this sense, Hmong in both Laos and the United States in my study did not have a commonly shared diasporic history as members of a decentered diaspora without a singular ethnic homeland. The various discursive claims and dissonant viewpoints about their ethnic origins indicate that Hmong are also the product of multiple migratory dispersals. Such decentered and dissonant histories have important implications for Hmong's ongoing diasporic consciousness and subjectivities, for they produce ambivalent identifications with the multiple countries in which Hmong have resided as ethnic minorities.

While it is unclear when exactly the Hmong dispersed from southwestern China to various Southeast Asian countries and started living in Laos, scholars note that since the late sixteenth century, during the Qing dynasty, constant conflicts and wars between the expansionist Manchus (the ruling group at the time) and various ethnic groups (including Miao) resulted in their forced migration farther to the south and southwestern provinces at the frontier of China (Diamond 1988; Hostetler 2000; Jenks 1994; G. Lee 2007, 2–3). In the seventeenth century, continuing ethnic conflicts killed and displaced a large portion of the Miao group and eventually forced them to scatter to other neighboring countries in Southeast Asia (Entenmann 2005; Tapp 1998; Tapp and Lee 2004; Tapp et al. 2004). Some earlier studies of Hmong outside China suggest that the Hmong people's migratory dispersal from China and their arrival in Southeast Asia (including Laos) occurred between two hundred and four hundred years ago (Geddes 1976, 27).

Although only limited sources are available about the status of the Hmong during the French colonial presence in Laos between 1893 and 1945, there are some documents about their social activities and ethnic interactions during that time (see M. Lee 2015; Wolfson-Ford 2018). Scholars note that Hmong were both voluntary and involuntary contributors to the Lao nation-state under French colonialism and subject to taxes and civil duties imposed by the colonial regime (G. Lee 2004,

441; Tapp 1989a). Some studies mention that the Hmong fought for the French government to repel foreign invasions, such as Japanese expansion into Southeast Asia in the 1940s (McCoy 1970, 68). It is also known that Hmong assisted with the French colonial domination of Laos because they hoped to realize their dream of establishing an autonomous and independent ethnic district for themselves in Nong Het, in the northern part of the country, in return for their cooperation (Chan 1994, 8).[12] According to the Hmong families I interviewed in California, some Hmong individuals lived in the capital city of Vientiane during French colonial rule and worked as government employees, especially those with some formal education.

Further Diasporic Dispersal: The Vietnam ("Secret") War and the Predicament of Homeland

In Laos the Vietnam War caused further diasporic dispersal of the Hmong, many of whom fled the country and temporarily stayed in refugee camps in Thailand. Despite its name, the Vietnam War should be understood in broader context as part of the larger international conflict that arose from the war and spilled over to neighboring countries, especially Laos. Since the signatories of the 1962 Geneva Accords declared the neutrality of Laos and agreed to refrain from foreign military interventions, US military operations during the war had to be concealed (C. Vang 2010).[13] However, Hmong in my study commonly used the term "Vietnam War" to refer to the war in Laos, which indicates they did not believe a war that impacted them so directly should be considered covert or "secret."

Most Hmong who fled to Thai refugee camps after the Vietnam War eventually migrated to and resettled in various Western countries (including the United States, Canada, France, Australia, New Zealand, France, Germany, Argentina, and French Guiana) as refugees after screening and interviews with foreign agencies and organizations without much consideration for their previous lives. Those left behind in the camps who could not be successfully relocated in foreign countries had to return to Laos, including many Hmong villagers in Dao Tha. This more recent geographical dispersal has provided an important reason for diasporic Hmong's ambivalent relations to various nation-states and also structured their transnational connections in the diaspora.

The impact of the Vietnam War and the subsequent diasporic dispersal it caused is still present in Hmong people's everyday lives in various ways, for both those who returned to Laos after residing in Thai refugee camps (including the Hmong of Dao Tha) and their families and relatives living apart as resettled ethnic minorities in various countries outside of Southeast Asia. The Hmong residing in other Southeast Asian countries (including many of those in the northern provinces of Thailand and Vietnam) had little connection to the Vietnam War and therefore may have different historical experiences from those living in Laos and the United States. In accordance with Cold War global geopolitics, the Lao nation-state was internally divided between the Royal Lao Government (the non-Communist successor of the former Kingdom of Laos) and the Pathet Lao, which initiated the Communist regime that eventually established the current Lao People's Democratic Republic (Lao PDR) after the US withdrawal that ended the Vietnam War. Such severe national political divisions at the local level also created ethnic divisions among Hmong in Laos as well.

The majority of Hmong who initially migrated to the United States in the 1970s as refugees were known to have fought for the Lao Royal Army with the support of the US CIA against the Communist Pathet Lao under the Hmong General Vang Pao's leadership (Conboy 1995; C. Vang 2010).[14] The history of Hmong during this period has been complex and controversial, especially in terms of the motives and positions taken by different Hmong leaders and followers. According to Hmong interviewees, not only did the CIA recruit Hmong soldiers for the Lao Royal Army, but so did the coalition between the Communist Pathet Lao and North Vietnam, whose representatives went to some Hmong villages and mandated that at least one or more sons of each family should participate on their side of the conflict. In this sense, Hmong villagers in Laos were recruited and even compelled to fight for both the Communist and anti-Communist sides. As many interviewees put it, the war was remembered as "the worst thing that can ever happen in one's life that one never, ever wants to see happen again." They also said, "These tragedies occurred because of America and the Soviet Union and had nothing to do with Laos."

The Hmong who were recruited by the CIA to fight for Laos against the Communists had to flee the country after the war to avoid persecution by the new Communist Lao state and ended up in refugee camps in Thailand before they migrated to the United States and other Western countries. In contrast, other Hmong soldiers who fought for the Communist Pathet Lao remained in Laos after the war and are currently recognized by local Lao governments as war veterans. A limited number of them, including two of my interviewees in Laos, received a small military pension from the government. The historical legacy of this intra-ethnic political conflict can still be observed today in many Hmong households in the diaspora. For example, Hmong villagers in Vang Vieng had pictures of their Communist political leaders and the Vietnamese leader Ho Chi Minh at the center of their main wall at home, whereas pictures of General Vang Pao were frequently found at Hmong homes in California.

The Hmong people's historical cooperation with multiple political factions, including the French colonial administration, the Royal Lao Government (prior to the Communist regime), the Communist Pathet Lao, and the US CIA, is related to the different political motives of the Hmong leadership, including to gain independence from political domination by different ruling groups, establish a future Hmong homeland, or dream about returning to a united Laos, and so on. Because they were ultimately unsuccessful, Hmong in my study in the contemporary diaspora no longer seemed to support such efforts and commented that establishing an autonomous Hmong district in Laos (as a homeland) is not possible nor justified (see the introduction).

The internal political differences among Hmong have important implications for their current transnational relations and continuities in the diaspora. The historically constituted political divisions between Hmong who stayed in Laos and those who went to the United States as refugees have not prevented or impeded them from developing strong lateral transnational socioeconomic and cultural connections with each other across borders (see chapters 3–5). In fact, because of the diasporic dispersal after the Vietnam War, the cross-border social and cultural relations in the Hmong diaspora are not with the supposed ancestral homeland of China (which was lost after the earlier migratory dispersal) but between co-ethnic communities scattered in different countries during different phases of diasporization (e.g., between Hmong in Laos and the United States). This is the historical foundation of the transnational flow of socioeconomic capital and culture that accounts for the decentered nature of the contemporary Hmong diaspora in the absence of a coherent territorialized homeland.

Displacement and Life in Refugee Camps in Thailand

When Hmong who collaborated with the US CIA fled from Laos due to the Vietnam War, their families crossed the border from different parts of Laos, especially from the northern areas of the country, where they were most heavily affected by the war. They were then housed in different refugee camps in Thailand, where many of them remained as protracted refugees for years. In fact, some lingered there for decades before they were eventually resettled in the United States or sent back to Laos later in the mid-2000s. As a result, Thailand became another country in which Hmong resided for a significant period during their diasporic journey across borders, creating a subjectivity based on partial affiliations with the country that remain significant for some of them to this day.

Most Hmong interviewees in the United States recounted that leaving behind their homes in Laos was extremely sudden and difficult. Families could not discuss their plans to escape the country with others but had to "flee by night," abandoning their homes with considerable fear, anxiety, and uncertainty. For example, Steve Thao, a successful businessman in Sacramento, was only a child when his family escaped from Laos. Crossing the Mekong River in complete darkness, his oldest brother, who was a young soldier under General Vang Pao, was shot in his leg on the Lao side of the border. As soon as the family reached the Thai border, they urgently took the brother to a nearby hospital for treatment, but one of his legs ended up permanently unusable.

Similarly, Peng Xiong, another 1.5-generation resident in Sacramento in his forties, still vividly remembered the devastating thirty-day journey his family took to Thailand without proper directions or transportation. With no maps, Peng's family simply followed the mountain ranges in the darkness and slept in the bushes. He described a night that was particularly dreadful:

> People would whisper to parents with little kids crying in the middle of night, "You either silence your kid, or we will all be killed, because the military soldiers could hear the noise and find us." In fact, that happened to one of my little nephews. We had to feed him opium to silence him during our escape. We were able to revive and save him later, but he could have been almost killed. . . . If we hadn't done that to him, I am sure he could have been a much smarter person now. But yes, we all could have died.

Those Hmong who fled Laos ended up temporarily in a "stateless" condition in refugee camps in Thailand with uncertain futures. Under the authority of United Nations High Commissioner for Refugees, Hmong refugees were housed in several campsites in Thailand, such as Ban Vinai (the largest refugee camp), Chiang Kham, Nam Yao, and Phanat Nikhom, as well as the Buddhist temple Wat Tham Krabok.[15] Each family spent different lengths of time at these camps, depending on when they were designated for resettlement and how quickly the family decided to leave.

It is important to note that the refugee experience at Thai camps also varied and was remembered differently by individuals in both Laos and the United States.[16] For example, Xou Her, a tuk tuk driver who spent about five years at the refugee camp and then returned to Laos (instead of resettling in the United States), recalled the hardship, especially the uncomfortable living situation with limited space and freedom to move around. Life in the camp for him was very much confined, compared to his previous life in Laos:

> Life at the camp was very difficult. You could not go anywhere. Once a week, UN and Thai officers distributed food for us to eat. There was no independent house for each family. Everyone lived in the same place together. Some were relatives, but some didn't know each other at all. They [Thai officers] randomly grouped us and made us live together under the same roof. After living like that, coming back to Laos was more comfortable. It was difficult to buy a piece of land, a car, a house, or find a job after arriving here, because we had no savings.

For many Hmong resettled in the United States, the camp experience was also remembered as a time of extreme hardship and difficulty. For example, Chong Her shared his memory of suffering in the refugee camp, which eventually made him convert to Christianity as a way to survive in the face of both destitution and illness. His family moved three times to different camps within Thailand until he ended up in Ban Vinai, where he spent five years before eventually moving to the United States. Houa Lee, a retired man who resettled in Sacramento, also recalled the poverty and difficulties of survival during his refugee camp experience:

> In the camp we basically had difficulties with everything. At the very beginning of our arrival in Thailand, we had no support agencies that helped us with water or food. When our pocket money ran out, we had to beg the people at the Catholic charity groups or the monks at the temple. If that also became impossible, we had to go to Thai neighborhoods. [With their permission,] we worked for Thai people to get some money, like cultivating their lands or cleaning the weeds. If not, there was definitely nothing to eat. In that case, everyone just starved and got skinny. We also had no houses, of course. I don't know how else I can fully describe the hardship of my life in the camp.

On the other hand, there were other individual Hmong who shared positive memories, which were not simply about trauma, impoverishment, and desperation. During an interview with Chi Her, a young first-generation Hmong residing in Sacramento, spoke about differences in refugee camp life:

> Well, yes, life wasn't easy at the camps, but there was also fun. Hmong sometimes say that Soun Vinai [the largest refugee camp in Thailand] was a village of "heaven," like having festivals every day, because there were a lot of natural social gatherings. I mean, people had different experiences and memories. For some people whose parents had more money than others, the refugee camps could be a place for fun and good memories. But for other people, who had hard journeys and were poor, life in camp must have been miserable, like my uncle. I can understand that the degree of danger and hardship varies a lot, depending on the way individuals remember it.

Chi's view indeed resonates with those who made more positive remarks about their refugee experiences, especially among Hmong returnees in Laos and some Hmong in the United States who experienced the camp as young children. Young Hmong girls in their late teens in Dao Tha who spent their early childhood in Thai refugee camps recalled that they actually "enjoyed" being there because there were more opportunities for them, such as learning the Hmong alphabet with Western missionary volunteers and making pocket money by selling their embroideries.

Similarly, those Hmong in California who experienced the refugee camp as young children described their camp experiences as "fun," because they had "nothing to worry about as a kid," unlike their parents. Steve Thao, for example, who experienced a precarious border crossing at the end of the Vietnam War that severely wounded his older brother, repeatedly spoke about an enjoyable moment in the camp because of his brother:

> You know, my [oldest] brother is a good-looking man. Because of that, I was popular among many female nurses at the camp in Thailand. They were interested in my brother so [they] treated me really nicely. Whenever I was waiting in line for distribution of a meal, they would smile at me, wave their hands secretly, and call me to come see them. I got extra chocolates and candies that no other kids could get! [*laughs*]

It is possible that this seemingly "enjoyable" childhood memory has become a coping mechanism for Steve that can mitigate his traumatic refugee memories about his brother. However, Hmong I met during my research emphasized that they did have a life in the camps despite their confined refugee status. Some of them met their current spouses, dated,

Hmong Diasporic History and Multiple Homeland Narratives   61 and married in the camps, which indicated that the life of hardship and uncertainty at least briefly turned into special moments for their personal lives. Undoubtably, such positive memories did not dilute the fact that the war and subsequent refugee experience were the most traumatic part of the Hmong people's recent diasporic history.

As another country that is deeply involved in their long and dissonant history of multiple dispersal and displacement, Thailand was imbued with both positive and negative emotions as part of the diasporic consciousness of US Hmong who lived in the refugee camps. For some younger 1.5-generation Hmong, especially those born in the camps, the country is a refugee homeland of sorts to which they feel a certain level of attachment. This may be greater than any affiliation to their ethnic homeland of China, which is lost in ancient history, or even Laos, a country their parents fled as political exiles (S. Lee 2019, 225–26).

The End of Camp Life: Resettlement Abroad or Return to Laos?

Because refugee camps in Thailand could provide only temporary shelter, Hmong again confronted uncertainty about being resettled and relocated to another country (Hillmer 2010, 215–20; Long 1993), which became the final stage of their diasporic journey of further dispersal. The options they were given included resettlement as refugees in different countries, such as the United States, or a return to Laos. During the refugee screening process, Hmong were also asked for their personal information, such as name, date of birth, and village of former residence in Laos, in order to determine the extent to which they had been affiliated with anti-Communist military forces during the war. This subsequently influenced their chances of resettlement in the United States and other Western countries, as those who fought against the Communists with the CIA were given priority.

However, for many Hmong the seemingly simple questions were not easy to answer, because the way they remembered their personal information did not always meet the universal standard required by international agencies. For instance, many of them did not know their exact year of birth or age in a Western calendar–based system. Nonetheless, if Hmong refugees did not give the "right" types of answers, they were often suspected by officials of providing false accounts of their participation in the war. As a result, some of them were not allowed to leave the camps but were left behind, while other members of their families were separated and resettled in different countries.

On the other hand, there were rumors and horror stories about life in the United States that spread through the camps, which made Hmong reluctant, even to the point of resisting migration and resettlement. Stories like the following told by some of interviewees were spread and shared by many Hmong refugees in the camps: "When Hmong people were still in the camp, they watched movies and saw tall, giant Americans. They started believing that those Americans will turn Hmong into food and eat them! Hmong had a lot of fears and hesitation to leave for the US." Some elderly Hmong feared that they would be forced to give up their former tradition of polygamy and that families would be broken apart immediately after resettlement to Western countries.

Over time, the remaining Hmong who could not be resettled to other countries or refused to leave for the United States became protracted refugees and lingered in some of the Thai refugee camps for decades. This was especially the case in the Wat Tham Krabok temple, which housed the last group of Hmong refugee families. Many of them eventually moved to the United States between 2004 and 2008, joining their family members already living there. According to interviewees in Laos, those who wished to be resettled in a third alternative country (outside of the United States or Laos) were sent back against their wishes to Laos, making them feel uncertain about their future at the time.

I often had conversations with Hmong in Vang Vieng about their experience of repatriation and resettlement in the village. For example, Pao Her, a fifty-year-old resident, shared his experience of returning to Laos in the mid-1990s after spending decades at Thai refugee camps with his family and relatives:

AUTHOR: At that time in the refugee camp, you didn't want to go to America?

PAO HER: Well, I wanted to, but it was because the [resettlement] project ended. I mean, the UN did not continue to help the remaining people go to the US. They said there are no more countries that will take us, and we have to go back to our hometown in Laos. They also told us that if we go to America, everything will be very difficult. We will have to depend on the government's help, which may discontinue anytime, and we don't know the language so can't freely move around. They said we will end up being drug addicts! [*laughs*] I kept thinking about it and thought to myself, "Okay, if they still send us to America, I will go. But since the resettlement is over, well, that's okay, since I am a Lao citizen." I decided to come back to Laos.

It is also reported that Hmong families who returned to Laos often suffered from the sudden death of their babies with no explicable reason soon after repatriation. I realized that families initially did not mention children who died during their return to Laos and would only talk about them later when discussing past memories. The loss was "too painful to remember," as those parents who lost their children remarked. The Hmong residents of Dao Tha mainly consist of those who initially fled Laos after the war, lived in Thai refugee camps for decades, and then had to return to Laos because they could not (or did not wish to) be resettled in a third country. As will be discussed in the next chapter, they have continued to experience socioeconomic and ethnic marginality as minorities in rural Laos and feel they do not fully belong to the nation-state as diasporic peoples.

Refugee Arrival in the United States

Tou Lee, a Hmong man in his sixties living in a small city in Northern California located three hours away from Sacramento, recalled his arrival as a refugee in Washington, DC, in August 1978. He spoke about the temporary shelter he lived in and the difficulties he faced:

> At that time, the IRC [International Red Cross] took my family to the eighth floor of a hotel, which had just a very small room. I lived there for one month. Some days I didn't even have anything to eat. I only knew the Lao and Hmong languages, but the person who came as an interpreter was a Vietnamese. I had a lot of children, too. But I didn't know how to go to the market to buy things or how to make money. When my babies were so hungry and crying, there was no one to visit or take care of us. Oh . . . I was so frustrated! . . . About a month later, I started a job washing dishes at a big factory from sunrise to sunset. My life back then was very difficult.

Tou Lee's difficulties as a resettled refugee in the United States resonated with many other Hmong interviewees, and such historical memories of continued dislocation were ingrained in their diasporic consciousness. Hmong have been in the United States as refugees for more than four decades since their first official arrival in the country from different refugee camps in Thailand in the late 1970s. In reality, the resettlement process from Thailand to the United States took decades, because Hmong families came from multiple refugee camps at different times. Upon arrival, many of them initially gathered in Chicago and were then sent to various cities and towns depending on their sponsoring agencies, which were mostly religious and charity organizations, or the location of relatives who had already resettled in the country. Eventually, they again moved internally within the country to join family members and relatives in cities with larger Hmong communities.[17] When reflecting on the stories from the people I met and interviewed, I realized that their "true" hardship was not really over after they fled Laos and left Thai refugee camps. It continued as resettled refugees in the United States.

As illustrated in Tou Lee's story above, many of the Hmong experienced economic hardship and had difficult memories of their initial period of resettlement, which certainly did not feel like life in the "land of opportunity." When Hmong families first arrived in the United States, they were put in temporary governmental housing, and there was not enough support from those assisting with their refugee resettlement. The language barrier made overall communications difficult between Hmong families and their caretakers, which often discouraged them from explaining their needs or problems.

Sao Lee, one of the earlier Hmong refugees, who later became a well-established scholar, shared his experience of helping many Hmong families with the transition and resettlement process in American society. Soon after his arrival in the United States, he became an informal social worker for newly arrived Hmong refugee communities because of his previous role assisting foreign medical volunteer teams in a Thai refugee camp. Sao spoke about the difficult adjustment process of Hmong families to a completely new life in America in the early 1980s. As former rural peasants from Laos, they lacked basic knowledge about living in urban America. One day Sao visited a Hmong family and found out that the family did not know how to use the stove in the kitchen. Because they could not cook at all and barely ate any food for days, they got sick. On his daily visits to different houses distributing food stamps and aid items to them, he also made sure to explain and teach families that the water in the toilet is not drinkable. Even for some Hmong professionals who held reputable positions in the community because of their successful careers, their frequent stories of early hardship and struggles were not that different. Chue Yang, a public school administrator, spoke about how his family was initially rejected for government-sponsored low-income housing because they were "too poor to be qualified." He was laughing when talking about this as if it were a "fun" memory from the distant past.

Mai Lor, a program coordinator at a local Hmong community organization, also laughed about the difficult memories she had of her childhood after resettlement. In Utah, the first state where her family resettled before moving to Sacramento, Mai remembered that their lives back then were "kind of dark," because they could not go anywhere and simply stayed home. The weather was brutally cold, and they could not speak English that well. One day her parents talked about driving a car and said, "To go somewhere, we need a car. Every time I look outside, I see everyone drives. I mean, if everyone can drive, why can't we?" Her parents managed to borrow a car from her neighbor and tried to drive it right away. They almost crashed into the garage door and were barely able to stop the car. These stories of hardship resonate with many other Hmong's experiences and memories of resettlement, which were often narrated in a playful manner. Apparently, Hmong immigrants in the United States have come a long way since their early difficulties as refugees, and some of them have become economically independent and successful, especially those members of the older 1.5 generation in their forties.

Laos as a New "Ethnic Homeland": The Heart of the Recent Hmong Diaspora?

Hmong in my study who resettled as refugees in the United States (especially those of the first and older 1.5 generations) have continued to feel emotional longing for their homeland of Laos as the origin country where they were born and raised (see G. Lee 2006; S. Lee 2016). Nonetheless, as part of their consciousness as displaced, diasporic people, they also have developed ambivalent feelings and perceptions about their former homeland and sometimes feel they can never return, despite their nostalgic longings for it. Because the contemporary Hmong diaspora is also the product of a more recent dispersal from Laos after the Vietnam War, Laos is not simply the natal homeland for first- and 1.5-generation Hmong I interviewed in the United States (i.e., their country of birth) but also functions as an ethnic homeland (a country of *ethnic* origin to which they feel an emotional attachment) (see Tsuda 2009, 342).

Although Laos is one of the Southeast Asian countries in the diaspora to which Hmong initially dispersed from China centuries ago, there is now a more recent Hmong diaspora constituted by the post-1970s migratory dispersal from Laos to various Western countries as resettled refugees. For this more recent diasporic community, Laos is especially significant as an ethnic homeland of sorts, given that Hmong do not firmly identify with China as a definite country of ethnic origin. For other diasporas constituted by multiple dispersals during different historical periods, certain countries may have this dual nature as both diasporic host societies as well as homelands. In some ways, Laos was perceived as an ethnic homeland by diasporic Hmong in my study, especially among some US-born Hmong Americans who designated Laos as their "ethnic homeland" (see S. Lee 2019). As discussed earlier in this chapter, some of the older Hmong I met in the United States have a nostalgic longing for Laos as their former homeland, which they believe is a source of ethnic "authenticity" for cultural traditions that are practiced in the diaspora, such as the Hmong New Year festival (see chapter 6).

Contemporary diasporic Hmong communities in countries (such as the United States, France, Germany, Australia, and Canada) can also be centered on Laos as an ethnic homeland where their ethnic group recently originated. Nonetheless, there continues to be some ambivalence toward Laos among older Hmong in the United States. Their perceptions of this recent "ethnic homeland" were divided between those who expressed almost unconditional emotional affiliation with Laos and those who also had negative opinions, especially because of its political system and underdeveloped national economy. Even for elderly, first-generation Hmong interviewees, we cannot simply assume that Laos is the natural center for the more recent Hmong diaspora that evokes a homogeneous sense of nostalgic longing.

Some Hmong research participants in the United States had visited and stayed in Laos years after they left the country. However, many other elderly Hmong still felt they could not return to their ethnic homeland. Despite their continued nostalgic longing for the country, they were worried that the Lao government might not let them in because they had fled the country due to their anti-Communist military affiliation with the US CIA during the Vietnam War. They still had memories and images of the repressive Communist state they left behind and were worried there might be negative consequences, such as political persecution, if they return. In fact, there were negative stories about the political conditions and dangers in Laos that circulated among US Hmong communities based on fearful rumors. This disconnect between their longing for their former country/homeland and alienation from the state was further elaborated upon by, for instance, Tou Lee, a first-generation man in his sixties:

If Laos becomes a democracy tomorrow, I will return tomorrow. I miss the life of nature. This country [United States] is very rich; we all know that. But people like me, we still remember the small things in life, such as nature. For people who were initially from there [Laos], if that country becomes a democracy, I would say about 95 percent of us will want to go there. But we can't go right now. As you know, everything over there is Communist. All we can do is just talk and think about it. We can't help but just miss the life in Laos in the past.

Similarly, Sao Lee shared with me his emotional reaction when he recently traveled to Thailand and arrived at the land border between Laos and northern Thailand. It was the first time he had glimpsed Laos from the Thailand side since he fled as a refugee in 1979. Sao said "technically" he did not enter Laos because he was afraid that the Laotian immigration officer would mistake him as a former Hmong soldier who fought against the Lao Communist Party. He recounted his strong emotional affinity to his homeland:

I put one foot on the so-called land of Laos and the other foot still on Thailand, and I was crying. [*laughs*] My older brother [who accompanied him] said, "You are crazy! [for crying]." I said, "No! This is the land of my birth. But I cannot step into my country!" I wanted to go see the village where I was born, and maybe the last place that my school was in. . . . I really have a dream to return there someday before I die.

Like Tou, Sao spoke of a possible future when Laos becomes a "democratic society," allowing him to return to the country. He even pictured his life in the "true" homeland of democratized Laos and said, "With my ability and knowledge, we can contribute more to that country." In this sense, Sao's emotional connection to his homeland and nostalgic desire to return is predicated on Laos becoming a democratic society.

Although the nation and state are used interchangeably (as in "nation-state"), it is important to remember that when diasporic peoples express a nostalgic longing for their homeland, they may feel an emotional attachment to the country (as a nation) but not to the state, which they may dislike for political reasons. This is the basis for the conflicted relations that diasporas often have with their homelands. Nonetheless, during interviews in California, some Hmong noted that even if their dream of a democratic Laos comes true, a permanent return to their former homeland would still not be possible, because they have been living for such a long time in the United States as naturalized Americans and have enjoyed the benefits of life in a rich, developed country.

In fact, an expression still lingers in my mind from a focus group interview with elderly Hmong residents in Sacramento: "I still feel like I belong over *there*, even though my body is *here*." Despite their affinity to Laos as an emotional ethnic homeland of the Hmong diaspora, they were well aware of the impossibility of permanently returning to that country after such a long separation. As one of them remarked, "So I buried my *homeland* in my heart because my *home* is here." Such ambivalence and inability to fully embrace and return to the homeland is one of the important features of diasporas that face politically difficult homeland conditions. Similar examples can be found in Zlatko Skrbiš's study of Croatian residents in Australia and their refusal to return to the homeland due to their concerns about ongoing political tensions there (Skrbiš 1997, 443; see also Winland 2002). The ambivalent feelings and perceptions of US Hmong about their homeland has become an important component of their diasporic consciousness based on dislocation and exile as well as partial belongings/affiliations to multiple nation-states.

Conclusion: Being Hmong and a "People without a Country"

Undoubtedly, because of a long history of trauma and dislocation, the historical consciousness of Hmong scattered around the world is ingrained with memories of war, persecution, multiple displacements, loss of homeland, and dis/connections to the multiple nation-states where they have resided as marginalized minorities. These conditions constantly evoked a diasporic consciousness among Hmong in my study as a dislocated people who are without a "true" homeland and nation-state of their own. In this context, and given the uncertain nature of the documentary record, the purpose of tracing the Hmong people's diasporic history was to illuminate multiple (and sometimes conflicting) narratives and voices instead of subsuming them under a singular, authoritative account that can never fully capture the diversities of diasporic lives and histories. While navigating through people's varied memories and lived experiences about homelands, numerous dispersals, and refugee dislocations, one is struck by the continuous nature of survival and loss throughout the process of diasporization.

It is therefore not surprising that Hmong in my study have various theories about the location of their ethnic origins. Because of this continued uncertainty, their diaspora does not revolve around a strong affiliation to a definitive ancestral homeland. As shown in this chapter, even those Hmong who believe it is China felt an ethnic connection to

Miao in the country but did not affiliate with the Chinese nation-state. For others, their ethnic ancestry continues to be shrouded in doubt, speculation, and numerous possibilities for places of origin. Although Laos is technically an ethnic homeland for post–Vietnam War Hmong diasporic communities, including those residing in the United States, their complicated political and national concerns toward the country have rendered diasporic return difficult, if not impossible, thus compounding their sense of loss.

As a result, the dispersed Hmong diasporic communities I studied in Laos and the United States have been sustained by lateral transnational connections and cultural continuities between co-ethnics instead of ties to an original, territorialized homeland. This is the sense in which their diaspora is decentered. In addition, because it is a product of multiple migratory dispersals to numerous countries as refugees, their conscious- ness as a displaced diasporic peoples also includes complex and ulti- mately ambivalent relations to the multiple nation-states to which they have scattered throughout their diasporic history and where they cur- rently reside. This is especially the case with some US Hmong who view Thailand as a refugee homeland of sorts and regard Laos as an ethnic homeland instead of simply a country in the diaspora. Although Laos and the United States have become long-term, if not permanent, homes for Hmong, they have continued to remain ethnic minorities who partially belong in these countries. The following chapter will illustrate the cur- rent ethnic and socioeconomic status of Hmong communities in Vang Vieng and California as necessary local contexts for understanding their diasporic experiences.

2

Locating the Hmong Diaspora in Ambivalent Local Belongings

The diasporic condition can be characterized by various experiences of marginality, exclusion, and partial belonging in the countries where diasporic peoples and immigrants live as racial and ethnic minorities (see Parreñas 2001; Portes and Rumbaut 2001). Although Hmong in my study are citizens or permanent residents of the countries where they currently reside, many of them continued to feel that they were "partially" integrated into these nation-states for various socioeconomic, cultural, and historical reasons. This partial sense of national belonging also varies depending on generational status and explains how they have developed ambivalent affiliations to these countries. Diasporic peoples' marginality in respect to nation-states is an important part of the diasporic condition because it can evoke a desire to maintain cross-border affiliations and emotional attachments with co-ethnic communities dispersed elsewhere in the diaspora as an alternative source of transnational belonging.

Because there is a substantial connection between Hmong people's everyday experiences in local, national contexts and their persistent transnational diasporic consciousness, it is important to examine the specific local contexts that constantly produce feelings of marginality among them as ethnic minorities. The term "marginality" better captures both the changing levels of partial belonging and limited social mobility among Hmong in both Vang Vieng and California compared to "marginalization," which indicates greater levels of direct discrimination and constant social exclusion.

For Hmong in Dao Tha, experiences of marginality were initially based on a lack of economic opportunities in an underdeveloped national economy where they have long been economically confined to subsistence rice farming and do not have sufficient sources of income. Many Hmong families relied on unstable and irregular transnational remittances from their co-ethnics residing in the United States (see chapter 4). In addition, both their former political position against the Communist government during the Vietnam War and their cultural minority status continued to position Hmong of different generations at the margins of the Laotian nation-state to varying degrees.

Compared to the older generations, Hmong youth in Dao Tha may have become better integrated into mainstream Lao society through public education and greater economic opportunities (e.g., employment growth in the prosperous tourism economy of Vang Vieng). They have also interacted more often with people of different ethnicities at school or in the workplace. However, they continued to be subject to employment insecurity and ethnic marginality as minority workers in a rapidly changing Lao national economy while increasingly becoming vulnerable to the control of foreign capital and multinational corporations in the tourism, manufacturing, and mining industries.

In California, first-generation (and some of the older 1.5-generation) Hmong in Sacramento had trouble finding stable and well-paying jobs after their initial resettlement as refugees due to their lack of educational qualifications and language barriers. Their initial employment opportunities were limited to work in factory assembly lines and other low-skilled occupations. In addition to their persistent economic hardship, feelings of marginalization among older Hmong are also based on their emotional difficulty and distress adjusting to new lives in the United States. Many of them expressed concerns about spousal conflicts, health problems, drastic cultural differences, and the struggles of Hmong youth, all of which are inseparable from their lower socioeconomic condition in the United States as former refugees. Although some of the young 1.5-generation and US-born second-generation Hmong American interviewees had better economic opportunities and received college educations, they seemed to have experienced racialized exclusion to a greater extent at school, the workplace, and various public spaces, as well as from other minority peers because of their greater social interaction with mainstream American society.

The marginal status of the two Hmong communities examined in this chapter may be different from the partial national belonging of Hmong in other parts of Laos and the United States. It is possible that in major cities of Laos, Hmong in urban settings (especially youth) may have experienced more economic and educational integration than those in rural villages like Dao Tha. In the United States, Hmong communities in other parts of the country—for instance, in the Midwest—can be situated in a different political environment with greater social activism that demands inclusion in local and national communities. This chapter therefore ethnographically highlights two specific localities in Dao Tha and Sacramento and at the same time recognizes that they do not necessarily represent the entire Hmong community in Laos and the United States. The goal here is to demonstrate how the various living experiences of Hmong in each locality are connected to the desire for diasporic belonging beyond national boundaries.

Experiences of Marginality among Hmong in Dao Tha, Laos

The 2015 census published by the Lao government estimates that there were about 595,028 Hmong living in Laos, making them the third-largest ethnic minority group in the country and 8 percent of the national population.[1] Unlike neighboring villages that consist of only one ethnic group, Dao Tha's residents are of three different ethnic groups: Hmong (officially named "Lao Soung," which means "highlanders"), Khmu ("Lao Theung," or "upper middle-landers"), and Lao ("Lao Loum," the majority Lao ethnic group known as "lowland" residents).[2] Although official demographic data at the provincial and district level is not available except for major cities, Dao Tha's oldest residents and village leaders estimated that there were about 250–300 people living in the village.

The village was strategically established by the government in the late 1990s in order to resettle Hmong returnees from Thai refugee camps and attempt to ethnically integrate them with the Khmu and Lao Loum residents. The majority ethnic group, the Lao Loum, came to Dao Tha mainly because they were unable to live in other nearby villages, which were already occupied by older residents, while the ethnic minority Khmu villagers were forced to relocate from their mountain farmlands.[3] During my very first visit to Dao Tha, in 2003, the village was still considered new and extremely poor, compared to other Lao Loum villages that are ethnically homogeneous and were established more than thirty years ago.

Despite local government policies to enforce multiethnic housing and residential arrangements, the three ethnic groups live in adjacent but ethnically segregated communities in the same village. The majority ethnic Lao community was located closest to the main Song River, while the

Locating the Hmong Diaspora in Ambivalent Local Belongings   73

Hmong community extended into the hills across the main road. The Khmu community was located to the north, farther away from both the Lao Loum and Hmong communities. Unlike the Lao or Khmu, a good number of Hmong households were able to purchase their own rice fields but only because of financial support from their families and relatives residing in the United States. These fields were located far away from the Hmong residential community in the mountains, invisible from the main road.

The head of Dao Tha must be annually elected and rotated between the three ethnic groups in the name of "equal" political leadership and to prevent disputes over power. However, because none of the three ethnic groups in the village had wanted to live with one another, it was very difficult for the villagers to collaborate, whether for implementing new community rules or reaching a consensus for village development projects. This certainly contributed to discontent and problems among Dao Tha's multiethnic residents. Ever since my first visit to the village, many elderly residents repeatedly told me that I should be aware of the subtle ethnic tensions in the village. At times, the ethnic Lao Loum villagers continued to perceive Hmong as former anti-Communist "guerillas" from the Vietnam War and also ethnically stereotyped them in other denigrating ways.

Being Ethnic and Minority: Racialization and Cultural Stereotyping

The Hmong villagers in Dao Tha were often racialized as minority peoples and subject to cultural stereotypes. The following episode illustrates the stereotypical images that other ethnic groups had about Hmong. One chilly morning in early December during my fieldwork, I woke up feeling sick and had no appetite. I came out of my room, went inside the kitchen for some leftover steamed rice and hot water, and then sat at a large family table outside. I did not take any side dishes, sauces, soup, or cooked vegetables to eat with the rice. Kham, the distant niece of my Lao Loum host family, saw me eating and suddenly started to laugh out loud. Pointing her finger at me, she exclaimed, "Sister, you eat like Hmong!" Instead of explaining to her that this is how I used to eat at home whenever I felt under the weather, I simply responded to her in a joking manner by saying, "Yes, I eat like Hmong because I look like Hmong." Kham's brief statement felt harmless to me but also confirmed a typical and prevalent cultural racialization about Hmong based on a process in which specific cultural meanings (usually stereotypes) are ascribed to perceived racial and phenotypic differences (Omi and Winant 1986, 64).

The Hmong in Dao Tha were racially visible to a certain extent as a distinct ethnic minority. I often witnessed how non-Hmong, especially Lao Loum, made numerous remarks about the distinctive East Asian racial appearance of the Hmong. I initially thought Hmong women were ethnically differentiated by other residents based on the accessories they wore, such as silver earrings and scarfs with colorful embroidery patterns. However, when I accompanied them in Dao Tha to public areas, such as local markets, sellers and bystanders frequently referred to all of us as "Hmong girls" with no hesitation, apparently because of our supposedly similar racial features and appearance. This also indicates how the racialization of ethnic minorities is often accompanied by assumptions of cultural difference. Given what I heard about how Hmong youth were criticized for not knowing or properly speaking the national Lao language, I felt that people probably did not hesitate to single us out as "Hmong" in public, because they assumed we would not understand the language.

On another occasion, I was at the town market with two young Hmong women. A middle-aged Lao Loum man followed us and murmured to himself, "Is it because Hmong look like Chinese? *These* girls look so Asian! [meaning East Asian]." I could not help but giggle. From my outsider's point of view, everyone in Laos is supposed to be "Asian," and it was not necessary to racially differentiate between those who looked East Asian versus Southeast Asian. Indeed, local people do refer themselves as *kon Asi* (Asians) in Lao and thus pan-racially group all Laotians together regardless of ethnic differences, but only in relation to the *farang* (white) tourists from Western countries.[4]

Because Hmong apparently do not look like Lao Loum or other "typical" Southeast Asians from the perspective of other local residents, particular cultural traits and stereotypes were ascribed to them based on their "race" that appear to be different or even "strange." This includes images of Hmong as "poor" people who eat "impoverished" food, such as plain rice in hot water, as implied in Kham's comment earlier. Other cultural stereotypes were frequently based on their rituals, different language, or simply their distinctive names.

Such racialization has sometimes pressured Hmong to change their cultural practices in order to avoid possible discrimination. For example, Hmong youth in Dao Tha often told me that they no longer wear traditional ethnic clothes on a daily basis because they do not want to be "picked on and teased" by other ethnic groups as "old-fashioned rural people [*kon ba:nno:k*]." One of the youth in the village, Xou Her, further explained:

> In our real Hmong culture, we are supposed to wear traditional dress in daily life. I also have a set of daily clothes for men—simple black pants and a top. But Hmong no longer put it on every day, because we are shy in front of Lao [Loum] people. Now we only wear traditional dress and take pictures for special occasions like the New Year. . . . I know we shouldn't be ashamed, because it is our culture, but we can't do that all the time, because others will think Hmong are people from the distant past [*kon gao*].

These experiences were shared by another Hmong villager, who said "If you are the only person wearing Hmong traditional cloth, it is embarrassing! Everyone will ask, 'Oh, you wear the old traditional Hmong dress wherever you go?' They will mock you." Given that jeans were most favored and desired by all youth, the stigma of Hmong ethnic clothes may not be the only reason why Hmong youth feel discouraged to wear traditional dress on a daily basis. However, it certainly shows that they have become conscious of the negative cultural stereotypes imposed on them as a racialized ethnic minority.

There has also been increasing pressure on Hmong ethnicity and culture at the state level. It is well known that Hmong cultural practices have continuously been the target of national assimilationist projects designed to minimize and reduce ethnic differences by "unifying" (rather than "eradicating" from a state perspective) various ethnic cultures through new national regulations and policies. Although the Lao government encourages ethnic minorities to participate in national events, such as sports games, beauty contests, and national festivals, in the name of Lao national cultural "unity," it is debatable whether this attempt to foster "unity through diversity" has been a multicultural policy that promotes ethnic difference or actually results in cultural assimilation (see Ovesen 2004, 215; Pholsena 2002).

The Lao state's ethnic unification policy has affected the daily lives of Hmong, including young students from the village. For instance, I remember how surprised I was when I learned that they started to modify their Hmong last names, which are notably short and distinctive, to make them sound more like standard Lao names.[5] The students were now required to register with their newly created Laotian last name at their current school and official documents. They have done so by usually merging their first and last Hmong names as their first name and adding a new last name that is similar to a Lao name. For example, a student with the first name of Naly and the last name of Vue would use Nalyvue (first and last Hmong names combined) and adds Boupao (Lao-style name) as a last name. In addition, the government has also required that Hmong shorten their traditional New Year celebrations from at least one full week to a maximum of three days including the weekends so as not to reduce their educational and economic productivity (and their contribution to the national economy) (S. Lee 2022). The Hmong in Dao Tha have again complied, leading to an impoverishment of their public celebrations.

Jan Ovesen argues that the reason Hmong in Laos were disadvantaged despite inclusionary efforts by the Lao state to improve their status is because of their cultural and political/historical differences from the majority Lao population (1995, 14–15). However, the daily experiences of Hmong in Dao Tha in relation to mainstream Laotian society and the state constantly reaffirm that their feelings of marginalization were not simply caused by cultural differences per se but by hierarchical relations that placed the Hmong people in a relatively marginal ethnic minority status.

At the Margins of the National Economy

Not only were Hmong in Dao Tha subject to racialized stereotyping as an ethnic minority, but they also continued to suffer from considerable socioeconomic marginality and poverty in an underdeveloped national economy. As one of the few countries in the world that remain steadfast as a Communist state regime, the Lao government has relied considerably on foreign donors to support the national economy (see Case 2011, 204; Ireson and Ireson 1991; St. John 2006, 175–76). Nonetheless, the United Nations Development Program (UNDP), which is heavily involved with the domestic economic development, classified Laos as one of the forty-eight "Least Developed Countries" (LDCs) in the world until recently. In 2018 the UNDP projected that Laos may be eligible to "graduate" from the LDC status by 2024.[6] However, the most recent report, in 2020, indicates that this has become uncertain again due to the negative economic ramifications of the COVID-19 pandemic.[7]

Although the Lao national economy transitioned from agricultural subsistence to the limited development of industry and tourism, it still provided Hmong (as well as minority Khmu) in Dao Tha with limited educational and occupational opportunities and unstable socioeconomic mobility. The main source of viable income for Hmong continued to be irregular remittances from their families and relatives in the United States, which may have placed them in a somewhat better economic position than other impoverished residents, especially Khmu, who had no access to transnational financial networks and support from co-ethnics abroad. However, remittances have not been a sufficient way to build long-term and stable economic wealth for Hmong in the present or the past.

During my first visit to Dao Tha, the vast majority of the houses in the village were shacks made of wood (wild bamboo) and thatch. By 2012, homes built with sturdier wood or construction materials like cement, concrete, and bricks were primarily owned by a small group of Lao Loum families, with only about five Hmong households (who received remittances from extended family members residing in the United States) and a couple of Khmu families living in such homes. Most Hmong in Dao Tha continued to live in shacks with dirt floors or unfinished cement houses with no sanitation or running water and very limited electricity. This was true even for the limited number of Hmong households who built better homes using remittances from the United States.

Although Lao Loum families could afford and usually ordered big bottles of filtered water and had them delivered to their homes, both Khmu and Hmong villagers had only public water taps shared by multiple households. Certain Hmong households started to connect individual hoses to two of these public water taps and diverted water to large water tanks or small buckets at the back of their houses. This usually caused frequent daily water shortages for the entire community. In the past, many of the Dao Tha residents walked to the Song River in the evening to bathe, wash their clothes, and draw water for daily household use. However, because of water pollution resulting from rampant tourism and the activities of tourists, the river became no longer usable by the villagers.[8]

Transnational financial support (remittances from relatives in the United States) has been critical for Hmong communities in general, as it enabled a small number of the households to run their own businesses (e.g., as store owners at the town market or tuk tuk drivers). However, such opportunities were not readily available for most Hmong rural villagers, especially for those in Dao Tha. Many were predominantly subsistence rice farmers who grew their own food on plots of land farther away from their village homes. Because swidden (slash-and-burn) farming was banned, the size and shape of cultivable land was insufficient for the Hmong villagers. Although there was slight variation in the socioeconomic status of various Hmong households in the village, their livelihoods relied on rice farming, small vegetable gardens, and raising chickens, as well as cows (owned by about one-third of the families as communal livestock), around their houses.

Farming and tending livestock were not sufficient sources of income, as Hmong villagers usually faced a shortage of rice at the beginning of summer, forcing them to buy it on the market at fluctuating prices. A small group of Hmong mothers would occasionally go to the local market to sell their garden vegetables, such as corn, cucumbers, eggplant, squash, and lemongrass during the harvest season. However, because there was an abundance of the same type of produce during that part of the year, they usually faced considerable competition at the town market and their income was quite limited. Despite increased employment opportunities because of the advent of global tourism and mining (see below), the Hmong in Dao Tha continued to experience ethnic marginality in the labor market and the workplace as well as restrictions on their economic status and social mobility. Many elderly Hmong villagers noted that Hmong are not merely "the poor in an already poor country," but their economic condition has been hampered over the years because they have limited access to financial resources and economic capital in a national economy subject to inconsistent foreign aid, problematic development schemes, and exploitive multinational corporations and global tourism industries.[9]

The Social and Ethnic Marginality of Hmong Youth in the Local-Global Economy

In contrast to older Hmong, younger Hmong in Dao Tha had more economic opportunities in the local Lao economy to earn incomes as wage laborers instead of simply relying on remittances or rice farming. The majority of young Hmong in the village, who still did not have much education, eagerly sought low-skilled and low-status jobs at mines and factories of multinational corporations as well as in the tourism industry. Although these jobs were not necessarily highly respected, they paid much higher salaries compared to other occupations and were more economically attractive.

For instance, the monthly salary of a low-skilled daily laborer at Australian-owned mines was usually over US$120 (and upward of US$200 depending on the project), compared to salaries of only US$55/month for public school teachers at that time. In this context, many formerly unemployed Hmong youth with limited education were willing to endure the inadequate and exploitative working environment in the mines. Similarly, three young Hmong women in their early twenties had short-term work experience in the garment factories of the capital city, Vientiane, for fifteen hours per day (8 a.m. to 11 p.m.). Local staff positions in nongovernmental agencies run by foreigners offered better employment opportunities but were limited to a very small group of youth of all ethnicities, not just Hmong.

In reality, however, even these jobs did not lead to significant and sustainable upward mobility or real socioeconomic integration in mainstream Lao society. Most Hmong youth toiled on the margins of these expanding industries and were often vulnerable to the temporary, insecure, and precarious nature of their jobs. Since 2010 an Australian mining company has launched multiple satellite project sites around the Vang Vieng district and started to excavate mountains and hills that surround the villages in order to develop new mines for copper, gold, and silver. This initially seemed to create new opportunities for local workers and improve the employment rate of the young villagers in Vang Vieng, including the Hmong in Dao Tha. However, Hmong youth working at this mine soon experienced employment insecurity as well as increasing tensions with workers of different ethnicities.

The foreign owners of the mining company, who have little understanding of local ethnic relations, hired and appointed majority Lao employees as managers and directors of lower-level workers, mostly ethnic Hmong youth. Not surprisingly, many Hmong workers I spoke with complained about misunderstandings with their foreign employers resulting from mistranslation or unfair assessments given by their Lao supervisors. They also reported that contracts for Hmong workers were terminated at different sites without any notice, regardless of their work ability and diligence, because their productivity was not fairly graded and reported by their Lao managers. Such experiences of ethnic and socioeconomic marginality seemed inevitable and persisted in other jobs that were globally operated and managed by foreigners.

In fact, the Australian mining company is merely one example of the many ways that foreign corporations, which have already commandeered the Lao economy, have an adverse impact on other local Hmong villagers, perpetuating their socioeconomic marginality. For example, there were concerns about the extent to which the exploitative nature of Chinese,

Thai, Vietnamese, and other foreign multinational companies would eventually jeopardize the sustainability of the local economy. One elderly Hmong man pointed to three different types of power transmission towers that were indiscreetly built in the village mountains and said:

> You see the gigantic electricity poles on the mountain? The first one, pretty old, was built to provide limited electricity to Lao people, and the second, new one was shared by both Lao and Chinese people. The last one is so new, it doesn't even have wires yet. I heard that one will extract electrical power from Laos and then export it to China directly without benefiting Lao people.

A similar remark was made by Yer Lee, another Hmong villager in his mid-twenties, who once told me about a new cement factory in town that will produce cement not for local use but for export to China directly. Yer added that unlike the two other previous cement factories, also funded by China, the new factory brought their own migrant workers directly from China and did not hire any local townspeople. He then asked my opinion about Chinese economic domination, which has gradually deprived the lives of villagers in rural Laos: "So what do you think? Do you think China will 'eat [*gin*]' Laos in the future?"

Although a thriving global tourism economy has fully penetrated Dao Tha and Vang Vieng in general, economic disparities among the villagers have widened along ethnic lines, leaving many Hmong in a state of marginality. The most immediate (and perhaps the real) beneficiaries of tourism were the Lao Loum villagers who lived the closest to the Song River, the only place in Dao Tha where the tourists visited and spent time. They also had resources, skills, and connections to local government officials and authorities who presided over the tourism industry. As a result, all the tourist bars that completely lined the river were owned by Lao Loum. Despite the rapidly changing village and town economy of Vang Vieng, the socioeconomic status of most Hmong (as well as Khmu) villagers remained more or less the same as before, and they have not benefited that much from tourism. Unlike the Lao Loum, who quickly transitioned from peasant farmers to prosperous bar owners, none of the Hmong or Khmu residents in Dao Tha established their own bars along the river. It was a daily routine for little children in the village to swim in the river looking for dropped money and belongings from bar tourists who got drunk and unconscious after hours of drinking.

The only way Hmong (and Khmu) youth in Dao Tha could benefit from tourism was by working as employees hired by Lao Loum owners of the river bars. Some youth who could speak good English were able to get part-time jobs in tourism businesses in the town of Vang Vieng as restaurant cooks, hotel and guesthouse staff, and tour guides (see S. Lee 2023). The wages for tourism jobs were relatively high, and the only required qualification was English proficiency. Working as tourism employees was also preferred by youth because it enabled them to interact with foreigners and access tourist goods.

However, as was the case in the mining factories, Hmong youth who worked in the tourism industry were still subject to income insecurity and socioeconomic marginality, and their income gains were generally temporary. Many of the global tourists who came to Vang Vieng wanted to enjoy a wild time by drinking and dancing at the river bars with loud music, taking drugs, and eating cheap local food (including food with hallucinogenic ingredients like mushrooms). Despite such disruptive and illicit tourist activities, local government officials in the past did not intervene, as tourism was an incredibly lucrative and thriving industry for the local and national economy.

However, right before the ASEAN (Association of Southeast Asian Nations) Summit in 2016, held in Vientiane, the Lao government closed down all the tourist river bars in less than a week, apparently worried that such tourist activity would tarnish the progressive image of national development and prosperity it wished to project to international leaders. Because the Lao Loum bar owners were forced to go out of business, they had to lay off all of their minority workers. Although those who were working in tourist businesses in town did not necessarily lose their jobs, global tourists have now been deprived of one of their favorite activities (getting drunk and doing drugs at riverfront bars), and Vang Vieng may be facing a long-term decline of tourists. In addition, the 2020–2021 coronavirus pandemic caused the temporary collapse of the remaining tourism industry, which again led to an immediate loss of income for village youth employees (S. Lee 2023). Even in 2023 the post-pandemic recovery of tourism in the area remains uncertain. In this sense, Hmong villagers continue to be subject to socioeconomic precarity caused by the vicissitudes of the global economy, international politics, and the globalization of infectious disease.

In short, although more young Hmong in Dao Tha were able to pursue better economic opportunities that were created by global capital, this has not sufficiently improved their socioeconomic status or ethnic marginality to increase their sense of belonging to the Lao nation-state. There were some Hmong individuals in higher-level occupations, such as teachers, governmental officers, and post office workers; however, only a small number of interviewees had such jobs, and they also experienced economic insecurity, often expressing concerns about their unstable and low incomes. Although such occupations were valued and desired in general, they simply did not pay well (as noted above, miners were paid much more than public school teachers). Such jobs were therefore respected not because of their competitive salaries but because they required higher education and were indicators of social mobility and status.

Reaching Out to the Diaspora: Searching for Alternative Forms of Belonging

Despite being Lao citizens, the ethnic and socioeconomic marginality that Hmong in Dao Tha have experienced made them feel that they were not "full" members of the Lao nation-state. This partial sense of belonging led some of them to search for transnational forms of affiliation in the diaspora and explicitly express a simultaneous, double-sided sense of diasporic belonging. While they nationally affiliated with Laos to a certain extent, they transnationally identified with the broader diasporic community as ethnic Hmong peoples who never truly had a country of their own. A good example was Nia Her, a Dao Tha resident in his late thirties who talked about his sense of belonging and ethnic identity: "As I said, I was born and live in Laos, but I am Hmong; that will never change. Those living in England, France, or America can be the citizens of those countries, as they achieved legal citizenship/nationality [*sansat*] after they migrated. But before that, they are always ethnic [*sonpao*] Hmong who just happen to live in that country."

Nia's sense of national belonging to Laos as defined by birth and legal citizenship is qualified by his consciousness of membership in the Hmong diaspora, which is perceived as the "true" source of Hmong ethnicity. For Hmong I studied in Laos, their national affiliation was conditional and based on the fact that they remain Hmong, regardless of their citizenship and the actual countries in which they happened to live. In this way, one can reconcile the discrepancy between a sense of belonging to current territorial nation-states and a sense of deterritorialized and transnational belonging to a diasporic ethnic community dispersed in multiple countries.

In fact, Nia further made a distinction between his own individual homeland and the common homeland for the entire Hmong diaspora during our conversation:

NIA HER: I would say my homeland is here in Laos for me. [*laughs*]

AUTHOR: What about other Hmong dispersed in many different countries?

NIA HER: Well . . . there is no homeland for all of us. I was born here, but I guess for those born in America, America will be their homeland. But if I think about every Hmong in Vietnam, China, Laos, Thailand, France, I would say there is no such Hmong homeland for all together.

In another interview, Xao Lee, an elderly villager, had a similar understanding about the current diasporic condition of the Hmong and expressed his regret about the absence of a coherent ethnic homeland that can unite the diaspora and create a strong sense of ethnic solidarity among Hmong scattered in numerous countries. In fact, he became emotional and teared up when he said, "My feeling is that if you were born as Hmong, you are Hmong regardless of where you reside currently. I am very sad that Hmong have no country, so everyone has to live wherever they are."

Based on the sense of socioeconomic and ethnic marginality, Hmong in Laos have continued to feel that they still live in a diasporic state and that none of their current countries of residence can fully incorporate or accommodate their co-ethnics dispersed around the world. Inevitably, their affiliations to Laos (and other nation-states where Hmong live) remain partial and ambivalent and cannot really encompass their common diasporic, ethnic identity as Hmong. Laos is one of many "homes" for such Hmong communities dispersed in different countries to which they may feel the closest and most attached, especially since it also serves as an ethnic homeland of sorts for the contemporary, post–Vietnam War diaspora. In this regard, it is not surprising that the sense of partial national belonging among Lao Hmong in my research was shared by those I studied in California, who also had experiences of socioeconomic, racial, and cultural marginality as ethnic minorities in the United States.

Partial Belonging among Hmong in Sacramento, California

One day in November, I was visiting California State University, Sacramento, to give a presentation about my research in progress to the Hmong student association on campus. I walked to the student union building with Melau, one of the members of the group, who accompanied me as my guide that day. As we entered the building, Melau directed me to the elevator and said, "So you will first meet the board members of our association. They are on the third floor in the 'Hmong village.'" I suspected that I misheard the word "village," so I asked her, "Did you just say we are going to the Hmong *village*?" Melau laughed as if she expected my reaction and said, "Yeah, no one knows why, but we call the lounge area where we hang out the 'Hmong village.' A lot of Hmong students are there, hanging out, doing homework, or just waiting for classes."

As soon as the elevator door opened before us, more than three groups of students were sitting at tables set along the round wall in one section of an open lounge area. I glanced around this "Hmong village" located inside a modern, renovated university building. They were chatting, listening to music, browsing the internet, working on laptops, or eating their lunches while checking their cell phones. Melau said hi to one of the groups and gestured to me to join her so that she could introduce me.

"Hmong Villages" in Sacramento: Ethnic Enclaves in Urban Spaces

While I certainly had not expected to find a "Hmong village" in the middle of an urban university campus, the term aptly reflects the residential marginality and ethnic segregation that Hmong communities in Sacramento experienced. Local neighborhoods with high concentrations of Hmong often resembled both mini ethnic enclaves in American cities and Hmong villages in Laos. Certain streets, intersections, school districts, and sections of the city are heavily populated by Hmong residents and located near Hmong markets and ethnic businesses. Many Hmong in my study lived in the northern and southern parts of the city of Sacramento in predominantly nonwhite minority communities that included other Southeast Asians, Hispanics, and African Americans. Those Hmong families who have become upwardly mobile moved to Elk Grove, a newer residential community with more expensive homes south of the city.

Living in the same city and neighborhoods, Hmong families found it convenient and easy to visit and interact with each other, not only for Hmong cultural activities and large ethnic events such as New Year celebrations, weddings, and funerals, but also for American holidays and small gatherings. As a result, many Hmong in Sacramento were able to live spatially and ethnically together (like villagers) despite being urban residents. However, this can also indicate their relative marginal status and lack of ethnic integration in the cities where they live.

As illustrated in the previous chapter, since their arrival as refugees, many first-generation Hmong in Sacramento have experienced economic hardship, racialization and discrimination, and various social problems, even though they have greater material affluence and economic resources when compared to their previous lives in Laos. Although younger Hmong Americans of the 1.5 and second generations are generally known to be more socioeconomically integrated, a certain amount of socioeconomic, cultural, and racial marginality persisted for those in my research. Despite their legal status as citizens or permanent residents in the United States, their sense of partial belonging has continued across the generations and discouraged some of them from fully affiliating with their country.

Socioeconomic Marginality and Health Problems among First- and 1.5-Generation Hmong Immigrants

In general, Hmong's low socioeconomic status and level of education in the United States have long been a major concern of scholars as well as community leaders and members (Chan 1994; Hein 1993; Y. Xiong 2013; Zucker 1983). According to an analysis of the US Census published by the Hmong National Development organization, the overall poverty rate among Hmong in the United States was estimated at 25 percent in 2010, which was considerably higher than the 11 percent poverty rate for the overall US population that year. The poverty rate of Hmong in California was 31 percent compared to the overall rate of 11 percent for the state.[10]

After they arrived as refugees, first-generation Hmong in my study were not able to continue or start their educations. As most of them were older and at least in their twenties upon their arrival, they missed the chance to enroll in schools simply because of their age or family obligations, whereas their younger 1.5-generation siblings took ESL classes before they became eligible for low-skilled jobs or could pursue further education. The current level of educational attainment among Hmong has been considerably lower than other immigrants, especially in terms of higher education, despite gender differences.[11] For example, in 2017 only 14 percent of Hmong had a bachelor's degree compared to 30 percent of other Asian groups and 19 percent of Americans in general.[12] As noted in the introduction to this book, most of the elderly Hmong immigrants in my study did not have any substantial education, never held stable jobs in the United States, and had been supported by government welfare programs. Half of my working-age interviewees had less-skilled jobs or were unemployed.

Hmong of the 1.5 generation who were born abroad and migrated to the United States as children or youth generally had higher socioeconomic status and were in their late thirties to early fifties, except for younger college students. However, there was considerable disparity in terms of their socioeconomic status. Some of them held professional jobs and were working as insurance or real estate agents, teachers, health-care employees, or social workers. In contrast, the income level of 1.5-generation working-class Hmong was often barely above the poverty line. This reality was very clearly addressed by Chi Her, a 1.5-generation Hmong who has been working on a factory assembly line for the past decade:

> Oh, life in America is very difficult! Everything is under government economic control in terms of the household. . . . It's like we are getting poorer, especially for those people who have less education. If you are really poor, you might get a little help. Otherwise, you can be super rich so that you aren't affected, even if there are many things to pay for. But it's very difficult for those people in the middle, who aren't the poorest but are far from being well-off either.

Economic hardship is not limited to poor families with low incomes; it can also be pervasive among other community members of higher socioeconomic status. As one interviewee put it, many of them are "not poor enough to qualify for social welfare and government support, but they definitely do not have enough to fully support themselves." Although first- and 1.5-generation Hmong families who consider themselves "middle class" may be better off relative to other households, they felt they were also in a somewhat precarious economic situation, which resembles the concerns of the lower-middle-class Hmong.

A good example is Shoua Yang, a 1.5-generation woman in her forties who has been working as a nurse at a county hospital and described her own family as a "typical" American middle-class household in a new suburban area of Sacramento away from segregated Hmong communities. Unlike other Hmong families in my study that have multiple children, Shoua has only two children, both in high school. When she started talking about her daughter, who was about to go to college that year, Shoua inadvertently said, "In this country, even if you are middle-class, life is very difficult." She was concerned about her daughter's college tuition and expenses, which the family could not afford, therefore limiting her daughter's educational choices. It was very clear that because middle-class Hmong families do not qualify for financial aid, the educational future of their children is not simply determined by their academic performance or aspirations but rather constrained by the limited economic means of their parents.

Through my repeated visits to the same Hmong community in Sacramento since 2008, I observed people's worsening economic condition over the years, especially during the Great Recession. Many Hmong women who had multiple part-time jobs to take care of their family were laid off. Men who used to work at assembly plants, food processing factories, or in other types of manual labor lost their jobs due to the rapid economic downturn. Some of those who were still employed in these companies continued to work from as early as four in the morning to the late afternoon and were barely paid a minimum wage (less than twenty-five hundred dollars a month).

Many families also lost their homes during the housing market crisis because they could not continue to make their mortgage payments. Both elderly and unemployed Hmong asserted that their life did not seem possible without social welfare assistance, such as Supplemental Security Income and other government financial aid programs, which had also been reduced because of government budget cuts. In this sense, despite internal class differences, many first-generation Hmong and their families have continued to suffer from relative levels of socioeconomic marginality.

Such economic struggles coexist with persistent social and psychological problems faced by US Hmong communities, including those in Sacramento. Their traumatic memories and difficult experiences of war, displacement, and refugee resettlement have had lingering effects on their family lives. Mia Vang, a 1.5-generation mental health therapist at a local hospital in Sacramento, summarized and explained the general social distress found among many older Hmong immigrants based on her observations:

> My patients are kind of middle-age, like my parents. Because of their social struggles of adjustment, language difficulties, and differences in cultural acculturation with their kids, we are not just dealing with mental illness but with all these factors. I feel like it's more difficult than the general population, which is able to get more support. Knowing that I am Hmong, my patients tell me everything: parenting issues, spouses, these all can play into depression. It seems like their treatment is slower, because there are so many important . . . environmental and social factors that affect their mental health.

In addition to mental health issues, the deteriorating physical health of elderly Hmong has also been identified as a major community concern, including in scholarly studies and government-funded research. During my fieldwork, elderly Hmong complained that they frequently suffered from noncommunicable diseases like diabetes, heart attacks, and high blood pressure. Obesity is also reported as a growing concern in the local Hmong community across generations (see Mulasi-Pokhriyal and Smith 2011). Meeting people with such health conditions and their families, I realized that they call their symptoms "American diseases," which they believe were never found among the Hmong in Laos.

Mor Lee, a retired first-generation man in his sixties, expressed his concerns specifically about the dietary and health environment of the United States. He said, "If I can live as I wish, living in Laos would be better. Nature there is just the same as when I was born. I am used to that environment. Food here is not natural/organic at all. You have to put it in a freezer and it is full of chemicals. It's not natural food. Like fruits in this country, there are not a lot compared to Thailand or Laos. Nothing is fresh here." Similarly, elderly first-generation Hmong who spoke about health problems attributed them to the particular lifestyles and environment in the United States, which they characterized as "no exercise because of lack of physical labor, too much artificial food, and too much stress," in contrast to their previous lives in Laos.

This does not mean that elderly Hmong feel much more affinity with Laos and indiscriminately think of the country as "better" (see chapter 7). However, the health difficulties that Hmong have *currently* experienced in the United States made them nostalgically long for a *past* life in their ethnic homeland of Laos. In fact, according to recent research, some elderly Hmong in the United States reach out to their homeland of Laos to seek traditional forms of medical treatment for difficult health conditions and to alleviate a sense of displacement they have experienced with their lives (see Thao and Bochaton 2022; Schein and Vang 2021). Others seek shamans in Laos for spiritual/religious and medical healing through transnational interactions between the two countries (see chapter 5).

Family and Social Problems: Perceptions of Cultural Crisis in America and Public Hypervisibility

In addition to socioeconomic marginality and health problems, many local Hmong families also struggle with difficult familial relationships, domestic violence, and social problems particularly related to gangs, drugs, and crime in the community. Elderly Hmong frequently expressed emotional distress about such problems and attributed them to the loss of what they believe to be their "traditional" cultural values. They engaged in essentialized discourses and self-criticism about how "Hmongness" ("what Hmong should be like") is threatened by the negative social environment of the United States. As a result, some of them have developed a sense of diasporic longing for a life in the past when they were "free" of such problems and were more "peaceful" and "more Hmong-like" (see G. Lee 2007).

For instance, Steve Thao, a 1.5-generation Hmong in his mid-forties, talked about difficult marital relationships as a community problem, which he believes is a product of an American culture that values excessive freedom: "Mid-age marital life crisis is also an issue. Spouses again claim freedom and say, 'Hey, you know what—if I am not happy with you, you are free to leave me and I am free to leave you. And I am not willing to work something out.' That's a social trend found in the Hmong community here and the reason why the divorce rate is going up fast." Ultimately, Steve emphasized that such social problems are a result of the American living environment that makes Hmong behave in ways that are contrary to what he believes to be their supposedly "traditional" culture and values. He continued:

> Hmong people are really "against" divorce. They will do anything to try to work out their problems and keep the relationship and marriage together. But because they exercise too much freedom here in the US, they don't go to the Hmong elders to consult and resolve the problems anymore. A few people might go to the Hmong elders, but the couples won't accept their cultural mediation during family meetings. I don't want to be negative about it, but that's the truth.

As part of familial concerns, the issue of marriage and divorce between spouses naturally connected to problems about Hmong youth. When I asked about it during my interview with Steve, he reacted by saying, "Okay, you want to talk about the most challenging things here," and observed, "The young kids, when they abuse the word 'freedom,' they can get into a lot of trouble. Not being in school, not getting good grades, getting in trouble with the law." This issue was also commonly identified during interviews with first-generation Hmong parents and grandparents and in surveys I conducted with young 1.5- and second-generation Hmong college students.

Some first-generation Hmong also believed that the American social environment has exacerbated parent-child relationships. Moua Xiong, an elderly man in his seventies, for example, was particularly concerned about US-born second-generation Hmong Americans:

For people like me who were born in Laos and came to the US at an older age, life [with children] is not that difficult. Only my youngest daughter was born here. But when I look at other families who have more than two or three children born here, they have so much difficulty. My kids [who were born in Laos], they respect and listen to us. When we taught them, "You don't steal other people's belongings, you don't do this or that," they will listen and not do such bad things. But oh, right now, the young children in the US, we all have such headaches! Look around the neighborhood here and Hmong families. They are not my real children, but they still worry me a lot.

Moua then compared Hmong lives in Laos and the United States: "[In terms of] the economic standard of living, I would say it is about seventy percent better in America [than Laos]. But the problems of youth are a much bigger issue here. Social problems like crime are much worse in America than Laos."

Other elderly Hmong and parents of Moua's age similarly attributed social problems among Hmong American youth to generational tensions and the greater difficulty that parents face raising and controlling their children in the United States. For instance, Mor Lee, another first-generation Hmong in his sixties, became disillusioned with the American social system, which supposedly protects the rights of children but, ironically, denies parents their right to engage in traditional and strict childrearing practices. Mor said, "In Laos, when the children do not listen to their parents, they can teach or correct their children. But here, you cannot say anything. If you do something to the children, they will tell their teachers and cause problems. You know, democracy gives you many rights in this country, but not for the parents. I don't like it."

As my fieldwork progressed, it became clear to me that gang activity among youth has been one of the common concerns shared by local Hmong communities. When visiting different families in Sacramento and other cities in California, I often looked closely at the family photos hung on the walls in living rooms. During one such visit, I unknowingly pointed to the youngest boy in a family photo and realized that I had never seen him or been introduced to him by the interviewee, Seng Her, the eldest daughter of the family. I casually asked her, "Who is he?" She paused and answered in a low voice, "My youngest brother. He is locked up [in prison]. He used to be the smartest, most beautiful one in our family."

I came across a good number of families with a child who was either a gang member or the victim of criminal behavior. Initially, Hmong parents never explicitly mentioned or introduced children who were

Locating the Hmong Diaspora in Ambivalent Local Belongings 91 involved in criminality or in jail. Other family members secretly noted that these parents could not include the children in their conversations, because "they loved the children deeply in their heart and therefore had to disown them." Later on, the parents expressed their disheartening emotional disappointment and sadness about the criminal acts of their children or Hmong youth with troubled lives.

In fact, parents of children who were criminal offenders or victims of rival gang conflicts were subject to considerable trauma. While some parents suffered from the metaphorical loss of their loved ones (to gang activity or imprisonment), others had actually lost children who had been tragically killed by gang activity. Hmong elders and parents wondered why gangs have become a serious problem in the Hmong community and suspected that it is because they live in "America," a country that does not "allow them to maintain 'real' Hmong culture" or "the way they used to be in their former [natal/ethnic] homeland" of Laos.

It is important to note that such concerns interviewees had about Hmong youth should be carefully differentiated from how these problems have been portrayed by the American public and the mass media. While issues like gang involvement and criminal activities discussed here were fully recognized by members of the Hmong communities I studied, what troubled them was the American social and cultural context in which they had been placed (which they believed caused difficult family relations and exposed youth to negative social pressures). The discussions about "failing" Hmong youth were not intended to directly blame youth themselves as fully responsible for such problems. They were rather frustrated about how such internal community struggles are uncritically portrayed by the public as "Hmong cultural problems" based on overgeneralizations.

Hmong communities have been grappling with the frequent criminalization of Hmong male youth at school, in their neighborhoods, and among the general public (e.g., see S. J. Lee 2002; Lo 2018; Vue, Schein and Vang 2016), which is often subject to misrepresentation by the mainstream media and popular culture, especially in the 2008 Hollywood movie *Gran Torino* (Eastwood 2008; see Schein et al. 2012).[13] Scholars have analyzed public discourses and cultural representations about Hmong gangs as a racialized project that portrays minorities like Hmong as inherently violent in order to (re)produce and restore (heteronormative) white masculinity as well as racial hierarchies (Schein 2007). This can be related to public understandings of homosexuality among Hmong, which indicates how hegemonic norms of hyper-heterosexuality in the United States have racialized and demonized Hmong as a "deviant" subject (Pha 2017).[14]

Although Hmong in general suffer from a certain level of social invisibility in American society, such negative "hypervisibility" (Schein and Thoj 2008) based on criminalization and racialization can be equally problematic, leading to racial profiling and police brutality against them in ways that deem the Hmong American community as perpetually incorrigible.[15] This was illustrated by critical responses from Hmong interviewees about *Gran Torino*. In the movie, "a lot of things were really disappointing," according to Chia Xiong, a Sacramento resident in her early thirties. She noted, "That's what they try to do [portray Hmong], but they got the Hmong people wrong. It's really not me." For Xou Her, a college student, the movie intentionally selected gangs to represent troubled Hmong masculinity and "kind of tuned it up and overdid it for the audience." Having "kind of mixed emotions" about the movie, Xou said, "It's good that Hmong are exposed to the public [audience], but at the same [time], they didn't do it correctly."

Lor Vang, another college student, was bothered not only by the movie itself but also by its impact on the members of the Hmong community who are made publicly visible through racialized and sexualized misrepresentations. Lor critically noted:

> You know, I hate it when other people ask about this, and some ignorant Hmong youth say, "Oh you don't know who Hmong are? Go watch *Gran Torino*!" That really bothers me! That doesn't make sense. A lot of Hmong youth, they don't know what to follow in terms of Hmong identity. So sometimes they refer to movies, other histories, something that other people do with very generalized ideas. But that generalization from the movie is so biased. It stereotypes us. I don't want that.

In sum, such negative public images of Hmong customs and supposed criminality contribute to experiences of ethnic marginality that produce an ambivalent sense of national and social belonging among Hmong I interviewed. In fact, some older Hmong constantly dream of a life outside the United States (namely, back in their homeland of Laos) or some unidentified (diasporic) "third place" outside the nation-state where they can freely practice their ethnic culture without public pressure. Such romanticized desires are part of the diasporic condition based on a yearning for an alternative place and time.

Continued Socioeconomic and Ethnic Marginality among Young 1.5- and Second-Generation Hmong Americans

Despite their generally greater level of social integration in mainstream American society, young 1.5- and second-generation Hmong I studied described how they have continued to be subject to socioeconomic and racialized, ethnic marginality, making them feel like partial citizens who do not fully belong to the nation-state. Compared to first-generation Hmong, 1.5- and US-born second-generation youth are known to be more culturally assimilated and better educated, which can lead to higher socioeconomic and occupational status. The young Hmong Americans in my research had finished high school, and many of them were also attending local colleges and universities. However, they were not the "norm" and are different from other Hmong youth, especially those who experience low educational achievement or get involved in gangs and are in danger of joining the American underclass. In this context, the common struggles and problems faced by young Hmong were the central topic of my interviews and conversations with them.

In addition, 1.5- and second-generation Hmong may be exposed to greater ethnic discrimination, racialization, and ethnic prejudice in their daily lives compared to older, first-generation Hmong immigrants, who tend to live more ethnically segregated lives. This sense of ethnic marginality is related to the Hmong community's decades-long struggle against their social invisibility and lack of recognition in their own American "home." In addition, they do not have control over which aspects of the Hmong community are selected and made visible by the public in generalized ways to represent them (such as criminality and socially disapproved cultural practices).

On various occasions, young Hmong spoke to me about how they were bothered because relatively few Americans know about the Hmong in general. For example, Lor Vang, a senior in college, gave me a detailed story about his experience of racialization and invisibility:

> I was waiting at the light rail station and there was a guy who kept looking at me and asked whether I am Chinese. I said no. Then he went through other Asian groups, like Japanese, Korean, Vietnamese, to find out who I am. I said, "I'm Hmong," and he looked confused. He asked right away, "What is that?" I was like, "Okay, where should I start?" So if I usually start with how my parents were initially from Laos, then people respond right away, "Oh, so you are Laotian." Well . . . not really . . . long time ago, Hmong people lived and came from

China. Then they go, "Oh, then, you guys are Chinese!" Oh, well, I have no idea what to say!

The lack of visibility about Hmong in American society was an ongoing issue, even to a thirteen-year-old boy such as Ryan Thao. One day, a couple of Ryan's friends at school asked him, "What is Hmong?" Because he could not give a succinct definition, he and his friends decided to go online to search for information about Hmong. Instead of "Hmong," his friend typed "monk" in the web search engine. Ryan stopped his friends and said, "What are you typing there? I am not a monk!" He added that his friends teased him about how an ethnic group called "Hmong" sounds "stupid."

Many other 1.5- and second-generation Hmong youth I spoke with had similar daily encounters associated with their marginalized racial and ethnic minority status that was caused by the lack of knowledge among mainstream Americans about Hmong, even though they are the ninth-largest Asian group in the United States, with a population of 299,000.[16] Despite being racialized as "Asians," my young interviewees have felt that they are still not known among ordinary Americans. Some of them believe they lack social and political visibility in America partly because there is no recognizable homeland called "Hmong" that can anchor their ethnic identity, unlike other Asian Americans.

For Hmong youth who learn about US history at school or those who study it for their citizenship tests, the erasure of the historical contribution of their own ethnic group seems to be particularly perplexing. According to them, the history of the United States, which is supposed to be about *all* Americans, neglects the critical contributions of their parents and grandparents during the Vietnam War. Indeed, Hmong in my study did not simply think of themselves as one of many immigrant minorities that happened to reside in the United States. They considered themselves a "special" group, who sacrificed themselves for the American nation and were exiled from their natal homeland as a result. Lily Moua, a US-born college student, spoke about this historical marginalization of Hmong from her country's national history:

> You know, in history classes, they [books] talk about Russia, America, and all other countries but almost always avoid Laos. I always wondered why they don't teach about those Southeast Asian countries like Laos. Even if they talk about the Vietnam War, they never really talk about Hmong and how we contributed. I've always wondered why they do not teach that.

Sai Lee, another second-generation college student who complained about the ethnic invisibility of Hmong, said, "It sucks in high school, you learn histories about all other races, but we never see anything about Hmong."[17] Another young interviewee talked about how this absence of Hmong from American history is perplexing. "It is true that for other immigrants, they came to the US because they told themselves, 'I need to work hard to make myself better,'" she noted. "But we came to America because Americans first came to the Hmong [in Laos] and kind of disrupted and destroyed our lives."

Many of the ethnic struggles that young Hmong participants in my study experienced are related to this historical exclusion that produces subtle, racialized microaggressions rather than explicit discrimination or blunt racism. This is perhaps why some elderly and young Hmong said they did not have "harsh" feelings about their ethnic minority experiences and felt like they could "deal with it" or "ignore it." However, at the same time, they continued to articulate these concerns and problems they experienced in their daily lives as members of an apparently "forgotten" ethnic minority group. Indeed, ethnic marginality is not always based on overt processes of oppression or discrimination of minorities by the majority group but can also be caused by the deliberate exclusion of these groups from a country's national history and nation-building projects (see Eriksen [1993] 2002; Jonsson 2001, 2005). In this sense, the process of marginalization from the nation-state has as much to do with historical amnesia as it does with explicit ethnic discrimination.

In addition, prejudice from other ethnic minorities in their neighborhoods has also become a critical issue that 1.5- and second-generation Hmong American youth have confronted in terms of interethnic dating and marriage. For instance, the oldest son of one interviewee had long been dating a Vietnamese American girlfriend but faced uncertainty about the future because of her family's serious objection about his Hmong ethnicity, which continued for years. Likewise, Tony Cha, a college student, also shared with me his difficulties in his romantic relationship with his Filipino girlfriend and attributed it to ethnic prejudice against Hmong:

> When my girlfriend first brought me to her dad, he was saying to her in front of me, "If you date a Hmong guy, you are going to suffer. A lot of Hmong guys, they tend to simply use girls." I was like, I'm trying to get away from that stereotype about Hmong men using girls. Throughout my life, if I date a girl, I will try to be loyal to that one girl. I guess her father thought that if she dates a Hmong guy, she would just be heartbroken.

As these examples illustrate, the discriminatory experiences of Hmong youth not only come from mainstream society but often originate from other equally marginalized, ethnic minorities, such as other Southeast Asian and African Americans (see Hein 1995). According to college student Sai Lee, "Growing up in Stockton, I guess everybody didn't like Hmong people. Even other Asians didn't like us. There were a lot of Cambodians in Stockton, and they always picked on Hmong people, and then Vietnamese picked on us, and African Americans did that, too." Ironically, the government assistance that Hmong in Sacramento received as former refugees led some African Americans and other Southeast Asians to develop negative perceptions of them as competitors for social welfare and limited job opportunities. Such ethnic tensions with other people of color exacerbates their relative alienation in the United States and reminds them of their continued ethnic minority status at the margins of the nation-state.

Conclusion: Transnational Diasporic Belonging beyond "Partial" Homes

In sum, historical and cultural exclusion, socioeconomic struggles, and tensions with other minority groups have contributed to a sense of racial and ethnic marginality among Hmong in my study across the generations. Despite better educational opportunities and socioeconomic and cultural integration, their national membership was often questioned in ordinary interpersonal interactions, evoking a sense of ambivalent national belonging. However, it is an open question how much the marginal status of Hmong in each locality discussed in this chapter is representative of Hmong communities elsewhere. Even if their socioeconomic and ethnic positioning may be somewhat similar, such experiences may not always have the same outcomes and therefore lead to partial detachment and incomplete affiliations with nation-states.

For instance, in his study about Hmong American political movements, Yang Sao Xiong (2022) analyzes how Hmong's commonly shared marginality can actually motivate them to politically mobilize through a collective voice and agency. In fact, Hmong American communities located in other parts of the United States, especially in the Midwestern states of Minnesota and Wisconsin, seem to have been more active in terms of civic engagement and the exercise of political power (e.g., Wong 2017). As they are among the largest Asian American groups in some of these communities, their demands for rights and social inclusion can become a different form of political belonging. Lori Lopez's (2021) recent research on Hmong American "micro" ethnic media shows how they were able to use various media platforms, which can challenge their marginality in mainstream media.

Unfortunately, there has been a lack of research that focuses on Hmong livelihoods and their local ethnic experiences in other regions of Laos. Without further empirical studies, it is hard to assess the extent to which Hmong's experiences of ethnic marginality vary across the country. It is possible that there are growing internal differences among Hmong living in rural regions versus urban areas as well as those in the northern part of Laos, known to be heavily populated by Hmong. Unlike the case of Dao Tha, Oliver Tappe's (2011) study of a multiethnic community in Houaphan province, northern Laos, seems to indicate that the tourism economy made a more positive and beneficial impact on Hmong life. Moreover, it seems that some Hmong communities in different regions of Laos were able to utilize their social networks based on kinship for the development of transportation and infrastructure and to pursue socioeconomic mobility through agricultural businesses (e.g., rubber plantations) (see Baird and Vue 2017).

However, certain aspects of the ethnic marginality of Hmong discussed in this chapter are not necessarily unique to those living in Dao Tha but can be found in other parts of Laos (e.g., see Pholsena 2020 about multiethnic relations in southern Laos). Because the Lao nation-state has continuously prioritized economic development through its projects and programs, it has not only relocated ethnic minorities from the highlands but also resettled Lao Loum people in newly and strategically created villages (see High 2009, 2021). Hmong who live in such villages, regardless of whether they are homogeneous or multiethnic communities like Dao Tha, may experience similar economic constraints as well as (precarious) opportunities provided by the government-led development of global tourism and foreign investment by multinationals engaged in resource extraction.

It is therefore important to understand that ethnic marginality is one of many possible reasons why Hmong seek alternative forms of belonging beyond national boundaries and that such marginality can also instigate commitments to localized places as well. Although not all diasporic Hmong are situated in a state of marginality in their host nation-states in the same way, it has been difficult for Hmong I studied in Dao Tha and Sacramento to fully develop a sense of national belonging to their respective countries. Such sentiments of ambivalent and partial belonging to the nation-state are an important indication of their continuing socioeconomic, cultural, and historical exclusion in Laos and the United States. This further explains why Hmong I met still considered themselves to be a "people without a country": not only do they lack strong affiliations to a definitive country of ancestral origin; they also find it difficult to feel fully integrated into their current countries of residence.

This is an important part of the diasporic condition that encourages Hmong in my study to reach out to the diaspora and maintain transnational socioeconomic relationships and cultural affiliations with dispersed, co-ethnic Hmong elsewhere. In this sense, the next three chapters will explore how transnational social relations based on kinship and familial economies and cultural continuities in shamanism and spiritual rituals are sustained among the two Hmong diasporic communities in Laos and the United States. Such cross-border social interactions and shared cultural practices create a sense of co-ethnic belonging across national borders that is an integral part of diasporic identity.

PART II

Transnational Ethnic and Cultural Continuity

3

An "Imagined" Community
of Transnational Kin

Hmong Kinship Continuities
in the Diaspora

On a cloudy and humid day during my fieldwork in Laos, I was returning to Dao Tha from the town of Vang Vieng.[1] From a short distance, I recognized a Hmong man walking toward me who had arrived the day before at the farm guesthouse where I was living. He approached me and asked in the Hmong language, "Are you Hmong?" I replied in Hmong, "No, I am not Hmong." We both laughed.

The man's name was Moua Cha, a Hmong originally from Laos who had resettled in France after the Vietnam War. He was visiting and traveling around Laos by himself but was disappointed that the town had changed so much because of the tourist activities, and he could no longer deal with the noise from the bars along the river. As a result, Moua decided to leave the guesthouse that day and stay with his relatives in the village farther away from the river. Since I had come to know every Hmong family in Dao Tha by that time, I asked, "Who are your relatives?"

Moua replied, "I don't know yet, because I have never met them. But I found out where their house is."

"Didn't you just say that you will be staying with your relatives?"

"Yes, they are my relatives," he said.

Because he sounded so certain and firm, I had to inquire further. "But you never met them before and don't know who they are at all?"

"No, I don't. But I know they are my relatives for sure, because their last name is also 'Cha,' same as mine."

At first I thought Moua was joking, because I could not understand why Hmong with the same last name would be considered relatives, as they were not biological kin but complete strangers who had not even known about each other. It was not unusual to see Hmong families in Dao Tha host guests (including distant relatives) from outside town, but I had never heard of anyone there who had family and relatives in France. The next morning, I decided to visit one of the Cha family houses that I knew in the village to see if Moua had really found his "relatives" and was able to stay with them. Soon I ran into Chou, the father of the Cha family, who was sitting outside in a circle with Moua and introduced him to me by saying, "This is my brother from France." His son Yia added that the whole family was very happy to meet his "uncle from France" for the first time, so they shared food with Moua and allowed him to sleep at their house.

I initially found it hard to believe that the Cha family would extend familial hospitality to a stranger from France on the basis of their same last name, which simply indicates they are members of the same Hmong clan. One might wonder whether the Cha family in Laos was willing to be more hospitable toward visitors like Moua who are from rich foreign countries because of the expectation of reciprocal return, such as possible financial help in the future. However, as I repeatedly observed and heard about more cases of similar clan hospitality, I realized that such expectations of future economic or social reward were not always the case. Hmong I met in Laos hosted "strangers" with the same clan name from China as if they were family, and Hmong in California have done the same for Hmong from all over the world as well (see also Schein and Vang 2021).

* * *

On the first day of the annual Hmong New Year festival in Sacramento that started in late November, I attended the event with Sao Lee and his wife, Joua, whom I grew to know quite well during my fieldwork. I dressed up in a pink traditional Hmong New Year outfit that Joua lent me from her daughter. As a special event that year, the New Year Organizing Committee created banners for the eighteen Hmong clan surnames, which visitors could pick up and take photos with in front of a large model of a qeej installed at the main entrance gate. The assistant at the site asked for our surname, handed us the banner that said "Hmong Lee," and directed us toward the gate.

As we waited in line for our photo to be taken, Sao turned to me and jokingly said, "You are technically Hmong Lee!"[2] He was referring to my Korean last name, which is pronounced and spelled in English in the same way as his family's last name. His humorous comment made me

Posing with the Hmong "Lee" clan banner at the Hmong New Year festival in Sacramento.

laugh but also helped alleviate my slight unease about pretending to be a member of the Hmong Lee clan simply because I have the same last name. No one pointed out that as I am not Hmong, I should not hold the banner of the Lee clan.

Kinship as a Diasporic Hegemony

What makes Hmong clan kinship, based on a surname system, so dominant and inclusive that it allows Hmong to accept complete strangers as family? And what makes them willing to jokingly pretend that clan affiliation and hospitality can be extended to a non-Hmong like myself because of our similar-sounding last name? Because Hmong in my study felt they are ethnically and socioeconomically marginalized and do not fully belong to the countries in which they reside, they have sought communal affiliation across national borders with diasporic Hmong living in other countries. Since they lack a definite territorial ethnic homeland as a centralizing and unifying force in the diaspora, lateral transnational social relations based on extensive kinship networks between dispersed Hmong communities have become the key factor that keeps their diasporic community together.

Although Hmong have endured centuries of dislocation and migratory dispersal, the fundamental principles of their kinship system have persisted over time in the two communities I studied and have become a pervasive and entrenched part of their diasporic identity. As a prominent example of transnational continuity, kinship not only consists of both cultural beliefs and principles that structure how they interact with clan members (as well as marry) but also constitutes social/kin relationships across borders that sustain these cultural practices. In this chapter I will examine how Hmong I studied in both Laos and the United States have adhered to three main fundamental kinship rules that they perceive to be the core of their diasporic community: (1) clan hospitality (the cordial treatment of clan members of the same last name, as if they were family), (2) clan exogamy, and (3) ethnic endogamy. The transnational persistence and continuity of these kinship rules is based not only on immediate biological kin and genealogical ties but also on an extensive clan system, which is represented by eighteen Hmong surnames. Hmong clanship generates a socially constructed sense of familial affinity that has become an important source of transnational continuity in the diaspora. In fact, it was seen by Hmong in my study as a critical aspect of "being Hmong" that produces a sense of belonging to and identification with the broader diasporic community across national borders.

The extent to which members of the Hmong diaspora in my study conformed to these kinship principles across national borders is certainly remarkable. It was quite pervasive among men and women and members of the older and younger generations in both countries. Hmong Christians in California whom I interviewed for my research also strictly adhered to the kinship system, despite their reluctance to closely follow other traditional Hmong cultural practices such as shamanism and funerals (see chapters 5 and 6). In this sense, I will first demonstrate that the Hmong kinship system in the diaspora became hegemonic in a Gramscian sense—a pervasive, taken-for-granted, and uncontested belief system that individuals widely accept through their voluntary, implicit consent, which therefore *did not* have to be ideologically imposed on them by ruling elites. The kinship system has been culturally inculcated in each generation by the parents, who are the most invested in it.

However, diasporic hegemonies such as Hmong kinship are never absolute or impenetrable. In response to my questions, Hmong interviewees commonly pointed out that kinship principles "keep Hmong together" despite a history of geographical dispersal and separation. They engaged in extensive justifications of their kinship system based on biologized discourses and claimed that it is an "essential" aspect of being Hmong in the absence of a homeland. Such conscious efforts to defend and uphold cultural norms about kinship (which could have been instigated by the presence of an outsider anthropologist) may be an indication that the kinship system is no longer as taken for granted and habitual as it once was and that its hegemonic status may be more of a historical condition.

In addition, hegemonies can eventually become subject to contestation and critical awareness (Alonso 1994, 381, 389; Comaroff and Comaroff 1991, 24–25), especially when they are enacted in different national contexts in the diaspora. In the case of Hmong kinship, counter-hegemonic resistance seems to be emerging, especially among those of the younger Hmong generations I met in California. According to older Hmong, the rule of clan hospitality, which Hmong extend to strangers simply because they share the same surname, is considered to be in danger of weakening among the younger generations. In addition, some young Hmong interviewees in both Laos and the United States have started to question clan exogamy by pointing out the contradictory logic embedded in its theory of biological relatedness. Those in California also questioned ethnic endogamy, since they have been raised in a society where interethnic marriages are common. In addition, gradual increases in violations of kinship principles and changes in family structure among Hmong in California can also challenge the hegemonic system. Therefore, as kinship hegemonies have become susceptible to new disruptive forces in the diaspora, they may have become *ideologies* that must be actively defended and imposed by the "ruling elites" (in this case, the parents, elders, and the community).

Hegemony, Ideology, and Structures of Power

Hegemony has been mainly analyzed in the context of the state (Alonso 1994, 281) and systems of social class or gender (Budgeon 2014; Burawoy 2012; Hall 1986). In contrast, diasporas are often understood to be transnational social formations that can challenge and even subvert the power of nation-states. However, it is important to recognize that diasporic peoples can also develop their own hegemonies that are as effective as those produced by nation-states and other power structures.

Hegemony consists of pervasive and inscribed cultural beliefs that individuals obey through their implicit consent because they are assumed to be part of the natural order. Because hegemony is based on such "spontaneous consent" (Gramsci [1971] 1989, 12; see also Brow 1988; Burawoy 2012, 194–95; Glassman 2011, 32; Hall 1986, 16; Kunnath 2013, 51), it does not need to be actively and continuously enforced by coercive power structures, disciplinary institutions, or community sanctions (see also Comaroff and Comaroff 1991, 22–23). In fact, hegemony is so culturally inculcated and ingrained in everyday life that subjects do not perceive it to be a system of control and therefore are unaware of being dominated. In this sense, hegemony seems to contrast with ideologies, which are particular worldviews of ruling elites that are contested by subordinate peoples and therefore must be imposed on them by more direct systems of power (Scott 1985; Williams 1977, 109).

Nonetheless, hegemonies are still embedded in power structures, and those who benefit from the system perpetuate it through concealed forms of domination that are often not directly experienced as relations of power. For hegemonies to become widely accepted and entrenched, they must first be effectively inculcated in individuals through socialization, family upbringing, and other hidden forms of "soft" cultural power, such as education, mass media, and ritual (Comaroff and Comaroff 1991, 25). In the two Hmong diasporic communities I studied, kinship beliefs became effective as an unchallenged hegemonic system through repetitive teaching from parents to children. Through the socialization process, Hmong parents, who often wish to uphold and perpetuate kinship hegemonies, obtained their children's implicit consent, which obviated the need for them to constantly enforce kinship rules through overt compulsion once their children become young adults. In some sense, kinship rules are more liable to become hegemonic, because their apparent logic is often related to biologized notions of blood ties and family lineage (as discussed below).

Clans and Surnames: The Basis of Hmong Kinship

The Hmong kinship system consists of patrilineal clanship based on eighteen different surnames.[3] The clan includes (and even subsumes) smaller-scale, subclans that consist of different family lineages that are believed to be traceable from a paternal Hmong ancestor (see G. Lee and

Tapp 2010). Because there are multiple subclans in one large clan that have varying degrees of relatedness and differences from one another, it is impossible to find a common ancestor for the entire clan. Timothy Dunnigan (1982) observes that the agnatic sub-lineage (the eighteen clans) system eased the resettlement process for Hmong in the United States and helped them establish a successful economic network.

The Hmong word *xeem* (pronounced *seng*) refers to clans and is interchangeably used with the word "surname." This clanship is the basis for socioeconomic resources and remittances and the foundation for Hmong social organization in both local and transnational contexts. Indeed, exchanging last names is an important and basic part of daily life for the Hmong in my research, as they wish to identify their clan membership and make appropriate kin connections. Whenever Hmong met another Hmong for the first time, their very first question was usually "What is your Hmong last name?" (*"Koj yog xeem dlaab tsis?"*). This question is especially important when Hmong youth explore possible romantic relationships, because they have to find Hmong from another clan to date (the principle of clan exogamy). In other words, the simplified Hmong clan system based on last name expands the primary meanings of biological kinship to much more flexible, nonconjugal social groups.

Hmong kinship practices initially reaffirm scholarly efforts to define kinship more extensively and analyze it as a social and cultural construct that consists of systems of symbolic meanings based on social relations rather than a naturalized system based on biological blood ties (Parkin 1997, 3; Peletz 1995, 356–57; Schneider 1980, 4–6). The boundaries of kinship membership become flexible and are constantly blurred as demonstrated by scholars who redefine and reconceptualize kinship through their ethnographies (Carsten 2004; M. Clarke 2008, 155; Schrauwers 1999, 314–16; see also Kuper 1982, 81).

The next three sections will examine the three hegemonic principles of Hmong kinship (clan hospitality, clan exogamy, and ethnic endogamy). I will demonstrate how prevalent they initially were among Hmong I studied in both Laos and the United States because of their widespread behavioral compliance with these principles in terms of their interactions with clan members and marriage choices. I will then discuss how these kinship principles are already becoming less hegemonic and more ideological by examining how Hmong interviewees actively engaged in discursive justifications of their kinship system, which indicates that the system is not as habitually ingrained as it may have been in the past.

Clan Hospitality toward "Strangers"

One of the hegemonic kinship rules among diasporic Hmong is to provide family-like hospitality and support to members of the same clan, even if they are complete strangers. For example, an elderly villager outside Dao Tha, Poa Moua, spoke about the broad sense of common clan identity and transnational kin affiliation across national borders: "For example, if you are of the Vang clan, it doesn't matter which country you live in or which city you choose to reside [in]. You are just the same Vang like before. This is not something that you can change. You should love other Vang and you will be beloved by other Vang."

Because of this emphasis on surname as the arbiter of one's clan identity, Hmong interviewees broadly assumed that they have kin connections to anyone who shares the same last name, regardless of their country of residence, even if they have never met before or will never see each other again. For example, Bea Her, one of the villagers in his late fifties in Dao Tha, said:

> In Vietnam, there will be a lot of Hmong people whose last name is like mine, "Her." The last name Her does exist in China, too. When some Hmong from China came to Laos to sell things, I asked them whether there are Her families in China. They would answer, "Of course, there are a lot of Her people in China." So that means there are many of my Her family and relatives living there.

Indeed, many Hmong shared with me their experiences as either the recipient or the provider of family-like hospitality and support after they unexpectedly encountered Hmong in other locales who were part of the same clan. Cha Vue, another interviewee in a different Hmong village, willingly served as a host for a Hmong (Miao) peddler from China whose surname was also Vue:

> The unity among the same clan is very strong. There was a man from China whose last name was also Vue. When he came to this village, he asked people around for the Vue family and heard about my family. We were really happy to see him for the first time, so we let him stay in my house, killed a chicken to cook, and treated him well. We felt like real brothers. The bond among the members from the same clan is so strong and special like this.

Such experiences among Hmong interviewees in Laos resonated with those in the United States, who also strongly believe in the continuity of kin affiliations and clan hospitality across national borders. For example, Lena Thao, a 1.5-generation woman in Sacramento, spoke about this system:

> We have an extended clan system, and we value our kinship very much. Although we have been separated for many years, we know that we are still related to each other. If I go to Germany right now, I will try to find a Thao family first. I know they will treat me as a family. I would call them aunt, uncle, and so on, even though I don't know who they are.

Lena believed that such kinship principles extend to Hmong in other parts of the diaspora and speculated that Hmong (Miao) in China must also retain their last names. "Although sometimes they may be forced to take on Chinese names in order to work in the cities, they must still preserve their clanship," she concluded.

In a different interview, Ying Thao, an elderly resident of Sacramento, similarly explained that the hospitality provided to clan members with the same surnames is a fundamental principle that has sustained diasporic Hmong throughout their history:

> It is the last name that makes us Hmong. Even if I never knew you from before, if you mention that you are from the same Thao family, I will treat you like a real family. Generation after generation, Hmong should never forget where they are from, what family they belong to, and our Hmong nationality. I am sure you hear Hmong saying to each other, "When you travel, I don't want you to spend money for hotel, food, or transportation. You should stay with us [member of the same clan]." Nobody provides free food or a free room like the Hmong. Many other people call us "jungle people," because Hmong have poor knowledge since the war, but we have a good mind and good heart.

The younger generations of Hmong in both countries generally learned the rule of clan hospitality from parents by following their behavior toward members of the same clan from a young age. During my fieldwork in Laos, I repeatedly observed youth who actively upheld clan hospitality by doing most errands and taking care of their clan relatives and family guests from other parts of Laos as well as the diaspora (mostly from Thailand and the United States and more rarely from Australia and France). In fact, I was constantly impressed with how Hmong people's clan hospitality was mutually assumed and universally practiced during first encounters with clan strangers, indicating that at the level of behavioral compliance, it was quite widespread and hegemonic. When Hmong

An "Imagined" Community of Transnational Kin   111

(Miao) scholars from China visited US Hmong communities, they were immediately welcomed by those who share the same surname, as if they were a member of their families. For instance, one such scholar, Fei Yang from China, was introduced to members of the Yang clan in the local Hmong community by her (non-Hmong) research advisor while holding a temporary academic affiliation as a visiting scholar at a university in Colorado. Since her arrival in the United States, Fei received extensive support from the local Yang community during her visit, including airport pickup, accommodations, local transportation, and meals.

Other activities were arranged and provided by various members of the Yang clan in the area, none of whom she had met before. Fei's subsequent visit to California was also arranged by members of the Yang clan network in Colorado and California who wanted to welcome her and develop a kin connection. I ran into Fei multiple times during my fieldwork at different Hmong community events in California. During each encounter, she was with a different Yang clan member who guided her around and introduced her to me by saying she is "like" their niece, aunt, or sister, and so on. We joked that the US Hmong community was treating her like a VIP.

"To me, it's like a mystery!" Fei remarked. In fact, she was half Hmong and could not speak Hmong properly. Her father is Miao/Hmong while her mother is ethnic Han Chinese. Fei said she actually does not feel completely related to the entire Yang clan in the United States because of her different cultural and personal background as well as her nationality. According to Fei, although she mentioned her different background to the many Yang clan members she met, she was still assumed to be and treated the same as a Yang family member, simply because she inherited the last name from her Hmong father.

The application and expansion of clan-based kinship was so inclusive and broad that Hmong could sometimes hypothetically embrace a complete foreigner like myself based on my last name (and my similar racialized appearance), as illustrated at the beginning of this chapter. Sometimes, elderly Hmong asked for my "Hmong" last name. I initially made it clear that my last name sounds identical to the Hmong clan name of "Lee" in English, but the correct Korean pronunciation is "yee," so I am actually not a member of the same Hmong clan! But later on, after being asked the same question numerous times, I ended up answering that I am "Hmong Lee" from Korea, which made people laugh.[4] This led to amusing discussions about whether to include me in their clan system as a new "Korean Hmong."

Clan Exogamy

Clan exogamy seemed to be more hegemonic than clan hospitality among Hmong during my research. The principle strictly prohibits both Hmong men and women from dating or marrying members of the same clan who have the same family name, even if they have never met and are complete strangers from other countries. This is because it is believed that everyone in the entire clan could hypothetically be genealogically related if they trace their ancestry back to the original clan founders in antiquity. Because of such reasoning, clan exogamy was considered extremely important by Hmong in my study as a "tradition" that must be passed down to all the descendants in the diaspora.

Among individual interviewees in both Laos and the United States, none of them had married or dated within their own clan. The surprisingly low number of clan exogamy violations may have been the result of conducting research among members of relatively cohesive and large Hmong communities in California as well as in rural Laos, where the cultural inculcation of this kinship principle and potential community sanctions against violators can be considerable. Nonetheless, clan exogamy's hegemonic status was confirmed by its pervasive acceptance, at least among diasporic Hmong in my research sample in the two communities.[5]

In fact, only one violation of the clan exogamy principle was (repeatedly) mentioned to me, which apparently happened some time ago. A young Hmong couple in the United States initiated a same-clan marriage despite severe opposition from both sides of their extended family. As a result, the couple was "disowned" by both sides of the family and shunned from the Hmong community. This story has been constantly retold by Hmong interviewees in both Laos and the United States as a disgraceful example of marriage that jeopardizes Hmong cultural identity. Interestingly, a few Hmong mentioned that in rare cases when young couples do marry someone with the same last name, one of the spouses intentionally changes the original last name to something completely different, inventing a new kind of surname. For example, the history of the new last name "Hang" or "Feng" was mentioned as an example of a name adopted by spouses who married another person whose last name was also "Vang."

Youa Her, a Dao Tha villager in his fifties, stressed the power of clan exogamous dating and marriage rules and how diasporic Hmong obey them unconditionally as a hegemonic principle despite geographical separation and national differences. By emphasizing family relations among the same clans, Youa said:

> Let's say I am a single man and go to America to marry a Hmong woman over there. When I see a beautiful woman, I must ask first of all, "What is your last name?" If she says "Her," then I would respond right away, "Oh, my sister!" I can't create a family with her. This is a Hmong cultural rule that is observed in the same manner in Thailand, Vietnam, America, Australia, every country. If they have the same last name, it means they are brothers and sisters, even if we have been separated for so many years.

Since the clan surname is understood to be the key to defining a Hmong cultural and ethnic identity in general, many Hmong in my study expressed their confidence in the hegemonic continuity of the clan exogamy marriage rule into the future. For example, a fifty-year-old man, Cha Lee, in Dao Tha said, "We still preserve the clan like our ancestors did in the past. For example, I am Hmong Lee, so if I go to Thailand, the same Hmong Lee clan will still uphold the marriage rule. This rule is what has been preserved the most, the longest. And we can never change this in the future."

Although hegemony is so entrenched and widely accepted that it does not have to be continuously enforced by coercive forms of power, as mentioned earlier, it does need to be inculcated and ingrained in each new generation through the mechanisms of soft, cultural power, which ensures the compliance and consent of subjects. For Gramsci ([1971] 1989, 12, 60), hegemony is based on the power of intellectuals of the ruling class. However, I argue that hegemonic domination relies on a more diffuse and pervasive power embedded in everyday social relations and experiences (e.g., see Foucault 1995), which cause hegemonies to be inscribed as part of the habitus (Bourdieu 1977). Such symbolic power resides in schools, families, and communities; is based on everyday routines, exercises, rituals, and bodily disciplines (see Comaroff and Comaroff 1991, 25); and may not be experienced as actual power at all. In this way, Hmong kinship principles elicited the consent of the members of both diasporic communities I studied and therefore retained their hegemonic status.

Nonetheless, the implicit and hidden systems of cultural power involved in learning and socialization are still based on power relations. In their everyday lives, clan exogamy principles (and other kinship rules) were culturally inculcated in Hmong children as part of their upbringing by their parents, who wish to uphold the kinship system. This ensures that hegemonic beliefs became ingrained and fully accepted by their children at an early age, making future resistance among youth less likely.

Interviewees in both Vang Vieng and California emphasized the need for intentional parental education in order to pass down their cultural and kinship traditions to their children in the diaspora. For instance, one of them spoke about the importance of instilling the clan exogamy rule in his children:

> Absolutely, I taught my kids the [kinship] rule when they were little. I told them that it doesn't matter whether the person is pretty or handsome. If you have the same last name, it means you are siblings, so you never get involved. That's been taught for many, many generations and we still believe in it very strongly. We need to tell our kids, "You are family by the same last name, so you are not allowed to date or marry."

Such parental education appears to have been successful in the past, since my research seemed to confirm the hegemonic status of clan exogamy among young Hmong in both Laos and the United States, at least in terms of outward behavioral compliance. During my daily visits with Hmong youth who worked at a community center in the village of Dao Tha, I started to notice that many teenage girls frequently received phone calls from unknown Hmong men asking them for a date. The phone calls came from men not only from different villages, cities, or provinces in Laos but also internationally from other countries like the United States, France, China, and Thailand. When a teenage girl named Meng Xiong, for example, received calls from these potential future boyfriends, the very first thing she said right after the initial "hello" was "My surname is Xiong. I am Meng Xiong in Vang Vieng," which indicated that the caller's first question was about her last name. Such exchanges of surnames are to make sure that they are not from the same clan and are therefore qualified to start a romantic relationship.

Likewise, young 1.5- and second-generation interviewees in Sacramento shared similar views about clan exogamy as older Hmong. A college student, Neng Her, who migrated to the United States as a baby, expressed his strong belief in marital kinship practices:

> I want to keep the tradition going. . . . I don't want my generation or myself to mess everything up. I do have preferences [about dating partners] and they are simple. She has to be Hmong, her last name can't be the same as mine, and the last thing is she has to believe in shamanism. I am not offending any other ethnicity or other religion.

An "Imagined" Community of Transnational Kin   115

Of course, I can compromise [about differences] with them, but at the same time, I cannot be easy on them either.

Leng Thao, whose background is the same as Neng (born in a Thai refugee camp and raised in the United States), noted, "If you are from the same last name, it does not matter how much you love each other. You just can't marry. . . . If I had known or met a woman before who is also a Thao, I just can't do it [start a relationship]. She is my sister. That [this kinship norm/principle] will probably never disappear."

Ethnic Endogamy

In addition to clan hospitality and clan exogamy, ethnic endogamy is another kinship principle that initially elicited prominent hegemonic compliance among the Hmong I studied, despite national and generational differences. While the rate of intermarriage has been on the rise, especially among Asians in the United States, ethnic endogamy was quite prevalent among Hmong communities in both countries during my fieldwork.[6] In Laos I met only two Hmong men who had non-Hmong spouses and lived in the capital city of Vientiane. There were no other cases of interethnic marriage among Hmong families in Dao Tha or in other nearby Hmong villages in Vang Vieng. Of the sixty-three individuals I interviewed in California, only two of them were in interethnic or interracial marriages or dating relationships, although I occasionally heard of other cases secondhand. However, some interviewees pointed out that interethnic or interracial couples may not be visible because they tend to be disengaged from the Hmong community and may not actively show up to or participate in its events.

In Laos, even Hmong youth who initially seemed open to intermarriage in principle said they had no intention of pursuing romantic relationships with non-Hmong. Initially, I wondered whether the parents were using their power to strictly prohibit interethnic dating. On the contrary, it seems that youth were voluntarily complying with ethnic endogamy on their own, and it was not being actively imposed on them. Although it seems that Hmong parents in Laos would be the most invested in the kinship system, since it ensures their children will marry within the Hmong community, when I spoke to them, many said that they are not against intermarriage with non-Hmong and were tolerant about youth pursuing ethnic exogamy. Parental responses to my questions about this issue were surprisingly uniform. For instance, two elderly women, Yeng and Chue, both in their seventies in Dao Tha, expressed their tolerant attitudes toward interethnic or interracial marriages in a similar manner:

YENG: It is up to them [the youth]. If they [an interethnic couple] love each other seriously, then that is fine. If the farang [white foreigner] is going to marry Hmong, we only check if their last name is the same as the Hmong's. If different, then they can marry.

CHUE: As long as Hmong marry foreigners who don't have the same last name, it is okay to marry. But among the same Hmong clan, they can't marry each other.

However, this apparent leniency of Hmong parents and elders in Vang Vieng toward ethnic exogamy needs to be examined more carefully. First of all, the possibility that non-Hmong or foreigners would have the same last name as the Hmong is very remote (only some Chinese, and possibly Koreans, may share several surnames with coincidentally similar pronunciation). The other ethnic groups in the village, such as the Lao (Loum) and Khmu, have completely different family naming systems from the Hmong. In this sense, these parents seemed to be more willing to entertain the possibility of ethnic intermarriage for their children, as it would still sustain the all-important clan exogamy principle.

It seems that older Hmong people in Laos appear to be more tolerant toward interethnic marriage perhaps because they were certain that it is highly unlikely to happen anyway, given its hegemonic status. Because youth have complied with the hegemonic principle of ethnic endogamy for generations without the use of coercive force, parents may not see the need to overtly enforce the rule by using their disciplinary power. It is also possible that they can profess tolerant attitudes (especially to an outsider, foreign anthropologist) because they have observed that hardly any youth have ever married non-Hmong.

In fact, Hmong youth in the village expressed skepticism about their parents' lenient attitudes about ethnic exogamy. "It is definitely easier said than done," one of them emphasized and then elaborated:

They [elderly Hmong and parents] can maybe just say in principle that it's okay to marry foreigners or non-Hmong. But if it really happens, I am sure they will change their mind and seriously object. If you think about it a little more, there are many problems with marriage between Hmong and non-Hmong families [in Laos]. No mutual communication, no cultural similarities are possible. . . . They speak totally different languages to begin with.

As mentioned above, ethnic endogamy also appeared to be hegemonic among young, 1.5- and second-generation Hmong Americans in my study. According to a survey I conducted with eighty-three Hmong college students in the Sacramento area, most of whom were born and/or raised in the United States, the preference for ethnic endogamy was still strong among them. In response to a set of questions related to ethnic preferences about marriage and dating partners, twenty-three out of twenty-four Hmong students who were already in romantic relationships answered that their current dating partner's ethnicity is Hmong.

The young Hmong I interviewed who preferred someone of Hmong ethnicity as their romantic partners spoke about how they voluntarily consented to the endogamy rule, instead of having it imposed on them through the disciplinary power of their parents. For instance, Lena Thao, a married 1.5-generation woman in her late twenties, explained that her desire to marry a Hmong man was a personal preference and choice. "I don't think intermarriage would be a problem with my parents," she noted. "But it is my personal preference to date or marry Hmong. I wanted somebody that would fit well with my parents and Hmong culture. It is just something that I would like to continue." Similarly, in a different interview, a US-born college student, Lily Moua, expressed her attitude toward marriage in the following exchange:

LILY MOUA: Ah . . . I actually prefer a Hmong person but I am not a racist![7] [*laughs*] I mainly just want to keep our culture together. If I were to marry someone from another culture, I feel like I kind of lose my own culture.

AUTHOR: So what kind of culture can you keep if you have a Hmong partner?

LILY MOUA: I would definitely say the Hmong language. If I were to lose my language ability, it's like I lose myself, too, because my language is what determines who I am.

When Hmong of the younger generations spoke about their preference for ethnic endogamy, they conveyed that a spouse who is compatible with their own traditions and language was critical, which resembles the desires of their parents and of the older Hmong generation. In general, I was quite struck at the level of behavioral compliance with the ethnic endogamy principle during my fieldwork among Hmong youth in both Vang Vieng and California despite the multiethnic environment of the two countries and the relatively high rate of intermarriages among Asian populations in the United States.

Discursive Justifications for Hmong Diasporic Kinship Hegemonies

Despite the widespread adherence to kinship rules among Hmong in Vang Vieng and California, at least in terms of their outward practices, there are signs that some cracks have emerged in the hegemonic system at the level of their discourses. Hmong interviewees justified and legitimized their compliance with the hegemonic kinship system by giving biological explanations (i.e., family and blood ties) for their social clan relations. Moreover, they emphasized the need to comply with the principles of their kinship system because of the absence of an ethnic homeland that can promote and sustain Hmong diasporic unity and belonging across national borders.

Although individuals do not necessarily obey hegemonies mindlessly out of sheer force of habit, such active reflection and conscious efforts to justify the cultural principles of the kinship system indicate that they are no longer taken for granted by interviewees and assumed to be part of the natural order at the discursive level, even if they continue to elicit tacit and pervasive consent in terms of actual behavior. Nonetheless, the discursive statements I discuss in this section do not necessarily contest or challenge the kinship system. Although they indicate that kinship hegemonies have become subject to discursive awareness, they are not yet fully subject to *critical* discursive consciousness (which will be examined in the next section in the US context).

In addition, it is important to note that such discursive justifications were given by interviewees because I asked them why they continue to abide by the kinship system. As a result, they were obliged to explain their kinship system and legitimize its importance to a cultural outsider who was initially unfamiliar with it and surprised by their pervasive compliance with its principles. In their daily lives, however, I did not observe Hmong giving such explanations or discursive rationalizations of their kinship practices to one another throughout fieldwork.

Nonetheless, the rather passionate and strong reactions I received when I asked interviewees about their adherence with kinship rules may indicate that it is no longer as habitual and culturally ingrained in their minds as it once may have been (if it still is, they would not have understood my question or thought it to be strange). Therefore, kinship hegemony may have already been a historical condition that is gradually shifting to an ideology that has to be actively defended against contestations and ultimately enforced by coercion by those in power (see the next section).

Biologized Discourses about Kinship

Even nonconjugal, nonbiological kinship systems like Hmong clanship rules were justified in my interviews through naturalized and essentialized discourses based on genealogical and biologized reasoning. Although the kinship affinity that the Hmong feel toward other clan members is primarily a social construction, it is still based on biologized discourses that refer to blood-relatedness. Indeed, Hmong people's flexible inclusion of clan members as kin is made possible because they believe that the eighteen clans descended from one ancient ancestor and that they are therefore the children of the same parents. Clan members are referred to by familial terms such as "brother," "sister," "uncle," and so on. They become similar to members of a family in various ways, although they are not accorded equal positions as blood-related, immediate family members.

Based on this biologized logic, Hmong research participants believed that hospitality and financial support must be extended to all clan members because they are "like a family" and because to do otherwise is similar to rejecting a brother or sister (or another blood-related family member) who has come to visit or is asking for financial help. Likewise, Hmong are strictly prohibited from marrying a clan member with the same surname because that would be "like marrying a family member" and is therefore considered incestuous and taboo.

In this sense, Hmong clanship can be compared to the concept of "universal kin," which is defined as a unifying source in the African diaspora (Gilroy 1992; Hall 1990; Helmreich 1992). Since the national origins of the current members of the African diaspora are no longer known, these scholars suggest that its members can alternatively construct a common sense of kin identity as part of a unified African race based on a shared historical consciousness. This concept of universal kin is emphasized as a way for resettled African diasporic communities to overcome subordination and deliberate exclusion by nation-states (Gilroy 1987).

However, as Stefan Helmreich critically points out, the idea of universal kin has the possibility to resemble how nation-states naturalize their members, borders, and territories in the name of a single, unified national race. He further questions whether such pan-African ethnicity based on common, shared "black" experiences under colonization can be achieved without excluding individual differences and the othering processes of the nation-state (Helmreich 1992, 245). Nonetheless, as seen in the Hmong case, diasporas can develop and promote a unifying ethnic identity through notions of shared biologized kinship to counter nationalist exclusions and marginalization. Even nonconjugal and nonbiological forms of kinship are still conceived and taken for granted through genealogical metaphors by local peoples.

Diasporic Kinship and the Ethnic Homeland

In addition to biologized discourses of family that naturalize clanship rules, many Hmong interviewees in both Laos and the United States gave other discursive justifications for their unwavering adherence to their kinship principles in response to my interview questions. Their continuing historical consciousness as a formerly persecuted and dispersed "people without a country" who have lost their ethnic homeland serves as a compelling reason to legitimize their kinship practices across the diaspora. Because of the absence of a country of ancestral origin, they explained that their unquestioned allegiance to their clan and kinship system enables them to sustain ethnic solidarity and a shared diasporic identity across national borders.

About 90 percent of interviewees in both countries mentioned that their kinship rules are first and foremost "what make Hmong identify and maintain their ethnic identity despite their geographic dispersal and separation." They wished to conform to their kinship rules, believing "there is no other feasible, concrete way to actually maintain their [our] scattered ethnic community in the absence of a territorial homeland, an independent government, or global ethnic leaders." With the enduring power of their clan kinship beliefs, Hmong interviewees seemed to reaffirm and be reminded of what it means to be diasporic Hmong. This discursive justification of their kinship principles was repeated by an overwhelming number of interviewees regardless of gender or generational status. Although parents and elderly Hmong may be most dedicated to the kinship system as its beneficiaries, who want to sustain their ethnic "tradition," younger Hmong also invoked such discourses on their own.

Justifications of the clan hospitality principle in the context of the Hmong diaspora were especially prominent among parents and elderly in my research. Consider this following exchange with Thai Lee in Dao Tha:

> AUTHOR: For me, even if I unexpectedly encounter Koreans [my nationality] abroad who have the same last name as mine, we won't

express much special feelings toward each other unless they are really my family.

THAI: I guess it's probably because you guys have your own country. There are so many Koreans from Korea, so you are used to seeing other Koreans in foreign countries. For Hmong people, we are scattered all over the world, so far from each other.

Likewise, Nia Her, a senior villager in Dao Tha, explained:

In my opinion, I think the reason why Hmong stay together without a homeland is because of family ties, especially the last name. If families have the same last name, they treat each other better than people who have other last names. Going through the difficult wars in China [in past Hmong history], the clan system must have made Hmong stay together.

Malina Xiong, a Sacramento resident in her forties, made a similar claim:

AUTHOR: In your opinion, what makes Hmong people keep their Hmong ethnic consciousness and identity despite geographic separation, and how do they maintain it?

MALINA: It is our surnames. Even if I do not know the person directly, if that person is from the same clan, they are like family to us. Indeed, we know that we are somehow connected to each other, one way or another, even if they live far away.

Many interviewees also repeatedly claimed that shared clan exogamy principles enable Hmong to maintain their ethnic affiliations with other Hmong dispersed across the diaspora. This claim was succinctly stated, for instance, in the following quote from Sheng Her, one of the clan representatives in Sacramento:

I don't know why we are so attached to each other [despite geographical dispersal], but one thing that really keeps us together is, if you are of the same last name, it makes us the same family. If your last name is Thao, you never ever marry another Thao person. If you do that, it's taboo [incestuous]. Even if you are a Thao who lives in Korea, you are still considered as a family and a relative of Thao elsewhere.

In this sense, Hmong kinship principles have allowed interviewees to imagine a sense of kin affinity with their co-ethnics scattered abroad and reaffirm a common and persisting Hmong diasporic identity in the face of a long history of dispersion and the absence of a territorial homeland that can unify the diaspora. The strong consciousness of their diasporic history supports the existential legitimacy of their kinship rules and explains why they remained hegemonic throughout the process of diasporization.

Although such discursive kinship justifications were confined to my interviews, where I actively elicited such responses, and were not part of daily conversations and interactions as far as I could tell, there were a few possible exceptions. As described above, it is quite clear that within the family, parents actively taught these principles to their children by explaining and rationalizing their importance as part of the (soft power) process of socialization and cultural inculcation. In addition, Hmong living in the United States may find the need to engage in more active reflection and efforts to explain their kinship practices to others because of their greater cultural differences from American mainstream norms compared to Laos.

For instance, although clan exogamy has been practiced by Hmong in Laos for many generations, interviewees in California were quite aware that it is clearly different from standard American marriage customs. As a result, their hegemonic adherence to this kinship rule may have become a more intentional and conscious act, instead of simply an unreflexive or instinctual reproduction of a prescribed habitus. During an interview with a middle-aged couple in Sacramento, Chong Her and his wife, Soua Yang, we discussed Hmong marital customs, including that of surnames, which does not follow the conventional US conjugal practice where the wife adopts the husband's surname:

> My wife has kept her maiden name. In Hmong culture, when we marry, we don't change our last name. Some young [Hmong] women who were born and grew up here [in the United States] may have changed their last name [after marriage], but as far as I know, most still keep their last names. The reason behind this is that if you are a woman and marry and change your last name to your husband's, people will misunderstand and think you married your sister or brother [i.e., a person from the same clan].

Unlike the United States, in Laos, Hmong spouses do not have to explain why they have different surnames, because that is more standard practice in mainstream Lao culture. Therefore, this type of justification of a Hmong married couple's naming practices based on clan exogamy seems to have become more necessary in the American context, and it was repeatedly given to me on different occasions. Although Hmong were explaining their kinship system and principles to me, as a cultural outsider, the fact that such statements were often made in an unprompted manner is significant. This may be an indication that their previously habitual and hegemonic compliance with clan exogamy in Laos may have become a more conscious practice that needs to be legitimized in the different national cultural context of the United States.

Emerging Resistance and Challenges to Kinship Hegemonies

There are other important indications that the hegemonic hold of Hmong kinship as a naturalized belief system may be weakening among Hmong, especially in Sacramento. Their cultural principles of kinship are increasingly subject to not only discursive *awareness* but also to discursive *critique and questioning*, especially among youth. As a result, their kinship system may be transitioning from a widely accepted and uncontested hegemony to an ideology whose logic is actively questioned and may possibly be violated in the future.

Since hegemonies are never absolute or impenetrable, they are vulnerable to critiques and subversive challenges, eventually disrupting the implicit consent of subjects on which they are based. This is especially the case when they travel through the diaspora and are enacted in different national social contexts. Although hegemonies are threatened during revolutionary periods or by subordinate groups, such as the working class (Gramsci [1971] 1989, 210), migration can be an important source of hegemonic erosion in different contexts. When individuals move to other countries, they can certainly face new and conflicting social pressures that make them question their inherited hegemonic belief systems. If such resistance ultimately results in a significant number of individuals disobeying such principles, they become less hegemonic and are transformed into ideologies that must be defended and actively imposed by the coercive power of "ruling elites" (parents and elders in the case of Hmong kinship).

In fact, elderly Hmong in both Laos and the United States were not certain whether the younger generations would continue to adhere to the culture of clan hospitability toward extended kin members in the diaspora, which usually requires a considerable amount of time, effort, and financial responsibility. They claimed that Hmong youth are "no longer interested in their distant clan relatives living abroad" whom they have never met or known before. For instance, Long Her, an elderly woman in Laos, spoke about such concerns: "In our children's generation, it will be like 'I don't know them [members of the same clan] and they don't know us.' Whenever I think about this, I feel frightened [*tok jai*]. Hmong American kids will not know about their relatives in Laos. They only look at books to study about other people or pictures but do not come here to see or love us."

In the United States, a forty-year-old Sacramento resident, Cher Her, had a similar opinion. "I think in the future, Hmong will change and become more like the non-Hmong community," she said. "The young generations already do not want to call clan relatives to come and share food. Even when you are in the same place at family gatherings, they won't know who their [clan] relatives are and how they are related to each other." Both interviewees were quite worried that familial hospitality toward clan kin will be significantly reduced in the diaspora in the future and may eventually be limited to only nuclear family members living in close geographical proximity.

Hmong kinship hegemonies are being increasingly subjected to critical discursive awareness and contestation by Hmong youth in California, especially those who were born and raised in the country. Second-generation Hmong Americans I interviewed already started to openly question the legitimacy and contradictory logic of both clan exogamy and ethnic endogamy. Although very few Hmong youth have actually married Hmong of the same clan, they no longer take the clan exogamy rule for granted but express critical opinions about such marital restrictions in their discourses because they are virtually unheard of in mainstream American society. They especially question the logical consistency of the Hmong marital system, which prohibits marriage with a clan member with no blood ties but, incongruously, permits, if not encourages, marriage with a cousin (as long as the person has a different surname), despite the fact that such marriages have a greater level of biological relatedness. Again, these Hmong youth are influenced by their upbringing in American society, where cousin marriage is anathema.

For example, Koua Xiong, a second-generation Hmong American college student, critically discussed the contradiction between the clan exogamy rule and cousin marriage:

> In some sense, I disagree [with the Hmong marital system], because it allows you to date and marry your own cousins. If my siblings are married to different family clans, then their kids and my kids can marry each other. So that's okay because your last name is different, although you are related by blood? But if you are from the same clan and have the same last name, then it's not okay to get married, even if you are not [biologically] related at all? This does not make any sense.

An "Imagined" Community of Transnational Kin   125

Koua's comment was indeed shared by other young Hmong Americans who raised similar objections to clan exogamy. In other words, Hmong youth employed the same biologized reasoning that older Hmong use to legitimize clan exogamy by applying it to cousin marriage, exposing the logical flaw of the hegemonic Hmong clan exogamy system in their discourses.

Indeed, older Hmong constantly brought up the example of the young US Hmong couple who married within the same clan to express their concerns about the possibility that, in the future, later-generation Hmong may no longer comply with clan exogamy. One interviewee referred to this extreme case and noted, "The kids here in America today, they don't know. What can you do when they say, 'Here, it's America. You can do it'?" Some Hmong families may be somewhat more accepting than before of those who marry within the clan and may not completely disown them. However, the couple still has to move and live far way, isolated from their families and ethnic communities, according the Hmong interviewees.

In addition, more young Hmong American college students who were part of my research were starting to question the restrictive ethnic endogamy rule as well. They were born or raised in an American culture that is tolerant of interethnic marriage to a much greater extent than their immigrant parents, and they also have more opportunities to interact (and become romantically involved) with non-Hmong individuals than those living in Laos. As mentioned earlier, interracial marriage between Asian Americans and non–Asian Americans has become prevalent, and interethnic marriage between Asian minority groups has been on the rise as well (Min and Kim 2009). In addition, in areas outside California that have limited Hmong populations, one cannot assume that Hmong always adhere to the principle of ethnic endogamy.

Although the young Hmong in my research still seem to have overwhelmingly adhered to the hegemonic endogamy norm in practice, many of them were actually equally open to the idea of dating or marrying non-Hmong, at least in principle. In addition, a few Hmong youth were critical of the virtual ban on interethnic marriage. For instance, Tony Cha, a freshman at a local university in Sacramento, whose girlfriend was a Filipino American, faced objections particularly from his grandfather, the eldest and most influential member of his Cha clan:

> Whenever he [his grandfather] sees me, he asks when I will break up with my Filipino girlfriend. I never dated a Hmong girl, because I find they are like my cousins. To me, every Hmong person is related to each

other somehow, even if they do not share the same last name. . . . That's why I don't date Hmong girls. It's not because they are unattractive.

It should be noted that such resistance and challenges to Hmong kinship hegemony seemed to be primarily at the discursive level among US Hmong youth interviewees. Nonetheless, such emerging discursive challenges from certain Hmong youth raise the possibility that they may eventually engage in more overt forms of behavioral resistance by actively violating Hmong kinship principles and marrying non-Hmong or even members of the same clan.[8] This may indicate that the soft power of childhood socialization and parental teachings may not be enough to successfully manufacture widespread cultural consent. As a previous hegemony becomes an ideology that must be actively enforced in practice, Hmong elders and parents may have to resort to more coercive and punitive forms of power in order to impose Hmong marriage rules on youth. This may include threatening to disown them or forbidding them from showing up to familial or community events, which apparently has already happened in isolated cases where there were violations in kinship principles.

Conclusion: From Hegemony to Ideology

Hegemonies are not simply the purview of nation-states, ruling classes, or systems of gender domination. Although diasporas often consist of deterritorialized, displaced peoples, they can also develop their own hegemonies that have become removed from critical discourse and assumed as the natural order of things. Because hegemony has become so pervasive and culturally inculcated through the hidden, soft power of education and socialization, it no longer has to be actively imposed by oppressive structures and coercive systems of control. In fact, the initial hallmark of hegemony is that it is not experienced consciously as a system of coercive power and domination.

This chapter has demonstrated that the three principles of Hmong kinship that initially elicited widespread voluntary consent and behavioral compliance have been in a transitional phase from hegemony to ideology. Clearly, the Hmong who participated in my research have become more conscious of their hegemonic kinship principles and provided discursive justifications and compelling reasons why they must adhere to them faithfully instead of unreflexively taking them for granted (a process to which the anthropologist also partially contributed). In addition to employing biologized discourses about blood ties and descent, they regarded the persistence of their clanship and marriage systems across national borders as an "essential" aspect of Hmong (diasporic) identity that keeps their dispersed ethnic communities together despite the lack of an ethnic homeland. Although such discourses may have subjected previously hegemonic beliefs to active reflection, they legitimize the logic of Hmong kinship instead of challenging it.

However, the Hmong kinship system is not impervious to eventual contestation and critique. This is especially true for diasporic hegemonies, which must be reproduced transnationally in the face of different social and cultural pressures in various nation-states of residence. Therefore, hegemonies in diasporas have to be maintained not only through time (from one generation to the next) but also across geographical space (from one country to another). As a result, they increasingly come under discursive critique, especially among the younger generations in countries where these hegemonic norms are incompatible with the local, mainstream culture. It seems that the Hmong kinship system is therefore being transformed from a hegemony, whose pervasive dominance and assumed universality elicits unconditional compliance without explicit structures of control, to an ideology, a culturally relative belief system that needs to be actively imposed by those in power (parents, in this case) on subjects (children and youth) through direct forms of compulsion and punishment (see Comaroff and Comaroff 1991, 23).

Regardless of whether Hmong kinship principles will remain hegemonic or will simply become a dominant ideology that needs to be deliberately enforced, they remained entrenched in the two diasporic communities I studied, enabling Hmong to not only create "imagined" communities of transnational kin (see Anderson [1983] 2006) but to also sustain active social connections across national borders. As will be discussed in the next chapter, their clan-based kinship system has become the basis for an extensive familial and clan economy between Hmong in Laos and those in the United States. Such economic relationships enabled by social networks of kinship across national borders constitutes an important source of transnational cultural continuity within the diaspora.

4

Compassionate Money

Monetized Longing and Emotional Remittances in the Transnational Familial Economy

In the early afternoon of a warm January day in Laos, I had an interview appointment with Seng Yang, the owner of a small pineapple farm in Dao Tha. On my way to his house, I ran into a young friend, Yia Lee, who also knows Seng very well, and we walked to Seng's house together. Seng was at home, remembered that I was coming that day for an interview, and kindly brought out three small wooden stools from inside his house. Like many of the families in the village, Seng also had relatives who migrated as refugees to the United States after the Vietnam War. About four or five of them, including his older brother's son, were living in California and Minnesota. I asked him a rather obvious question: "Do you miss them?" Seng responded right away:

> Sure, of course I miss them. In Laos we miss them a lot, but we don't know if they miss us just as much as we miss them. Sometimes we call them and they pick up the phone. But they actually don't really call us. That is probably because they are not really interested in our lives anymore. That has become the reality between Laos and the US these days.

Because I sensed Seng's underlying regret and sadness about the decline in communication across borders with his family members, I asked how he manages his feelings of loss and longing for his relatives. Seng continued, "If I miss them, I ask for money. If I have no money, I miss them. So when I don't have money, I call them."

As soon as Seng told me this, I paused for a moment, recalling how many times I had heard similar answers from other Hmong. During my fieldwork in Laos, I was repeatedly told that when they miss their family members and relatives living in other countries, they ask for money. I finally came to realize that the desire to receive financial support as evidence of familial "love" among Hmong I spoke to in Laos was sincere, not simply a way to disguise their economic motives or pressure their families and relatives residing in the United States to send them money. They were truly equating money with emotions, familial love and care, and feelings of longing, all of which help connect separated families transnationally. Money therefore becomes not simply a financial remittance but an emotional remittance as well.

Affectionate Money:
Diaspora's Transnational Linkage

The extensive kinship networks and clan systems across national borders discussed in chapter 3 have also enabled the two Hmong diasporic communities I studied in Laos and the United States to develop strong transnational connections, which is an example of the social continuity and cohesion that can be maintained in the Hmong diaspora despite the absence of a coherent ethnic homeland. Economic transactions and remittances that flow through these kin networks are one of the most salient forms of transnational social relationships among diasporic and migratory communities (Conway and Cohen 1998; de Haas 2005).

It is clear that migrant remittances are important as a form of transnational capital, not just because of their economic value as a monetary transaction. Instead, the emotional values and cultural meanings of money (defined broadly as "love" by Hmong in my study) sent through familial and kinship networks provide the transnational social bonds and continuities that keep geographically dispersed diasporas like the Hmong together. Such emotional remittances help them maintain a sense of mutual ethnic affiliation and diasporic belonging to a broader transnational community.

The Lao term *kwaam hak* (translated as "love" in English), which was used by Hmong in both countries during interviews (with the exception of US-born Hmong Americans, whom I interviewed exclusively in English), has broad and multiple meanings. It signifies related emotional values, such as longing for geographically separated family members; nurturing, mutual compassion; and familial care. Even in English, love is such a versatile concept that can be associated with various meanings in different contexts beyond purely amorous or romantic sentiment. While this is also the case for the Hmong transnational familial economy, it is important to note that the meaning of love used by Hmong is based on social relations. When Hmong in both communities discussed and explained the roles of money, it was emphasized that those separated from each other should *kwaam hak peng gan* ("love each other" or have a relationship based on love). In this context, Hmong interviewees further elaborated how much they miss (*kithot*) and worry (*pen huang*, in terms of care) about family members abroad.

In addition to these variable emotional meanings that the word "love" can contain, remittances (money) as an expression of love were not always mutually understood or shared between Hmong senders in the United States and their recipients in Laos. Instead, they had rather differing interpretations about the meaning of money. Hmong in Dao Tha constantly requested financial support from their co-ethnics in the United States by associating money with familial love, nurturant care, and longing. In contrast, Hmong in Sacramento were generally less enthusiastic about such emotions and feelings of love expressed through money, seeing it mainly as an economic means of support. They felt remittances are rather an insufficient substitute for their physical absence from Laos and inability to directly take care of their family back home. Some also doubted the sincerity of emotional appeals from Lao Hmong relatives for money in the name of "love." In addition, because of global inequalities between the two countries, Hmong in Laos (who live in relative poverty) may have felt entitled to receive love through money from their richer US family members as a form of transnational redistribution and moral obligation among co-ethnics. However, because remittances flow predominantly one way (from the United States to Laos), Hmong in California sometimes felt that the "love" they send to family and relatives in Laos is ultimately unrequited.

In this sense, Hmong interviewees in Laos and the United States interpreted love and its relationship with money differently, because those in Laos perceived love as inseparable from and already embedded in economic relations, while their co-ethnics in the United States considered love expressed through money as insufficient and somewhat insincere. This indicates that the concept of love not only evokes and encompasses a variety of emotional meanings; it is also contested when expressed through money among families and relatives across national borders. Such differences between remittance senders and recipients in the Hmong diaspora about the meaning of money can be discerned through comparative, multi-sited fieldwork in both the migrant homeland and the host country.

At first glance, the sense of longing for familial members living abroad seems to be a purely emotional feeling that has little to do with material values, such as money. As Keith Hart notes, money is usually seen as impersonal and derived "from the anonymity of homogeneous individuals meeting in the marketplace, with price resolving their superficial differences" (2007, 13). However, the transnational familial and clan economy is far from impersonal, since they are embedded in diasporic communities and identities that consist of intimate family as well as clan members (that is, extended kin who are like family).

Many scholars in the social sciences have already argued that remittances are not simply a means of transferring financial resources but can also be a lens to understand the "social meanings" that are attached to transnational interactions and economic exchanges in migratory contexts (Dossa and Coe 2017; Levitt and Lamba-Nieves 2011; Thai 2014). In fact, money is not only inseparable from transnational social relations but often sustains them and inscribes different social and cultural meanings for the participants involved (Carruthers and Espeland 1998; Cheal 1987; LiPuma 1999; Parry and Bloch 1989; Zelizer 1998). As Viviana Zelizer (1996) notes, money can be "special," for it produces rich symbolic meanings by enabling people to interact, negotiate, and transform their social relationships.

This noneconomic value of money has been featured in a number of studies, especially in the scholarship about transnational migration. As shown in Hung Cam Thai's (2014) study about the Vietnamese diaspora, the Viet Kieu (overseas Vietnamese) and their families in Vietnam constantly engage in a discourse of familial love and obligation through monetary remittances despite their internal hardships and insufficient income in the United States.[1] As Leisy J. Abrego (2014) demonstrates, remittances are particularly significant, both emotionally and financially, for transnational families in which the parents (who migrated to foreign countries) are separated from their children (left behind at home). In the case of transnational Salvadoran families she studied in the United States, the emotional meanings of remittances are further complicated by the parents' undocumented status and gender disparities in the host country.

Similarly, Rhacel Parreñas (2001) argues that remittances are not only one of the most critical ways international Filipina migrants financially support their children left behind in the Philippines but also partially make up for their physical and emotional absence as mothers.[2] As shown in Cati Coe's (2011) study in Ghana, even for families who migrate internally, financial support can either reduce or create emotional distance between domestic migrant parents and their children at home. These studies commonly reaffirm that money is certainly commensurate with nonmonetary values and cultural meanings and is not simply a material substitute for social relationships among separated families.

Clearly, money sent across national borders holds symbolic power to express the emotions of love, familial care, and longing and often partly compensates for geographical distance and the physical absence of loved ones who have migrated abroad. While the emotional aspect of money enacted through transnational remittances among Hmong families who reside in the United States and Laos is the focus of this chapter, there are some important differences between this example from the Hmong diaspora in my research and other cases of economic migration. Unlike transnational economic migrants, diasporic refugees like the Hmong were forced to involuntarily migrate and disperse due to political conflict, war, and violence in their homelands. Hmong relocated as entire families rather than individual economic migrants, and after resettlement, they have engaged in a transnational economy as members of various cross-border communities of kin, not simply as individuals.

Because of such differences, remittances can be analyzed broadly as the product of transnational exchanges at the *collective* group level in terms of both senders and recipients, broadening analyses that are based mainly on individual connections.[3] In this sense, research on migrant remittances needs to better specify the actual participants who engage in the transnational economy of money and emotions. Existing studies tend to focus on (labor) migrants and the economic impact of their individualized remittances to their immediate families remaining in the homeland (see also Boccagni and Baldassar 2015; Brown and Poirine 2005; Lindley 2009).

Because the transnational economy of emotional remittances I analyze in this chapter operates through diasporic kinship networks based on an extensive system of Hmong clan affiliations, it often involves collective financial and emotional support, which is not confined to the level of individual migrants and their biological families. Not only did Hmong migrate as a group, but their kinship system also produces differing collective obligations toward family and clan members residing back in the homeland, which contrast with the generally more individualized nature of the remittances of most labor migrants. Such social and emotional relations across borders that constitute the transnational social continuity of diasporas need to be considered when theorizing about transnational economic relationships. Because participants are embedded in different

Compassionate Money   133

social systems and circumstances, their remittance patterns and ensuing meanings cannot be generalized, even if they are engaging in the same economic behavior.

The Collective Nature of the Transnational Economy in the Hmong Diaspora

Part of the diasporic identity of Hmong I studied in Laos and the United States has been developed through transnational familial social relationships based on their extensive kinship networks. These networks have enabled Hmong people to maintain contact with each other and engage in a transnational economy of financial and emotional transactions as well as the limited exchange of goods (herbal medicine, cosmetics, cultural artifacts, traditional clothes, and handmade embroideries from Laos).

When Hmong in my study identified members of families and relatives with whom they stayed in touch or assisted financially across national borders, they did not simply speak of their immediate, blood-related family members but usually included more extended kin members from the same clan as well. Among the Lao Hmong households in my research, all but two had at least one or more family members and relatives of the same clan residing in the United States. They not only maintained direct communication on the phone with them but also received intermittent financial support from them for various reasons. Among Hmong individuals I interviewed in California, only seven of them responded that all of their close family members had moved to the United States with them and that they had no substantial transnational relationships with Hmong in Laos.

Remittances were sent both individually and collectively, depending on the nature of the request from Laos. Hmong in the United States arrange and manage to send money when their relatives and clan representatives in Laos call, asking for money for different reasons. When Hmong sent money from the United States to their immediate family members in Laos, they used money transfer services, such as MoneyGram or Money Center (inside Walmart stores). They usually called other clan members in different cities and states to announce a request for funds and ask for additional monetary contributions in order to gather a larger sum to support the Hmong community in Laos, making remittances a collective endeavor.[4]

The focus of this chapter is this collective dimension of these remittances, which have been frequent but also irregular. Many of the elderly first-generation Hmong I interviewed who had the most immediate connection to their co-ethnics in Laos did not have jobs or regular income but relied on their limited savings, governmental subsidies, and social welfare to financially support their families in both Laos and the United States. Despite their limited financial ability to send remittances, extended family members of their clan, including those of the second generation, also contributed money and increased the amount they remit to Laos. However, since collective clan remittances were usually irregular and could not provide sustained income or substitute for regular wages, it was insufficient to improve overall life conditions for their Hmong families and relatives in Laos in the long term.

Kheng Xiong, a Sacramento resident in his forties, went to Thailand once in 1996 and again 1997, mainly to visit relatives and his childhood friends and to make video recordings of his trip. We talked about transnational familial and kinship ties across borders based on his own experiences:

AUTHOR: Do you still stay in touch with them [his Xiong clan members] in Laos and Thailand?

KHENG: Yes, we keep in touch, make phone calls, and listen to people there about how they are living.

AUTHOR: Are you really close to them as relatives?

KHENG: We are distant cousins. It's like my grandfather and their grandfather are distant brothers.

AUTHOR: When you mentioned that you still stay in touch with your family and relatives, do you frequently help them financially?

KHENG: Sure. In Hmong culture, because we are one family and we live as a group, whenever our relatives have some major events over there [in Laos], each of us here contributes maybe about twenty to fifty dollars to help them with the expenses. Also, a couple years ago, we collected money for our relatives in Laos to buy a tractor for their farm. We didn't buy it for individuals, but for all of them to share, so one family can pass it around. We do that all the time.

AUTHOR: So who is in charge of managing these transactions?

KHENG: Yeah, we have a contact person in our clan over here. Over there [Laos], in all the cities, we have the contacts too from the same clan. They will contact us and say, "Oh, we have an emergency. Can you help and send us some money?" So here [in the United States], you call everybody to collect money to send them.

AUTHOR: How often do you think this happens?

KHENG: Well, we only do this for the major events. We used to send money for the New Year's over there, several hundred dollars. We know some families are not rich in Laos. They may not have enough, so we contribute a little bit for them to share for major events like clan funerals or weddings.

Kheng's personal story of collective remittances sent through transnational clan relations outlines the general pattern of financial contribution from US Hmong to their co-ethnics in Laos and resonates with many similar cases. As revealed in the above exchange, the social relationship between the money sender and the recipient is established through close family and relatives and expanded by clan networks. The cross-border kin networks supervised by clan representatives in different diasporic communities also confirm how Hmong have successfully organized and institutionalized their kinship system and used it as the basis for the transnational remittance economy across national borders.

When extended family members across generations participate in collective transnational economic and emotional exchanges, there are several benefits. As many US Hmong in my study indicated, money may be the most "convenient" way for them to contribute collectively to those living in Laos, because in their words, "it is just money," compared to making frequent visits to Laos or maintaining regular communications in order to stay in touch. In addition, the Hmong kinship system also enables second-generation Hmong Americans to participate in the clan-based transnational economy with relatives in Laos without the pressure to maintain other substantial social commitments and obligations to them. In the case of the Sacramento Hmong community, when funds were collected as a group, only a small monetary contribution was expected from each of these young Hmong. Not only did this reduce the financial burden of remittances for individual Hmong families, but they could also avoid expensive international transfer fees that they would have paid if the remittances were sent individually.

Living on American Dollars in Laos through the Transnational Money Chain

Stereotypical images of Hmong as impoverished citizens in a poor Laotian national economy have persuaded US kin members to engage in an irregular yet persistent transnational economy of financial remittances. From a developmentalist perspective, Hmong people's living condition in Laos may be seen by their US co-ethnics as impoverished and their socioeconomic status as patently low and marginalized. As discussed in chapter 2, despite the thriving tourism and mining industry in the rural village of Dao Tha and the subsequent diversification of employment in the town of Vang Vieng, it is true that the economic activities and opportunities for Hmong were still very limited.

In this context, collective remittances from Hmong relatives in the United States provide critical funds for Hmong in Laos to cover a range of daily expenses as well as occasional special events, to buy pieces of land (rice fields), and, less commonly, to build a better (cement) house. One interviewee, Ying Cha, a villager in his mid-forties in Vang Vieng, spoke about how his economic condition improved with the help of his siblings and extended family members living in the United States. He juxtaposed familial love and economic support within the diaspora by saying:

> My father's younger brother's family in America helped my family here a lot in the past. They bought land and rice fields for us in three places and helped us to build two houses. For my own family, the total cost was more than 41,000,000 Lao kip [US$5,100]. If they had continued to be well off in America, they could have helped us more. This is how you really love each other as Hmong. But now their help has stopped, so we are poor again.

Usually, small-scale, irregular remittances tended to be used for daily necessities and subsistence but also for larger purchases and consumer items, such as TVs, DVDs, refrigerators, motorbikes, kitchen appliances, and furniture, rather than saved for future investments. Occasionally, they were used to fund the education of children, which enabled a limited number of Hmong youth to leave farming and pursue other careers. Remittances also allowed some Hmong households to establish capital for businesses, such as buying a tuk tuk or truck and opening shops at the market in town, although no Hmong in Dao Tha owned stores in Vang Vieng.

Financial support from Hmong in the United States was not limited to basic subsistence or business needs; it also provided funds for special events that are an important part of Hmong villagers' cultural life in Laos. Almost all cultural celebrations and rituals for both individual households and the broader community in Dao Tha were at least partially funded by the remittances and financial contributions of their co-ethnics in the United States. Without such a transnational economy, annual Hmong New Year celebrations and various spiritual rituals or funerals that require funds to purchase food and supplies would have been very difficult for Hmong in Laos to afford.

Compassionate Money   137

Finally, collective funds from the US Hmong community could sometimes be used by individuals for other personal reasons, such as luxuries like international travel. According to Xou Her, a Dao Tha villager in his forties:

> My relatives in the US are telling me, "Whenever you pass the interview at the Lao American embassy and you are ready, let us know. Each of us will collect little by little to get you the plane tickets to come here [the United States]. We can collect fifty to one hundred dollars from each household and perhaps a total of five thousand dollars can be given to you." The grandfather [Xou points to the house across from his] earned about twenty thousand dollars that way [which he used for travel].

On the other hand, US remittances have allowed some Hmong villagers in Dao Tha to buy illegal drugs, such as opium. During my daily visits to different households in the village, I continued to observe ill and deteriorating elderly Hmong suffering from the health consequences of opiate abuse. When I visited them, I brought them eggs (the most nutritious-looking food item on sale at the tiny corner shop on the village road) and checked how they were doing. Because they knew that I had met and would continue to visit their families and relatives residing in the United States, I often begged them to at least eat food by reminding them that if they starve and rely only on drugs, I will really have nothing positive to tell their families in there when I receive any questions from them.

In sum, remittances from the diaspora, especially American dollars from US Hmong, have been the most important economic resource for Hmong in Dao Tha regardless of whether they were used for daily subsistence, consumer items and luxuries, important cultural events, or to fund a drug habit. Such monetary contributions were an essential and feasible means for Hmong villagers in Laos to continue to engage in transnational relationships with their families and relatives residing in the United States.

Transnational Familial Love Expressed through Money

Although US remittances are a critical form of economic sustenance, their cultural meanings and emotional significance simply cannot be ignored. The importance of money is based on the social meanings inscribed on this transnational capital by Hmong in Dao Tha in the name of familial love, transforming them into emotional remittances. In fact, much of the emotional affection involved in cross-border interactions is based on the circulation of US dollars sent to families in Laos for various purposes on numerous occasions.

Nonetheless, as noted earlier, the meaning of money was not construed in the same way between Hmong I studied in Laos and the United States, since the two communities have shown different attitudes about the relationship between money and familial love. While Hmong in Dao Tha openly shared their economic hardship with their co-ethnics residing in the United States and explicitly requested monetary contributions as an expression of love (including familial care, compassion, and longing for family overseas), the US Hmong I interviewed did not seem to believe in this emotional discourse. Although money has become a powerful means to express familial love and affection across national borders in the diaspora, it is important to consider such internal differences among the Hmong communities in each country. In addition, we must further examine the factors that enable these Hmong families to continue their transnational economic relationships that constitute shared diasporic identities across national borders despite such differing views about what money symbolizes.

Money as Familial Love and Economic Survival for Hmong in Dao Tha

One day during my fieldwork in Laos, I was talking with three Hmong men from different age and clan groups sitting on a wooden bench outside a house in Dao Tha. All three of them confirmed that they have family members and relatives in the United States, including a daughter, sister, and uncle living in California and Minnesota. Their family and relatives had visited them at least once in the last twenty years. They have also received financial support from their family and extended clan relatives multiple times, especially when there were important family or clan events in the local community, such as *ua neeb* (shamanistic rituals), funerals, weddings, and New Year celebrations. At the same time, they also frequently received smaller amounts of money, a couple hundred dollars at various times, which they used for daily needs and living expenses.

One of our initial conversations was about how they continue to feel love toward family members in the United States despite being geographically separated for such a long time and clearly equated it with monetary remittances. One of them stressed with certainty, "Yes, we still love each other, of course. For example, my relatives in the US, they still send us money to help and care for us. It is because they love us." Another man emphasized how he cries when he misses his family members in the United States. He then added, "I miss my relatives so much, so I tell them to send money to help me."

In these discourses, there was no clear distinction between love/care/longing and money at all. It is not clear whether materialistic desire precedes emotional yearning and attachment to family or the latter leads to the desire to request material contributions and commodities. Regardless, two seemingly contrasting values—money, as a purely economic value, and an emotional sense of longing and desire for care—were conflated to produce materialistic familial love and monetized social relationships, a system that works especially well in transnational contexts when people are geographically separated. For Hmong in Dao Tha, the money sent from families, relatives, and clan members has already become emotional remittances that symbolize the transnational continuity of social and kin relationships, which are imbued with intimate affinity and love that makes diasporic identification and belonging possible across national borders.

For instance, Xia Her, one of the elderly Hmong men whose younger brother and clan members migrated to the United States as refugees and mostly live in Sacramento, frequently equated money and familial love and longing as inseparable from the very beginning. His emotional longing has grown even stronger after his adult son recently migrated to join his brother's family in Sacramento. In a brief but powerful manner, Xia shared his feelings:

AUTHOR: Do you miss your son, Tou?
XIA: Oh, of course I do.
AUTHOR: When you miss him, what do you do?
XIA: Oh, when I miss him, I can't sleep well. . . . I get up, sit, and keep thinking. . . .
AUTHOR: What do you think about him? Can you give me an example?
XIA: I see people driving a car, but I have to walk because I don't have a car. When I see other people drive, I miss my family in America and want to receive money from them so I can also buy my car.

Apparently, material desire (such as for a car) can evoke Xia's emotional longing for his family abroad, which then makes one wonder whether he would no longer miss his family as much if he could buy a car with remitted money.

On the surface, this seems to resemble a modified version of Karl Marx's commodity fetishism, where the relationship between money and commodities in exchange comes to represent and obscure social relations. However, if a commodity enables the Hmong in Dao Tha to represent their persistent sense of familial love and longing toward transnational kin, the material object (a car, in this case) transforms such intangible sentiments into a visible and concrete form (instead of obscuring the transnational social relations), making it even more meaningful and valuable than its original economic value. When the local economic conditions of Hmong in Laos are perceived as insufficient and impoverished, it makes sense that financial assistance from faraway family members is the best form of familial care, since it allows them to purchase commodities like cars that embody and express love on a transnational scale.

Hmong in California: Money as a Questionable Icon of the Heart

While Hmong in Dao Tha frequently expressed materialistic transnational longing by making inseparable connections between money and familial love, Hmong in Sacramento did not explicitly describe their transnational social relationships in such a manner. Although they believed and hoped that remittances could partially compensate for their physical absence in Laos and provide practical economic assistance for their co-ethnics there as a means to fulfill their expected commitments, there was no indication that money is seen as a sufficient way of showing their transnational love, care, and longing for their families. This makes the emotional meaning of money more ambivalent and its power rather questionable for US Hmong who participated in transnational economic relationships, especially when some of their family members in Laos expended remittances on illegal drugs, as noted earlier.

One reason why US Hmong I interviewed in California did not strongly associate remittances with love can be related to how they perceive remittances as simply materialistic, detached from its emotional values, in contrast to their co-ethnics in Laos. As a result, they did not feel that monetary contributions can fulfill their familial and social responsibilities to kin and clan members in Laos, which require physical presence and actual in-person contributions (including labor, support, and active participation) to local cultural events at the community level, such as New Year celebrations, religious rituals, and other social gatherings.

However, as is the case for most transnational families separated by diasporic migration, physical presence and simultaneous participation are no longer possible for important cultural activities and community events between the two countries. This is especially the case for Hmong in the United States, who left their natal homeland of Laos and migrated abroad as refugees, making it impossible for them to always be present at and participate in social events with their co-ethnics in Laos. Although simply sending money and material goods to Laos is not sufficient to make up for their physical absence, they often felt that there was no other way to (at least) partially fulfill their family/clan responsibilities from afar by assisting those back in the former home country.

As a result, this social role of money for meeting transnational family commitments produced ambivalent and incongruent meanings because it was not fully satisfying for Hmong interviewees in California and felt less effective than expressing "love" through actual participation in family and community events back in Laos. Thus, their remittances can still be emotional but may represent feelings of regret stemming from their physical absence in their home country more than family care and nurturance associated with their "love" per se.

There are other reasons why US Hmong in my study were less likely to associate remittances with love. In principle, if their family in Laos has demanded remittances in the name of love to compensate for their migratory absence, they should be free from such obligations when they travel to Laos and visit their families to be together (and can thus express their love and care directly in person). However, even when they return and are actually present in Laos to participate in local events, requests and demands for money from multiple members of their family and clan continue to persist, if not become stronger. Indeed, Hmong from the United States who have visited their families and clan relatives in Thailand and Laos discovered that they were expected to bring additional money with them even after having to cover their own travel expenses. This seems to have made my interviewees in the United States wonder whether money is really "love," or is just money.

In addition, the frequent appeals for money by family members in Laos in the name of love were also interpreted somewhat cynically by US Hmong interviewees as an emotional means to justify instrumental motives and, thus, not entirely sincere. Many noted that money is quite "insufficient and too materialistic" for them to express "real" love, which should be separated from economic considerations. They also mentioned that they sent remittances to family and clan members in Laos because they felt it was "the least" they could do and "the most convenient way" to help. However, they rather critically pointed out that money should not be misunderstood as a proper way of showing love, despite what their co-ethnics in Laos say. In fact, some of them indicated that they were sometimes reluctant to talk to their Hmong relatives in Laos too frequently because they would constantly be asked for money.[5]

The story of Cheng Her, a Sacramento resident, about his trip to Laos aptly illustrates such experiences. Cheng has a sister, a cousin's son, and a lot of other relatives living in a Hmong village in northern Laos. He not only has been in contact with them frequently but also sent money to them upon their request. He and his wife traveled once to Laos through Thailand for a total of one month, more than fifteen years after they came to the United States. As a father of eleven children living in California, this onetime trip meant a lot to Cheng, because he had to accumulate many years of savings despite the economic hardship he experienced as a wage laborer at a local assembly line. He estimated that he must have spent at least eight thousand dollars for the entire trip, including buying his flight tickets and providing funds for his relatives in Laos, along with paying for a cow and pigs for a feast to celebrate his visit to the village. Even before and after the trip, his monetary contribution and financial support continued. We discussed his financial support for his family and relatives in Laos:

> CHENG: The people living back in Laos and Thailand are very poor. If they are ill, they need money to go to the hospital or to do ua neeb [shamanistic rituals]. That's why I send them money. I gave them money for funerals, too.
>
> AUTHOR: Do you miss them?
>
> CHENG: Yeah, I do. When I call my sister, she cries every time [*he makes crying sounds and then laughs*].
>
> AUTHOR: What do you usually tell her if she cries?
>
> CHENG: I say, "It's okay, don't cry. I will send you a little money, so stop crying." Haha! [*laughs*] . . . There may be some rich families there, but that is not my family. My cousin, my sister, and my relatives have no money. They are still poor.

I sensed that Cheng had gotten a bit cynical about his family's reactions as possibly an emotional ploy by impoverished kin to pressure him to send more money. He constantly laughed during the interview, even imitating his sister's constant crying about missing him. Cheng later said he did not believe that his love and affection for his family in Laos can be expressed through monetary contributions to compensate for his physical absence, but he still acknowledged and accepted the way his family in Laos interpreted and valued such emotional remittances. Because he was the co-breadwinner for his sister's family in Laos and felt a moral obligation to help impoverished kin in a less-developed country, Cheng responded to the sister's emotional reactions and longing by assuring her that he would continue to send her money.

Similar cynicism was also expressed by other Hmong in Sacramento who would frequently receive calls from their elderly family members in Laos requesting "emergency" remittances in the name of love when in fact the money would be used for other purposes, such as day-to-day necessities, consumer items, and home goods, or even for opioid drugs. Most of the time, such emergency phone calls sounded urgent, as if the caller allegedly had to rush to the hospital because of their ill health. Hmong families in the United States would discuss such requests quickly, collect ten or twenty dollars from different clan members, and send the money to the person who received the phone call. One time, when a Hmong in Sacramento received such a phone call, I asked what it was about. I was told rather casually that it was "just another phone call that they need money for the hospital. But you know, I know what it is for [to buy drugs]." The indifferent reaction reminded me of some of Hmong I knew in Laos who did indeed ask for money for their illness but ended up spending it on new home appliances or other miscellaneous daily goods.

In sum, for Hmong in Laos, money followed the heart and represented emotional connections, familial care, and a sense of longing, all of which were translated into the term "love." However, the same money was not mutually understood in the same way by Hmong in the United States but rather as a convenient (but not always sufficient) method to meet social expectations and respond to familial monetary demands from afar. Nonetheless, money still plays a significant role and encourages diasporic Hmong to stay connected and maintain their social relationships across national borders, thus serving as a source of social continuity and mutual diasporic identification among those separated from each other.

Global Economic Inequalities and the Cultural Meanings of Remittances

The cultural meanings and emotional value of remittances is also structured by global inequities between nation-states. This helps to explain why my Hmong interviewees in California, who did not necessarily see remittances as expressions of love, continued to send money to Laos anyway despite their doubts and reservations. In fact, a 1.5-generational Laotian American woman I met during my fieldwork in Laos, who later became a good friend, was constantly surprised and asked me why Hmong in the United States do not get tired of the repeated requests to keep sending money from their families in Laos. Because her parents and relatives in the United States opposed such financial support, which simply "gives a man fish" but does not "teach a man to fish," they eventually stopped sending remittances (except occasionally to fund education and major events).

Awareness of global economic inequalities was one important reason why US Hmong I studied have continued to send remittances, even if they were not convinced by the emotional appeals from their families in Laos in the name of love. Despite their own economic marginality in the United States, they fully understood the greater economic resources they had because of their relatively privileged position in the global economic hierarchy and firmly believed that life in impoverished Laos is still incredibly hard in comparison. Their remittances could thus be an important means to fulfill their moral obligation to support families and relatives and alleviate their poverty in an underdeveloped national economy. Otherwise, they could be criticized as "not caring" but "greedy" by their families in Laos. In fact, even protracted refugees who live in long-term exile have been known to send "seasonal" remittances to support their homeland and diasporic co-ethnics abroad (see, e.g., Hajj 2021; Zuntz 2021).

However, because remittances usually flow from wealthier migrant-receiving countries to economically less-developed home countries, they are often one-directional. Like other migrants in developed countries, many Hmong I met in California usually remitted with no expectation of return from their co-ethnics in Laos. Although most Hmong in Dao Tha did express their gratitude by calling on the phone after receiving the money, the only material goods they sent to their US family members (upon request) included herbal medicine, tea, and handicrafts from Laos. In addition, this has increasingly become difficult because of the complicated process of international shipping, fees, and customs. Therefore, if money indeed symbolizes transnational familial love, such emotional remittances for Hmong residing in the United States have essentially become a form of unrequited love because they cannot be returned by co-ethnics living in less-developed countries that are lower in the global economic hierarchy. Nonetheless, even if remittances for US Hmong interviewees were not fully imbued with emotional meanings of love, they continued to send them because of their country's global positioning as a wealthy country vis-à-vis Laos.

Compassionate Money   145

In the example discussed in the previous section, Cheng assumed that Laos has a perpetually impoverished economy that provides insufficient living conditions for his family there. In Sacramento he has maintained a frugal life with limited economic means and a low income, but for family members in Laos he believed that his relatively small monetary contribution made a huge impact as a major source of income. This explains Cheng's unconditional willingness to continue financially supporting them. Likewise, another interviewee, Kheng, had a similar view about the Laotian national economy, which not only explains why he continued to remit money but also convinced him that a small amount of money is sufficient to support Hmong relatives in Laos. During the interview, he also noted, "Over there [Laos], they can still farm so they can survive. But here, we cannot survive without money. [*laughs*] So we need to only contribute for major events in Laos, not for everything. I think most other Hmong here contribute money to Hmong in Laos in the same way." Therefore, perceptions about the different national economic status of migrant host and home countries not only influences the cultural meanings of remittances but also the motivation to engage in transnational economic relationships.

Conclusion: "Love Accompanied by Money"— Transnational Continuities through the Familial and Clan Economy across National Borders

This chapter has demonstrated how the transnational social relationships between the two Hmong communities I studied in Laos and the United States have been partly enabled by monetized economic transactions that are sent through extensive transnational familial and clan networks. As Michael Hardt (2011) emphasizes, love becomes more powerful when it is beyond intimate or private relations and able to create social bonds in broader public and societal contexts. In this sense, money in the form of remittances to kin living abroad has become an indispensable medium to project feelings of love and maintain social and kin relationships across national borders for people living in geographically separated, diasporic communities. This also enables them to communicate, connect, and participate in each other's distant lives, producing mutual solidarity and a common identity as diasporic peoples despite different understandings about the meaning of money.

Such transnational continuities across borders would not be possible with either love or money alone. Simple expressions of love without money would lack a tangible and commodified medium through which it can be effectively transmitted across national borders as emotional remittances. On the other hand, money remitted without feelings of love would make transnational social relationships constituted by remittances less intimate and meaningful. In this sense, the familial affection and emotional connections that were developed and maintained by transnational economic relations among diasporic Hmong in my study require a material basis that cannot be merely dismissed as "inauthentic" or "materialistic." Love accompanied by money is an integral part of the transnational social connections that keep these Hmong diasporic communities together.

However, although remittances remained one of the most prominent transnational interactions in the Hmong diaspora, there was a notable discrepancy of meaning between senders and receivers of remittances. As shown in this chapter, the emotional value of love attached to money was more prominent for the remittance-receiving community in Laos. While Hmong in California found remittances a convenient way to maintain their transnational kinship ties with those in distant Laos, money was not seen as sufficient to express love, care, and longing. Instead, it enabled them to fulfill their moral responsibility to support less economically fortunate kin in the home country. Nonetheless, because requests for remittances were couched in the language of "love," it became a very powerful factor that pressured US Hmong to continue such economic transactions and provide financial support despite living in the United States for decades. This also means we need to take into account the factors that make remittances emotional instead of limiting our analysis to their contribution to national economic investment and development (see also Huennekes 2018). The connection between money and love through transnational economic exchanges should continue to retain its analytical value as a way to understand diasporic continuities and belonging.

For diasporic Hmong I studied in Laos and the United States, transnational socioeconomic connections organized by an extensive kinship and clan system have also enabled various cultural practices to become highly transnationalized and maintained across national borders. These include traditional religious practices such as shamanism, as well as funerals and New Year celebrations, which will be analyzed in subsequent chapters. While they have become cultural continuities that have produced and promoted a sense of ethnic belonging and diasporic identity, they have also become transformed as they are practiced transnationally in different countries.

Compassionate Money   147

5

From Local to Transnational

Hmong Shamanism and Spiritual Rituals across Borders

During my fieldwork in Dao Tha and other Hmong villages in Vang Vieng, I frequently observed two distinct types of shamanistic spirit-calling rituals, one for local Hmong villagers and another for their families and relatives living in the United States.[1] The most memorable of the first type of spiritual healing rituals was conducted by the oldest and most-respected shaman for a family whose mother had been ill and weak for a while. On the day of the ritual, I rushed up the hill to arrive at the Hmong community early in order to help the villagers prepare for the big event. Outside the house where the ritual was to take place, many people were busy running around preparing for a feast. They were trying to build a fire, pouring water into a giant silver metal pot, checking other pots that contained rice and pork soup, and placing tons of thick wooden chopping boards and knives collected from different households on a large plastic mat on the ground.

I saw several people I did not recognize, who must have been family members and relatives from other places, ranging from nearby villages to as far away as the northern part of Laos. The whole ceremony required sacrificing two full-size cows, a large number of chickens, and some pigs in order to make sure the ancestors' deceased souls would be fully fed when they visited and joined the feast. A choice cut of meat was also to be given to the shaman in return for his ritual services. Certainly, the large gathering and feast was expensive for the family members. But as I was repeatedly told, this was a way for them "to share food and reaffirm their communal bond and sincere respect for the ancestors of the entire family's clan."

The social activity and excitement outside the house were a dramatic contrast to the shaman's world inside the home, which was serene and rather peaceful. Joua, an elderly shaman, was sitting on a small, old wooden chair in the middle of the family's dark house in his black dress and nontransparent veil as he waited with two rattling bells in his hands. Soon the shaman's ritual began as he rattled his bells to the rhythm of his gong man, who was standing next him, in order to summon the spirits of the ancestors. I realized that he had entered into a trance while he communicated with the ancestors in some incomprehensible language, which was the highlight of the ritual. His voice started to rise slowly but powerfully, and his body trembled more and more and shook left and right, seemingly out of his control or consciousness. Hearing the high tone of his voice, which resembled shouting, I started to wonder whether his communication with the ancestors' spirits was going well or not.

The shaman eventually rose to stand on the chair, his face still covered by the black veil, while he continued his nonstop chanting at a high intensity. I became a little worried whether he might fall over because of the veil and the tiny chair, but the intensity of his voice deterred me from holding the chair to make sure it would not tip over. Both his high-pitched voice and the loud clattering of his bells and the gong flowed out through the half-open door and mixed in with the hustle and bustle of the participants outside, who continued to prepare for the feast. The spiritual ritual provided a lot of emotional comfort for the family and gave them hope that the mother would be cured.

Two months after this spiritual ritual, I ran into the same shaman, Joua, on my way to interview one of the Hmong residents in the village. Joua was under a tree on the side of the village road and was about to complete a spiritual ritual. Unlike the previous ritual, which was for a local Hmong family, this time he was conducting a transnational spirit-calling ritual for his six-year-old granddaughter, born and living in California, whom he had never met before. His daughter and relatives in the United States had told him that his granddaughter had fallen onto the floor and was injured and requested that he conduct a ritual for her remotely from Laos.

Joua had already conducted the healing ritual for her, and now that she was recovered, he was conducting another one, this time to thank the ancestral spirit. For both rituals, there had been no community gathering or feast. Instead, he was by himself, chanting in a low voice; spreading rice wine around the corner of the tree; and distributing cooked rice, pieces of boiled chicken, and two cooked eggs to feed the spirits of the ancestors. After he was finished, I asked whether such an individualized ritual in Laos would be able to bridge the souls of the living in the United States and those of the ancestors in the spirit world, despite the geographical distance across national borders. Joua responded right away and claimed, "Of course, my ua neeb [shamanistic ritual] worked very well. Living in a distant land or a foreign country does not matter at all! It's the same thing."

In a calm and confident manner, the shaman slowly walked down to his home with a tiny shot glass, two split buffalo horns, and a few half-burnt incense sticks. This was one of many transnational spiritual rituals I observed in Laos, which were private, small-scale, and informal, and had been developed to accommodate the needs of the shamans' families, clan members, and close friends residing in the United States and elsewhere. They often took place on the side of a road, in a corner of a house, under a tree, or in the middle of a hill. Despite the substantial geographic separation between the two countries, it is believed that the shaman's healing power remains effective transnationally.

Situating Shamanism Transnationally across National Borders

According to the Hmong people's emic perspective, ua neeb, in the Hmong language, can refer to both shamans and the healing rituals conducted by them (including spirit- or soul-calling rituals).[2] As is the case with many concepts used in Hmong cultural practice, this chapter does not consider terms such as "spirit" and "soul" as clearly distinguishable and translatable to English. Most scholars (and Hmong themselves who employ English terms) use both "soul" and "spirit" interchangeably in the context of shamanism, although recently ua neeb seems to be referred to more as "spirit" (rather than "soul") calling. While it is difficult to distinguish between the two concepts, I use the word "soul" in a broad sense to refer to not only human souls but those of various other living beings (e.g., animals and trees), since Hmong rituals also deal with the souls of the latter. "Spirit" is used in this chapter in relation to human ancestors; thus, ua neeb that invoke them will be referred to as "spirit"-calling rituals.

Some scholars have examined Hmong shamanism as religious beliefs and practices (Mottin 1984; Tapp 1989b), while others have focused on its medical impacts and efficacies (D. Cha 2003; Culhane-Pera et al. 2003). The latter is especially prevalent in studies about Hmong American communities as part of their experiences with Western biomedical systems (e.g., Culhane-Pera et al. 2003). In particular, Dia Cha's (2003) insider account helps us understand the Hmong's cultural perceptions about health, illness, and medicine and their experiences with American medical systems.

However, throughout my research, Hmong referred to ua neeb rituals as *both* religious and medical healing activities, so the two were often combined. Indeed, shamanism and ua neeb have become an integral part of their lives not only in local contexts and communities but also in the transnational religious, medical, and cultural lives of Hmong in the diaspora who believe in ancestral spirits. From an emic perspective, when someone becomes ill, that person's soul is seen as in trouble and lost. For example, Cha Thao, a senior shaman in his sixties in Dao Tha, explained to me how ua neeb works for treating specific illnesses:

> Let's say you fell in the river, and soon you became seriously ill. One minute, you feel so warm, and then another minute, you feel cold and your whole body shakes. In this case, your shaman should do ua neeb in the river [which is where the afflicted person's soul was lost]. You kill two chickens: one for your forefather and the other for your foremother. Take them to the doorstep of your house, ask your ancestor's spirit to call your lost [wounded] soul to come back, and offer the chickens to feed the ancestor's spirit [to thank them for their help]. Then you will get well.

Treating an illness through shamanism, therefore, is not simply a medical procedure but is based on religious beliefs and practices as well. The person's physical body that needs to be treated is seen as inhabited by the soul, as Hmong explained to me during numerous shamanistic and spiritual rituals during my fieldwork. Ultimately, because bodily/physical ailments and diseases are seen as the domain of the soul, it is the soul that must be treated in order for the body to be cured. Since shamans are believed to serve as the medium between the deceased ancestors and their living descendants, they communicate with the souls of both their clients (patients) and their ancestors in order to find the exact causes of the illness and request the assistance and guidance of ancestral spirits to help cure the ailment.

Because shamans seem to commune separately with these spirits during the ritual, some scholars refer to this as a "mind-body dualism" (see D. Cha 2003; G. Lee and Tapp 2010, 29; Symonds 2004). Based on her research with the Hmong community in Colorado, Dia Cha (2003) similarly suggests that Hmong seek treatments for their physiological and spiritual conditions separately (i.e., herbs and traditional medicine for the former and shamanistic healing for the latter). However, the fact that the cause of the bodily illness and its treatment is connected to the soul can also indicate that the body and soul are not inherently separate.

While medical healing is one of the major aspects of religious ua neeb, because of the extensiveness of the spirit world, ua neeb also assists people in other ways as well, which makes it more challenging to define Hmong "religion" in clear terms. Indeed, shamans I observed played multiple roles in people's ordinary lives as consultants, religious guides, and medical healers who provide assistance not only for physical and mental health (e.g., emotional distress, anxiety) but also for various individual concerns, such as financial instability and crisis, children's futures, family relationships, and other afflictions, through smaller-scale spiritual rituals. Likewise, a Hmong scholar criticizes the limited notion of shamanism in Western contexts because of the extensive roles played by shamans (Her 2018).[3]

The diasporic dispersal of Hmong from Southeast Asia to various Western countries after the Vietnam War did not just lead to an erosion or loss of their shamanistic rituals. In fact, researchers have reported that the beliefs and practices of shamanism have continued in multiple locations in the Hmong diaspora, including all over inland Southeast Asia, such as Thailand (e.g., Hickman 2007; Symonds 2004), Vietnam (Michaud 1997b; T. Ngo 2016; Ó Brian 2018), and Laos (S. Lee 2021; see also Culas 2004) as well as across the United States (e.g., Borja 2017; Capps 1994; D. Cha 2003; Conquergood 1989; Gerdner 2012; Her 2005; Zhang 2020). Outside Southeast Asia and the United States, studies also mention shamanism among diasporic Hmong in Australia (e.g., Julian 2004; Tapp and G. Lee 2004), Canada (e.g., Winland 1994), and French Guiana (e.g., Clarkin 2005).

While Hmong Christians who do not practice shamanistic rituals have rapidly grown in Western countries (Vang 2010, 86) and in parts of Southeast Asia (e.g., T. Ngo 2016; Rumsby 2021), my research focuses on non-Christian Hmong in Vang Vieng and California who have continued to be engaged in shamanism, making it an important shared cultural continuity in both communities I studied. Hmong shamans were present in both countries, and they continued to conduct various spiritual rituals for local patients and clients in each country, who are usually clan members.

More importantly, during my fieldwork, Hmong shamans in various villages in Vang Vieng provided their services transnationally for family members and relatives in other countries across national borders, demonstrating how ua neeb rituals have always been deterritorialized and practiced across national borders instead of being restricted or bound to a specific locality. This chapter focuses on how shamanistic rituals have been practiced transnationally between the two communities I studied in Laos and the United States because of Hmong cultural understandings about the birth of shamans and the mobile nature of souls, as well as their extensive transnational kin networks and social relations across national borders. In this sense, I also demonstrate that the transnational power and continuity of shamanism is based on two types of deterritorialization, which I will call "transborder" and "spatial."

In the two Hmong communities I studied, shamanism has been an important form of transnational cultural continuity based on social relations across national borders as part of their shared diasporic ethnic identity, which supersedes localities and overcomes their geographical separation. At the same time, as shamanism and spiritual healing rituals were practiced transnationally, important changes emerged in comparison to locally performed rituals and services. As shown by the vignettes at the beginning of this chapter, most spiritual rituals in Hmong villages in the Vang Vieng area, especially ua neeb, were a collective group activity that involves a large gathering and sharing of food among family, relatives, and clan members. In contrast, when shamanism was transnationalized across national borders for the Hmong community in the United States, it became individualized and commodified to some extent, indicating that practices that are considered "traditional" can be subject to constant modification in transnational, diasporic contexts. Therefore, the transnational continuity of Hmong diasporic culture does not mean that the same, homogeneous cultural practices persist in an essentialized manner across national borders. Instead, they are modified and adapted to different local contexts as they travel through the diaspora and are subjected to the exigencies of transnational life, which is another reason it remains resilient in the diaspora.

In this chapter, I also examine differences in terms of generation and religious affiliation to understand the extent to which those two factors caused local discontinuities in shamanism and whether this affected its transnational continuity. Younger generations of Hmong in Vang Vieng and California continued to engage in shamanistic practices based on beliefs about ancestral spirits while playing different roles in such rituals. Although Hmong Christians in California did not engage in shamanistic practices, they often recognized that the shaman's healing power is not always incompatible or in conflict with Christianity. Hmong shamanism can also coexist with Western biomedical practices and be effectively practiced with racial or ethnic others.

Religious Transnationalism, Shamanism, and Two Types of Deterritorialization

There has been a recent increase in studies about religion in transnational communities and its impact on the experiences of immigrants, refugees, and diasporic peoples in the host country. Religion plays a key role in transnational social relationships that enable the continuity of cultures across national borders (Cadge and Ecklund 2007; Levitt 2003, 849; McLoughlin 2013; Tapp 2013, 103). Scholars have also examined how resettled refugees convert to mainstream religions such as Christianity, which leads to changes in social and gender relationships (see Ong 2003; Smith-Hefner 1994; Winland 1994), and how changes in religious practices resulting from migration also influence cultural behaviors and ethnic identities as well as internal social relations (Vertovec 2001; Warner and Wittner 1998).

While these studies of transnational religion examine the continuing relevance of religions brought from the homeland or newly adopted religions in immigrant communities, they tend to focus on mainstream religions such as Buddhism, Islam, and Christianity. However, some scholars have also examined the transnational and global dimensions of indigenous and non-mainstream religious systems such as shamanism, which have not been globally institutionalized or based on universalist discourses. As researchers have pointed out, shamanism should not be seen as locally bounded, territorialized, or particularistic (Atkinson 1992, 307–308; Boyer and Bergstrom 2008, 113), but rather, it encompasses some global dimensions. There have been cases of indigenous shamans in Brazil performing rituals for clients outside their localities, including for those who are part of an international medical network (Langdon 2013). Shamanism also involves individuals who travel across borders. This includes shamans who travel to the United States from abroad and incorporate global music into their trance dance to appeal to a wider audience (Cox 2003), as well as Westerners who romanticize shamanism and visit the Peruvian Amazon to experience its healing effects (Fotiou 2016). Local shamanistic knowledge about living harmoniously with nature has also been appropriated by certain members of the global environmentalist movement (Vitebsky 2003).

Although these studies examine how local shamanism can be engaged with transnational and global forces, they do not always discuss the exact mechanisms that make shamanistic practices effective beyond specific localities and across national borders. Since religion is one of the most critical means through which diasporas maintain their transnational social connectivity and the continuity of their cultural practices, it is especially important to provide explanations for how Hmong shamanism has been able to transcend localities and successfully transnationalized by moving across national borders.

Research on Vietnamese ancestral worship indicates that the cultural concept of "mobile souls" explains why this religious practice has spread transnationally through the Vietnamese diaspora. Mobile souls are seen to accompany migrants abroad and also freely and frequently travel back to their homeland (Hüwelmeier and Krause 2010; Nguyen 2003). In addition, technological devices and social media can enhance the global distribution of small-scale, ancestral worship practices between the homeland and the Vietnamese diaspora (Hüwelmeier 2016). Similarly, the Hmong concept of mobile souls allows the shaman's power to be transnationally projected across national borders to Hmong diasporic communities overseas. It is believed that shamans can be born anywhere in the diaspora (and not simply in the homeland) and conduct spiritual rituals in multiple locations. As a transnational cultural continuity, Hmong shamanism was also sustained across national borders between the two communities I studied through active social connections based on extensive kinship networks, which enabled Hmong to communicate with one another and arrange spiritual rituals and services from afar.

The case of shamanism among Hmong in my research indicates that shamanistic rituals have been a significant form of transnational cultural continuity in the Hmong diaspora because it embodies two different types of deterritorialization that makes it well suited to migratory and cross-border social processes. The first is what I call "transborder deterritorialization," which refers to any social process that moves across national borders and is not attached to specific localities. Most discussions of deterritorialization in the transnationalism literature seem to refer to this first type (see Appadurai 1996, 4; Faist 2000, 210–11; Guarnizo and Smith 1998, 10–13; Gupta and Ferguson 1992; Levitt 2001, 202). However, there is another type of deterritorialization that not only crosses national boundaries but also transcends the limitations of territorial space itself (Kearney 1995, 553; Portes, Guarnizo, and Landolt 1999, 224; Vertovec 1999, 449). By using modern telecommunications, digital media, and mass media networks, individuals who are not in physical proximity can interact and communicate over long distances, enabling them to disregard the constraints of geographical territory and physical space. I call this "spatial deterritorialization."

Migration and Shamanistic Births across Borders: Transborder Deterritorialization, Generation, and Gender

Shamanism has been successfully transnationalized and has traveled across borders through the Hmong diaspora partly because of its transborder deterritorialization to numerous countries throughout its history of dispersal. Elderly Hmong shamans currently living in the United States, such as those in California, were mainly born in Laos and migrated across borders to the country as refugees, ensuring that shamans were present in both diasporic communities. Since their resettlement after the Vietnam War, there has not been much new Hmong migration from Laos to the United States, and perhaps the only notable current migratory flow consists of mainly Hmong women in Laos who marry Hmong American men. However, according to my interviewees, new generations of shamans continue to be born in any country where diasporic Hmong have migrated to and currently reside, ensuring its transitional continuity and prosperity.

Although scholars note that some individuals may be taught to become shamans through intensive training and knowledge acquisition from other senior shamans (D. Cha 2003; Mottin 1984, 103), Hmong explained to me that shamans are destined to be shamans by birth. Being born a shaman means that the person's soul is chosen and imbued with spirituality by the ancestors. Such understandings of a shaman's destiny were evident in the comments of many Hmong, including one interviewee in Laos who said:

> Anyone can oversee other customs like weddings and funerals if one is taught, but in terms of a shaman, you can't learn to become one. If you can learn, then anyone could become a shaman. Shamans are born, because their soul was selected by the ancestor spirit. Whether a shaman's power comes to you or not is totally uncontrollable and beyond natural explanation.

During one of the ua neeb ceremonies that I attended in Dao Tha, the mother of a young shaman who was visiting from the capital city recounted how her son became a shaman:

My son's birth was very special from the very beginning. He was born in twelve months, you know, much later than normal. When he was born, he was really small, like a fist. But because of his unusual birth, he became a very capable and famous shaman for the effectiveness of his ua neeb. My son became a shaman not because he was cursed but because our ancestors' special spirit treasured him so much and got into his soul when he was still in my womb.

This narrative affirms that the birth of shamans is unavoidable and even blessed because the shaman's soul is "selected" (literally, "possessed") by their ancestors and therefore "special." Later on, I came to wonder whether one can give up being a shaman after being chosen and what would happen if one refused the role. During an interview in Sacramento, a reputable clan representative, Neng Her, spoke about this: "Well, it may be avoidable in some cases. If you give up being a shaman, you just become really sick and your body will start shaking all the time, forever. But if you want to stop shaking and being ill, you have to become a shaman and just don't practice it. You just feed the spirit once a year, that's it."

The fact that shamanism is inherited by birth has important implications for the transnational continuity of shamanistic culture, because it means there is always a possibility that a new shaman will be born in any Hmong community, even if they are dispersed across the world in the diaspora. Thus, in principle, the presence of shamans and ua neeb was never really geographically restricted to one place but was always detached from specific localities, moved across national borders (through transborder deterritorialization), and eventually became reterritorialized as diasporic peoples migrated and gave birth to shamans in other countries. In fact, senior shamans whom I met in different parts of California expressed no concerns about the possible disappearance of shamanistic practices in the United States, since they believed that shamans would continue to be born among younger generations of Hmong Americans.

Although there can be differences in individual abilities, Hmong interviewees believed that anyone chosen at birth by ancestral spirits can become an effective and powerful shaman regardless of age, generation, gender, and territorial location (that is, whether the shaman lives in Laos or the United States). There can be very young shamans who perform spiritual rituals, whose services are regarded to be just as effective as those of senior shamans. One interviewee noted that there is a shaman as young as ten years old born in the United States, who is quite capable and beloved by elderly Hmong.

In terms of gender, both men *txiv neeb* ([pronounced *tzi neng*] father shaman) and women *niam neeb* ([pronounced *nia neng*] mother shaman) can become equally effective shamans. This principle was frequently confirmed by Hmong interviewees in both Laos and the United States, including by the daughter of an elderly female shaman I interviewed in Sacramento. In fact, a study about shamanism among US Hmong communities identifies a number of female shamans (nine out of a total twenty participants) (Helsel 2019). Stories of new generations of female shamans born in the United States have also appeared in some local newspapers.[4] For example, Hmong American organization reported about the aspirations and challenges of a young female shaman who was initially baptized into Mormonism but later became a shaman after a serious illness.[5]

Despite these cases, I noticed that there still seems to be a gender imbalance among shamans in practice, as it was predominantly male shamans who conducted rituals on numerous occasions, and I have not observed any performed by women in either Laos or the United States. Male shamans were omnipresent, and reaching out to them was very easy and common, whereas female shamans were not socially visible or readily identified as such. I received no clear explanations for the paucity of female shamans from Hmong people, which contrasts with the pivotal role that Hmong Christian women played in the earlier process of refugee resettlement (see Winland 1994).

Nonetheless, the possibility of diversity among shamans in terms of age, gender, and geographical locations alleviates concerns that the tradition of shamanism may eventually "die out" under the pressures of diasporic migration and modernity, especially in Western countries. Because of the migration and birth of shamans across borders, Hmong shamanism has been able to transnationalize through transborder deterritorialization and spread to different countries in the diaspora without losing its effectiveness.

Shamanism as a Spatially Deterritorialized Practice: Mobile Souls in a Borderless World

The transnational efficacy of shamanism is based not only on transborder deterritorialization but on spatial deterritorialization as well. Although there are shamans in the United States because of migration and births across borders, shamanistic powers can also be projected transnationally to other countries because the Hmong spiritual world transcends (to some extent) the constraints of physical space and geographical distance in the material world. As the ritual powers of the Hmong shaman are not confined to specific localities but have always been spatially deterritorialized in this manner, shamans in Laos can effectively perform their rituals transnationally for Hmong living in the United States by using the spirit medium, even if their clients were not in physical proximity.[6]

Because of the Hmong concept of "mobile souls" in the spiritual world, the power of shamans and their rituals are spatially deterritorialized and can overcome some of the limitations of territorial space, making them transnationally effective across national borders even without the physical presence of the shaman. Souls reside in a noncorporeal, spiritual world that is not constrained by the physical barriers and geographical distances of the material world, allowing them to travel freely and instantaneously across national borders to any physical location.

Although spatially deterritorialized souls are supposed to be present "everywhere" and can therefore be technically accessed from anywhere, it is important to note that the spiritual world still somewhat parallels the territorialized spatiality of the material, physical world. This explains why shamans must "call" and summon ancestral spirits and souls from the spiritual realm to specific localities and physical places, therefore temporarily "reterritorializing" them so that they can project their supernatural powers across national borders. Likewise, "mobile" souls actually need to travel in a territorialized manner, as shamans guide their journey through many specific locations from a small village of birth to large cities or countries. In this sense, shamanism involves a constant dialectic of deterritorialization and reterritorialization in the transnational process. Hmong souls can be seen as partly or somewhat spatially deterritorialized, since they apparently cannot completely disregard the limitations of physical space.

The processes of de- and reterritorialization are illustrated in oral folklore narratives told at Hmong funerals about the mobile soul's journey and how it must travel continuously around the world at the direction of a shaman until it reaches its ultimate destination, which is supposedly an unknown place where the ancestors reside (see chapter 6). During the funeral at the Hmong Palace Church in Sacramento,[7] Xia Her, the representative of the Her clan in the area, explained to me the movement of the soul after death:

> The soul first goes to the place you were born. When a baby is born, the family is supposed to bury the placenta under the bed on the ground. At this aunt's funeral, the chanting will send her soul back

to the house [her birthplace] in Laos where her placenta was buried. We don't know where the real homeland is, so the soul cannot really be sent to the homeland. For a lot of us here [the United States], our placentas were buried in Laos. So our souls will first be sent to Laos.

After the soul of the deceased goes back to its birthplace and collects the placenta, the journey continues until it reaches the next major location, China, where the Hmong supposedly originated. Once the soul reaches China, it then tries to cross the border again until it eventually arrives wherever the deceased ancestors are supposed to reside. In the process, the soul is advised to be especially careful while crossing the Chinese border, as there can be attacks by "the old Chinese enemy." While shamans narrated this process during the funeral rituals I attended in both Laos and the United States, joss paper was burned to symbolize an offering of money to the soul, enabling it to pay off enemies to ensure a smooth and peaceful journey.

However, even after the soul arrives at the right place and settles with the ancestors, the journey does not end permanently, because it still has to travel frequently back to where its descendants live whenever they offer food to it as well as when the shaman calls it back through ua neeb and other spirit-calling/summoning rituals. There are other examples of how the deterritorialized soul of the deceased constantly travels and comes back to where the descendants are living and is thus technically reterritorialized. These include spiritual rituals such as *hu plig* (a relatively small-scale ritual to retrieve spirits of the deceased ancestors for various purposes, which does not always need to be conducted by shamans) and *nyuj dab* (a cow/buffalo sacrifice for recalling and commemorating the ancestral spirit, which is conducted more than a decade after the parents' death). In addition, it is not only the souls of the deceased that are mobile. The soul of a living person can also be temporarily separated and detached from the body when the ua neeb spiritual ritual is performed and can instantly travel to any location if summoned by a shaman.

Because the souls of both the living and the dead are spatially deterritorialized but also highly mobile, the shaman is able to perform rituals for clients who have migrated and are living in other countries in the diaspora, even if they are physically apart. A shaman residing in Laos can therefore conduct spiritual rituals for Hmong clients in the United States by immediately summoning both the souls of the dead ancestors (wherever they happen to be) and the soul of the living client (in the United States) and communicating with them through spirit possession.

A spiritual ritual performed outside a family's house in a Hmong village in Vang Vieng.

This spatially deterritorialized power and transnational efficacy of the Hmong shaman was aptly described by a Hmong senior in Dao Tha:

> A Hmong shaman's power is absolute. His healing power can be effective all over the world and across countries [even if he doesn't live there]. In America, when people get really ill, they might go to the hospital, but they still do not get well, since they do not know the

From Local to Transnational   161

exact cause or reason for the illness. So they ask around their relatives and find an effective and well-known shaman who lives here in Laos. They will contact and talk to the shaman on the phone and send information about the symptoms of the patient. After hearing about the problems, the shaman in Laos will try to figure out what happened to the patient's soul—whether the soul had a bad dream, got into an accident, or fell into the water. . . . Once the patient gets well, the family will contact the shaman again and send updates about the recovery of the patient. Then the shaman in Laos performs the ritual again to thank the patient's ancestor soul, who guided his ua neeb and cured the patient. The power of the shaman still works just like before [even when it is enacted in transnational contexts].

In sum, even if Hmong shamanistic rituals are performed locally, they are not territorially bound to a specific locale, but their power can be transnationally projected across the Hmong diaspora because souls themselves are not spatially bound and are free to move across territories. Therefore, spiritual rituals can be arranged and practiced around the world regardless of where shamans and their clients actually live. This is another way shamanism has operated transnationally between Laos and the United States.

Transnational Continuity and Local Discontinuity of Hmong Shamanism in the American Context

Cultural understandings about shamanistic births and mobile souls certainly explain the ability of diasporic Hmong to transnationally maintain shamanistic practices between Laos and the United States through both transborder and spatial deterritorialization. Despite such transnational cultural continuities, it is equally important to examine how possible local discontinuities in shamanism have affected the US Hmong community. Although American-born Hmong youth and Christians can be considered groups that may discontinue practicing spiritual rituals, we need to examine the varying degrees to which youth still participate in shamanism as well as diverging perceptions among Hmong Christians about the practice.

In my research, shamanism remained prevalent among Hmong in California. Both small-scale spiritual rituals (performed, for instance, in the backyards of family homes) and large-scale rituals conducted in community centers (e.g., as part of funerals) were frequent. Since these rituals in the United States were arranged collectively by the community,

US-born second-generation Hmong Americans often had access to the rituals in various ways, including through family and relatives. Indeed, both small- and large-scale spiritual rituals I observed throughout my fieldwork in California were well-attended by Hmong of all generations, who played different roles in these rituals.

During various interviews, young 1.5- and second-generation Hmong in their twenties who believed in shamanism discussed their participation in various rituals. As college students, they faced some challenges when attempting to engage in Hmong cultural practices at the level of their parents and community elders. However, there was always a group of youth who were more actively involved and closely worked with and assisted shamans throughout their rituals. Among them, one interviewee who was particularly serious about shamanism regularly spent weekends visiting a local shaman to gain more in-depth knowledge about ua neeb. Many others helped with cooking, setting up the rituals, and doing errands for their parents.

Those Hmong youth who could not relate to the ritual because of the incomprehensible language and procedures simply attended the ceremony (and chatted with their relatives) knowing they were often followed by fun family gatherings with plentiful food. Although the main roles in the rituals I observed were played by senior men, I consider the above activities forms of youth participation in shamanistic rituals, in contrast to some studies that found shamanism to be increasingly marginalized in the United States because of resistance among US-born young Hmong and lack of participation from Christians (e.g., Franzen-Castle and Smith 2013).

Continued or "revived" youth participation in Hmong shamanism is also discussed by some scholars. For example, in Deborah Helsel's (2019) study, shamans in California commonly noted that young (US-born) Hmong patients have become more enthusiastic about shamanistic healing and actively requested such services because of the growing interest in traditional, alternative medicine in the United States. Some Hmong communities in Minnesota provide financially affordable and less demanding spiritual rituals in specific community locations (e.g., St. Paul's Temple of Hmongism), making it more relatable and accessible to local Hmong youth (see Zhang 2020).

It is true that Hmong Christians do not practice shamanistic rituals based on ancestral spirits. This contrasts with other Hmong ethnic traditions, which are not discontinued by them but instead appropriated and modified (e.g., New Year festivities and parts of wedding ceremonies;

see chapter 6). Such local cultural discontinuities in terms of shamanism were evident during services at a Hmong Christian church in Sacramento. Numerous sermons stressed how the Hmong community needs to leave behind "old traditions" like shamanism ("belief in ancestors and ghosts") and become a "new," "modern" ethnoreligious community in the United States (see chapter 6). Despite being influenced by such teachings, however, many Christian Hmong told me during interviews that they "respect and tolerate" Hmong shamanism even if they no longer believe in ancestral spirits. Although Christian Hmong did not engage with traditional shamans, they agreed with non-Christian Hmong I interviewed, who generally felt that such traditional spiritual rituals do not have to be incompatible with modern Christianity and can indeed transcend religious (and even ethnic) differences (see below).

Despite such *local discontinuities* in shamanism among one religious segment of the US Hmong community, shamanism was still practiced by the dominant non-Christian Hmong population in the various California communities that I visited. It thus remained an important *transnational continuity* between Hmong in the villages in Vang Vieng and cities in California despite their diasporic migratory dispersal after the Vietnam War, which is enabled by cohesive social kinship networks across national borders. Hmong in these two diasporic communities were able to effectively practice shamanism because they used transnational kinship networks to plan, communicate, and arrange shamanistic and spiritual activities between the United States and Laos. As discussed in chapter 3, Hmong kinship does not consist of only biologically related kin (family and relatives) but also involves a broader clan system based on shared surnames and clan exogamy that has remained remarkably resilient in both Lao and US Hmong communities despite migratory dispersal. Thus, shamanism is constituted not simply by cultural beliefs but also by social relations.

Therefore, the maintenance of the shamanistic tradition among Hmong in California did not always require them to extensively practice spiritual rituals in their local communities, because they can also ask for services from shamans in Laos through their transnational kinship networks. When they arranged rituals remotely in this manner, they mostly relied on shamans who were family or relatives in Laos. Those who did not have extensive and direct transnational family connections contacted members of their broader network in Laos in order to find and consult with a shaman who is a clan member.

For example, Hmong in Sacramento created contact lists of clan members living in different countries (which were posted on their walls, doors, refrigerators, or kept in notebooks) and used them to communicate with clan-based kin who are not part of their immediate family or relatives to obtain information, exchange economic resources, or receive assistance for urgent concerns such as illness. As discussed in chapter 3, even clan members who are not biologically related are obligated to extend familial hospitality and assistance to other clan members both locally and transnationally. Because transnational kinship networks are extensive, there were only a few individuals in California who found shamans in Laos completely outside their clan. While some scholars note that the difficulty of finding knowledgeable local shamans could have caused some Hmong to convert to Christianity (e.g., Borja 2017), the ability to arrange shamanistic rituals and services transnationally has enabled its cultural continuity across borders.

I observed that Hmong living in California were more likely to contact shamans in Laos through their kinship networks, whereas almost no Hmong in Laos sought out US Hmong shamans for transnational spiritual services. I asked why US Hmong chose to arrange spiritual rituals remotely in Laos instead of relying on shamans in their local community and why Hmong in Laos did not seem to demand US shamans' services as much. However, there were no really decisive answers or clear explanations. I was generally told that the decision to consult with a shaman locally or transnationally is totally "up to the patient's/client's family." None of my interviewees in California mentioned that they contacted shamans in Laos because they were "better," more reliable, "traditional," or culturally "authentic." Indeed, although Laos can function as an ethnic homeland for US Hmong (see chapter 1), and "authentic" cultural traditions are often seen as located in the homeland by diasporic peoples (see e.g., Jones 2002, 12; Tsuda 2016, ch. 7), I encountered no such discourses about the homeland authenticity of shamanism among Hmong during my research in either Laos or the United States. Interestingly, this contrasts with funeral rituals, where those practiced in the "homeland" of Laos were deemed more "authentic" by Hmong in both communities (see chapter 6).

It is possible that Hmong in Sacramento sought shamans in Laos mainly because it may have saved time and labor and reduced the cost of the ritual. Indeed, large-scale ua neeb rituals performed in the United States could be demanding, as it often becomes an extensive and collective event that involves the entire extended clan and includes a feast and an animal sacrifice.[8] In contrast, if the ritual is conducted transnationally from Laos for Hmong in Sacramento, an extensive gathering is not always a feasible option, so the ritual is often performed individually by the shaman in private (see below). In this case, because the Hmong family in the United States cannot be present to witness the shaman's spiritual rituals in Laos, they sometimes request photos or video recordings from the shaman to see how the ritual was conducted. However, this only partially explains the motivation of seeking transnational services, as US Hmong can still do so locally by considerably simplifying and modifying shamanistic rituals (see Helsel 2019; Zhang 2020).

Occasionally, if shamans in Laos decide that a large group gathering and feast are still necessary for the ritual, their US Hmong clients would have to arrange the feast either in their own local community or even travel to Laos. In fact, while in Laos, I met and observed a number of Hmong from the United States who were visiting their families and relatives in order to be present at spiritual rituals and fund the feasts, although their visit was also combined as part of larger trips or vacations. For example, Yang Lee from Michigan and his cousin Tou Lee in Dao Tha arranged over the phone an extensive spiritual ritual months before Kong took a trip to Laos with his wife. They discussed overall preparations and made sure everything would be ready (including the communal gathering and sharing of food). Tou's family in Laos bought and killed a cow and prepared the rice, chickens, joss paper, and drinks in addition to contacting the clan members in local villages to gather for the occasion. All of the subsequent traditional ceremonial procedures were followed, including the elderly shaman's ua neeb, conducted at home. Yang paid for the entire cost of the ritual, which was several thousand dollars.

Rarely, but equally interestingly, individual shamans from Laos were invited to Sacramento to conduct spiritual ceremonies and services. In such ways, Hmong have used international kin relations to successfully conduct shamanistic rituals transnationally across the diaspora. Even if the shaman lives far away, US Hmong in my research believed that such spatially deterritorialized shamanistic rituals are just as effective as those conducted in their own local communities. The best evidence of the effectiveness of the shaman's transnational power is of course when the patient recovers from the illness.

When "Traditions" Become Transnationalized: Individualization and Commodification

When shamanistic rituals that were initially conducted in local contexts traveled across national borders and were practiced transnationally, significant changes emerged in this cultural tradition. Although traditions are often assumed to be cultural forms inherited from the distant past and thus more "faithful" to original practices (Hobsbawm 1983, 8; see also Bendix 1997), it is quite clear that they have always been constantly altered and remade over time. Scholars have commonly argued that traditions are always in the process of recreation and subject to change because of contemporary agendas and pressures (Briggs 1996; Clifford 2004, 156–59; Graburn 2001, 10; Handler 1986, 2; Linnekin 1983). This is especially the case when previously localized cultural traditions are deterritorialized to multiple diasporic locations by migrants and practiced across borders and are therefore modified and transformed in new transnational contexts (Tsuda 2016). However, these practices continue to be perceived as "traditions" that have been maintained and passed down in their original form from the ancestral homeland. In this sense, they remain transnationally "traditional."

In the case of Hmong diasporic communities I studied in Laos and the United States, transnationalization made traditional shamanistic cultural practices more individualized and commodified so that they could accommodate both shamans and patients/clients living in each respective country. Indeed, the distinctive nature of cultural traditions is their adaptability (as well as flexibility) to modify and transform their procedures, logistics, and many other structural components, especially in the context of transnational migration.

Individualization

As Hmong shamans in Laos provided their spiritual services to the diasporic community in the United States, their rituals have become increasingly individualized. When US Hmong arrange for such transnational spiritual services, the client's family and the shaman are not in physical proximity as is the case for localized shamanistic rituals. Thus, a large group gathering of extended clan members in Laos is not convened since the client family is not present. In this case, the spirit-calling ritual needs to be performed by the shaman alone without the family and a large group of participants who witness and assist with the ritual (as described in this chapter's opening vignette). This also means that the collective activities of animal sacrifice, cooking, and sharing of food are abridged for this type of transnational shamanism.

For example, in order to arrange shamanistic rituals transnationally, the Hmong family in the United States would first call the shaman residing in Laos to discuss their concerns and problems. The shaman would then conduct an initial and informal spiritual ritual, which involves throwing buffalo horns, in order to "ask" and communicate with the ancestor's spirit and determine whether it is necessary to conduct a more extensive ua neeb for the family. At this consultation stage, transnational interactions and communications between the shaman in Laos and the family in the United States may occur exclusively on the phone. It is possible that the shaman can already divine the causes of the problem and provide instructions about how to deal with it without performing ua neeb.

If the shaman decides that a ua neeb ritual is necessary, he or she communicates further with the US family to discuss possible dates for the ritual, the logistics, and estimated costs. The choice of date for the ua neeb can be influenced by whether the family in the United States can actually take a trip to Laos and be present during the ritual. However, since it is believed that the physical presence of the client at the time of the ritual does not impact its effectiveness or ability to resolve the problem, when travel back to Laos is not feasible or possible, the shaman conducts the ritual in Laos without the presence of the family. Depending on the shaman, some objects that symbolize the client's body and substitute for his or her physical absence may be requested. For instance, one of the US Hmong clients in Sacramento mentioned that when his mother was treated for her illness and received ua neeb from a shaman in Laos, the shaman asked her to send him one of his mother's T-shirts, which would represent her body and symbolize her presence. The senior shaman in Dao Tha who conducted the ritual in the opening vignette of this chapter used a picture of his young granddaughter sent from Sacramento.

Another elderly shaman I met in Laos, Pia Lee, had also been conducting individualized and informal ua neeb rituals to cure sickness among his cousins and his sister's relatives living in different cities in the United States. Pia usually conducted the spiritual rituals by himself inside his house without any witness. Depending on the seriousness of the request and concerns, Pia could have done a more extensive ua neeb at his house, which would include sacrificing an animal and food sharing, but he noted that doing so was not necessary. "About ten days after performing ua neeb, I usually receive good news from the family on the phone that their situation and problems are resolved," Pia remarked. Because his successful ua neeb services could be provided transnationally and effectively, other clan members in the United States continued to ask him to conduct these rituals for various issues, especially when family members fell seriously ill and did not recover, even with Western medicine or surgery.

As these transnational shamanistic rituals conducted for US Hmong did not include extensive community activities, it has been transformed from a socially rich communal event to an individualized private performance by the shaman without the participation of extensive family and clan members. Nonetheless, this individualization of spiritual rituals, when conducted from afar, does not reduce its healing power as long as the shaman is reliable and experienced, and it is considered to be equally effective as the collective and localized version of the ritual.

Commodification

During my fieldwork, when shamanistic rituals were performed transnationally across national borders, they were not only individualized but also increasingly commodified. According to Hmong in my study, in the past, shamans in Laos who practiced for the local community asked the family to prepare certain items and buy animals for sacrifice but did not request cash payment for their services. After the ritual was over, the family was certainly obligated to give the shaman something in return, such as the head of the pig (as a symbol of worship) or the best part of the cow meat sacrificed during the ua neeb ritual. In this manner, the ritual was considered an act of reciprocal social exchange, and a gift from the client was an expression of gratitude for services provided. The shaman's services were not rendered as a commodity that could be bought and sold with money.

In contrast, when shamanism is practiced transnationally in the diaspora, it is not possible for the US family to directly arrange for an animal sacrifice or communal feast in Laos in their absence or to send fresh meat to the shaman in Laos. Because they cannot express their gratitude to the shaman for the services through reciprocal gift giving in person, they instead do so by sending money. When shamanistic rituals are performed across national borders among diasporic Hmong, the geographical separation between the shaman and client has inevitably led to greater commodification of the relationship. Instead of reciprocating through a gift (such as meat), Hmong families residing in the United States have found an alternative means to express appreciation by placing a monetary value on the shaman's services and sending a cash payment.

Interestingly, some Hmong interviewees in California mentioned that they were ambivalent about Hmong shamans in Laos receiving cash payment for performing ua neeb and other spiritual rituals transnationally. For example, one of the young Hmong in Sacramento, Xiong Lor, felt that Hmong shamans in Laos must practice "pure and genuine" ua neeb. According to him, in principle, shamans' services are supposed to be socially beneficial and benevolent, not a type of capitalistic enterprise done for economic profit. Hmong in Vang Vieng also confirmed that monetary payment to shamans has recently become more common in their local community. They observed how shamans in Laos became used to being paid by US Hmong for their transnational services (or have heard of other shamans being paid) and began to charge even local families in Laos a fee because it increases their monetary income (compared to simply receiving meat as a gift). In this sense, the transnationalization of shamanism in the diaspora works both ways. Not only did shamans in Laos influence Hmong abroad across borders, but Hmong in the United States have also changed shamanistic practices in Laos.

Although the transnational version of the ua neeb and other spiritual rituals has become an economic transaction whereby the client pays the shaman for their labor and services, such commodification of shamanism is precisely what has made its transnational practice possible in the diaspora. It has undoubtedly simplified the overall process of ua neeb for US Hmong and made it much more convenient, since they do not always have to spend the time, resources, and effort arranging an animal sacrifice and feast in their own local community. Instead, the transferring of money to the shaman resembles the economic remittances sent from families in the United States to those in Laos. If US Hmong were not allowed to replace the meat-giving practice with cash payment to shamans in Laos for their services, it would have become much more difficult for them to enlist the shaman's services across national borders and possibly led them to rely only on local shamans in their own community.

The transnational persistence and continuity of shamanism in different countries in the Hmong diaspora is certainly a result of its adaptability to various national contexts. Not only are souls themselves mobile and able to readily travel across national borders, but shamanism has also proven to be a quite flexible tradition, allowing it to become individualized and commodified in order to adapt to the pressures of transnational, diasporic life. Despite these changes, however, Hmong in my study continued to regard shamanism as an important ethnic tradition that has been passed down for generations from ancestors in the distant past, giving it continued cultural authority and respect even when practiced in diasporic contexts. In addition, shamanism has also shown an ability to coexist with other contrasting forces of "modernity," such as Western biomedicine and Christianity, while remaining racially and ethnically inclusive. This is another important reason for its cultural continuity and transferability across national borders in the Hmong diaspora.

Mutual Coexistence: Biomedical, Religious, and Ethnic Others

Although many scholars have claimed that religious practices among transnational migrant communities brought from the original homeland can create conflicts with the mainstream host society (Cadge and Ecklund 2007; Levitt 2003), Hmong in my study who practice shamanism believed it can coexist with Western biomedicine and Christianity and can be applied to ethnic others in multicultural societies. As a result, traditional cultural practices do not simply decline or eventually disappear under such forces of Western modernity (Graburn 2001; Tsuda 2016, 234).

While Hmong shamans I spoke with recognized that their traditional healing rituals are under pressure from Western biomedicine, they did not necessarily believe that shamanism is threatened by and in fundamental conflict with modern medicine. In contrast to depictions of Hmong shamanism in the United States as completely incompatible with and opposed to mainstream American medical systems (e.g., Fadiman 1997), many non-Christian Hmong in California themselves did not always resist or reject Western biomedical care but instead adopted a much more accommodating position. Among them was Moua Xiong, a senior shaman in Sacramento, who had served Hmong in Laos and the United States for nearly forty-five years. Moua said:

> Yeah, for me, it is completely fine to go to hospitals. Actually, my [US-born] youngest daughter is a nurse working at the hospital. In the past, she would not want to listen to me at all. She said, "Your way is old and incorrect." But right now, she says it's "fifty and fifty." She means that American doctors cannot be right one hundred percent of the time, just as ua neeb can't be one hundred percent right. . . . If a person is almost dying, the family will bring the sick person to practice ua neeb. There are cases that those people actually ended up living a normal life. Other people who couldn't be cured by ua neeb might go to the hospital and can get better.

This resonated with the personal opinions of many Hmong in my study, who did not consider the shaman's healing power to be "outdated." A Hmong pharmacist in Sacramento, who was a believer of shamanism despite his medical training, pointed out that shamans' roles as medical service providers are not valued from Western medical perspectives. According to him, this is because beliefs about ancestor spirits lack "research and development of scientific, accurate knowledge," not because they contain some kind of fundamental fallacy.

In Laos, Hmong people's healing practices were also increasingly under pressure from biomedicine during my fieldwork, especially since the country has been investing in the development of a Western biomedical system. In fact, the Lao government has financially supported the overseas training of medical students and invited foreign medical practitioners to develop modern medical systems in the country. Hmong shamans are apparently not recognized by the government and are outside the national interest. A young shaman his early thirties in Laos, Poa Moua, shared with me his struggles and dilemmas as a shaman in current Laotian society. He noted that the shaman's authority can possibly be looked down upon because their status is not approved by official and authoritative institutions, such as the government or other national organizations.:

> I am an herbal medical doctor, but because I am not a real medical doctor, my life is not always easy. For medical doctors, patients always visit hospitals to see them. But for a shaman doctor, I have to be the one who goes to visit each individual patient to practice rituals inside their homes. Medical doctors tend to get more respect when they treat patients because of their formal education and official degree in medicine.

Although there may be disadvantages to being a shaman in a society that is increasingly prioritizing Western biomedicine, my discussions with Hmong shamans in Laos indicated that they did not always perceive Western biomedicine as a threat to what they believe to be their "traditional" way of life. Instead, some Hmong medical doctors actually understood the complexities of both "traditional" healing and professional and "modern" medical systems and regarded them as complementary and coexisting. Thus, although tradition is often understood to be inherited from the distant past, it is not always incompatible with modernity (see Hefner 1998).

During a spiritual ceremony for a family in a Hmong village in Vang Vieng, a young man was proudly introduced to me by the elders as a promising medical doctor who had trained at a major hospital in Vientiane. The man shared his thoughts with me about the increasing criticism that Hmong healing rituals have been receiving:

> If someone is hurt or gets injured, Hmong will want to be healed by ua neeb rituals according to our customs rather than Western medical treatment. It is because Hmong value the ancestral power very much

and highly respect the spirit, as well as having deeper faith in their traditions. But doctors and new religions like Christianity dislike and criticize our tradition, because they believe that when someone gets sick or hurt, chanting and superstitious rituals cannot heal them. In my opinion, conducting rituals is based on an individual's faith and respect, and it is a voluntary action. So I believe the action itself should not be the target of criticism.

Christianity is another (Western) national influence that supposedly challenges the legitimacy of Hmong shamanism, especially because of the growing Hmong Christian populations in the United States who do not practice traditional spiritual rituals. However, many accounts from interviewees who believe in ancestor spirits and shamans indicate that Christian religious conversion within the Hmong community does not always have to conflict with shamanism. As senior shamans in both Laos and the United States claimed, in principle, "There is nothing wrong about being a Christian, since all religions are supposed to teach how to be a 'good' person."

The possible coexistence of shamanism and Christianity was frequently discussed during my interviews. One of the village leaders in Dao Tha regarded the conversion to Christianity among some US Hmong in a somewhat sympathetic manner. He noted that although Christians may face hostile reactions, in the end the religion has the "same" good intentions and outcomes as Hmong shamanism. Hmong Christians in the United States like Shoua Yang, whom I met at the Hmong church in Sacramento, agreed with non-Christian Hmong about religious coexistence even with their potential differences and divisions. She got along well with her mostly non-Christian Hmong friends at school despite the fact that her family members are all Christians. Referring to large Hmong gatherings in her neighborhood as "traditions," she said, "Even though we do not believe in the same thing, either shamans or Christians, we still meet up together because it is good to be in the culture together."

Likewise, Youa and Kheng, a 1.5-generation married couple from different religious backgrounds, had been able to manage possible conflicts. Youa was from a Christian family, and Kheng was the son of one of the prominent and senior shamans in Sacramento. According to Youa, "In my heart, I am a Christian. I was raised as Christian. [But] I would go to his [her husband's] family functions and be there even if I don't believe in it [shamanism] or practice it." She continued, "He [Kheng] knows how I am. I am not going to give up something that I don't want to. I believe in Jesus, and he can't make me change and believe in shamanism. So we kind of just learn to live with the difference. I let him do [what he wants] and I do my own things for religion."

In addition, the religious boundaries between shamanism and Christianity can be fluid and transgressive, as shown by religious conversions. During my fieldwork, there were even stories of shamans who converted to Christianity. Mai Lor, a staff member at a nonprofit organization in Sacramento, narrated the story of her father-in-law, who used to be a reputable shaman. During their time in a Thai refugee camp, Mai's little niece was seriously ill and showed no sign of improvement despite extensive Hmong healing rituals. The family decided to take the niece to a Christian group in the camp for prayers, which, she claimed, cured the illness miraculously. As a result, Mai's shaman father-in-law "gave up everything to save the granddaughter and decided to become a Christian." More importantly, religion is not always a choice between two binary worlds, as shown by the case of a Hmong Christian in Canada who was both a pastor at a local church and a shaman (see Winland 1994).

Indeed, religious conversion is not unidirectional (from Hmong shamanism to Christianity, as often assumed). Individuals can move across religious borders in both directions. Lena Thao, a professional in her late twenties in Sacramento, was from a family that converted to Christianity, but after her marriage, her husband's Christian family converted back to Hmong ancestral spirituality. A young 1.5-generation college student, Sai, had an even more dynamic family history of repeated, bi-directional religious conversion:

> Actually, when we first came to the US, we were still with shamanism, but we switched to Christianity [later]. When my father got sick and was dying, my mom switched back to shamanism [to try to cure him through spiritual rituals]. She really loved him and wished to do whichever that would make him better. After my dad passed away, we then returned to Christianity. We kind of switched back and forth.

Nonetheless, Hmong who practice shamanism could experience social tensions and disputes about it with Christian Hmong because of their disagreements about ancestor spirituality versus Christian worship of God. Indeed, such criticism from Hmong Christians about their shamanistic beliefs can be frustrating, just as Hmong Christians may find it unfair to be criticized for their apparent cultural incompetence in Hmong traditions and even be shunned by the community. Instead of direct religious conflict, there are various perspectives and individual differences among Hmong who believe in ancestral spirits and those who are Christians.

Finally, in addition to its religious inclusivity and its porous borders with Christianity, Hmong shamanism can also be practiced with people who are not Hmong and thus adapted to multiethnic and racially diverse societies. In other words, it operates across both territorial and ethnic boundaries. As Langdon (2013) notes, shamans have engaged in a "dialogical process" with their clients not only across geographic locations but across racial boundaries as well (see also Fotiou 2016; Taussig 1987). There have been occasions when Hmong shamans provide services to non-Hmong individuals in both the United States and Laos. Despite the particularism often attributed to local and indigenous religious practices, the shaman's power can be based on a discourse of universality akin to world religions like Christianity and seen as effective for all people, regardless of their race and ethnicity. The following story, of unknown origin, about an American doctor treated by a Hmong shaman in the United States was told by a senior villager in Dao Tha:

> Once there was a white American doctor in the US, who got into a car accident. After being treated and released from the hospital, he got seriously ill again. He went back to the hospital, took medicine, and did everything possible, but he still did not recover. The doctor thought to himself, "I am a medical doctor, but how come I can't take care of myself?" and he became sad. One day, the doctor remembered his Hmong friend and went to consult him. He told the friend, "I am still young. I don't want to die yet. But I am so sick, from sunrise to sunset." After listening to him, the Hmong friend said, "You should go to see our shaman. Perhaps our culture can do something for you." His Hmong friend took the doctor to a Hmong shaman. After some tests, the shaman said, "Your soul is troubled and very sick. It fell down from the airplane! Now you have to do ua neeb so that your soul can come back. Then, you will get better. I can help you." The shaman cured the doctor's soul and he recovered after ua neeb. Now the doctor respects the shaman like his parent, because he was once nearly dead but regained his life with the shaman's help.

Similarly, although Hmong shamanism is not recognized in Buddhist Laotian society, the shaman's healing power is known to other ethnic groups, and there are a few individual Buddhists who privately seek out Hmong shamans when they face limited options to treat their serious illness and health problems. In Dao Tha I was told about the friendship between a senior Hmong shaman and two Lao Loum men that began after they were once treated by the shaman for their illness and distress. I sometimes ran into these Lao men, sitting in front of the shaman's house.

When I greeted them and asked what they were doing, they laughed and told me, "Nothing, just killing time with friend [*laughs*]." One of these men also helped the Hmong shaman's family purchase a secondhand truck from a company in the capital city using his knowledge, personal networks, and business skills as a former tuk tuk driver. In fact, I should also count myself as a foreign patient who was treated by a Hmong shaman during my very first stay in Dao Tha, when my legs were bitten severely by mosquitos and I could barely walk.

These are important examples of not only how the shaman's power is transnational and compatible with the forces of modernity but also how it can be applied to medical, ethnic, and religious others. The ability of Hmong shamanism to coexist with Western biomedicine and Christianity and embrace those of other ethnicities and religious backgrounds certainly demonstrates its inherent flexibility. This likely enables traditional cultural and healing systems like Hmong shamanism to persist in transnational diasporic communities, despite being constantly subject to the supposed pressures of modernity and ethnoreligious diversity in various countries.

Conclusion: The Continuity of "Traditions" in Transnational Contexts

For diasporic peoples like the Hmong, who have scattered to numerous countries around the world in response to a long history of persecution and war, the continuity of ethnic cultures is of fundamental importance for both the persistence of their transnational communities as a form of diasporic belonging and as a marker of their ethnic identity. Despite centuries of dispersal and displacement, shamanism has remained one of the core diasporic cultural practices among Hmong I studied in Laos and the United States. It is not simply a place-based religion that is tied to specific localities, but it has always been effectively practiced in many countries as well as across national borders because it is able to constantly reinvent itself in transnational contexts as it relocates to other countries.

The spiritual practices of the Hmong are able to successfully transnationalize because of cultural beliefs about shamanistic births as well as the mobility of souls, which are an indication of shamanism's transborder and spatial deterritorialization. Shamans will continue to be born in the diaspora, allowing diasporic Hmong in the United States and elsewhere to enlist the services of local shamans. In addition, shamans provide spiritual services not only to clients who are in physical proximity but also to diasporic communities abroad, as they can project their power anywhere in the world in a deterritorialized manner. Because the spiritual world is not as bound by physical space or barriers, the shaman is able to instantly invoke the mobile souls of living clients and their dead ancestors, wherever they happen to reside. Finally, Hmong in my study have practiced shamanism as a transnational cultural continuity in the diaspora through extensive family relationships and clan kinship networks between Laos and the United States, which allows them to receive the shaman's healing power and ritual services from abroad.

Nonetheless, when cultural traditions like shamanism are transnationalized, they are also invariably transformed in the process as they move across localities. Although shamanistic rituals in local contexts are usually collective, community events based on social exchange, they become both individualized and subject to greater commodification when practiced transnationally across borders. In fact, what makes a cultural practice continue to be "traditional" is not its unchanging nature but its ability to adapt in the face of transnational modernity while retaining the essential elements that connect it to a distant and unknown past.

In addition, not only has Hmong shamanism effectively crossed national borders; it has also overcome ethnic and religious borders to some extent by encompassing non-Hmong and religious outsiders within its spiritual healing power while coexisting in a complementary manner with Western biomedicine. Jacob Hickman's anthropological study similarly shows that the adoption of Hmong shamanistic healing practices has been "syncretic" with biomedicine, furthering the possibility that such practices are adaptable to various host countries of diasporic resettlement (see Hickman 2007). Although we may still observe conflicts between these two healing systems, shamanistic traditions are not always threatened by the forces of modernity, but they can effectively incorporate the "modern" in order to remain relevant and even thrive in a globalized world. In sum, shamanism has an uncanny ability to operate in both territorialized and deterritorialized contexts by embracing continuity and change as well as medical and ethnoreligious diversity in various contemporary societies.

However, despite the importance such transnational cultural continuities supported by cross-border social networks, which create a sense of ethnic belonging among diasporic Hmong I studied, it is equally important to realize that diasporic cultures and experiences are filtered through the nation-states where they are situated. While Hmong in both Laos and the United States have strived to maintain a shared ethnic identity through kinship networks, economic relationships, and common cultural traditions, significant national differences in cultural practices have also emerged among them. The Hmong people's diasporic identity should therefore be understood as based on simultaneous affiliations with both the different nation-states where they reside and their transnational ethnic communities across borders. The next two chapters will examine the presence and ongoing impact of the nation-state and national differences, which will complete the holistic analysis of diasporic identity.

PART III

Cultural Difference and Discursive Fragmentation

6

Cultural Differences in the Diaspora

Hmong Funerals and the Nation-State

During an interview in Sacramento, Moua Xiong, an elderly Hmong shaman in his mid-seventies, explained to me why he believes Hmong in Laos and the United States have remained "similar" despite their long geographical separation in different nation-states since the Vietnam War:

> Our culture depends on where we live because Hmong have no homeland. We do not have a country of our own, so we don't have a special place in America where we can practice Hmong rituals, like funerals, together. Whatever we want to do here, we need to borrow a place from *them* [by which he meant the government, or the non-Hmong mainstream society]. This is the same in Laos, as Hmong must always follow what *they* say. There has been no real change in this situation. [emphasis mine]

Moua believed that Hmong in Laos and the United States are not that different, because as a people without their "own country," both are situated as permanent ethnic minorities in other people's countries and therefore must seek permission from "them" when practicing Hmong cultural customs. Although he made a poignant point that the Hmong's positionality as a minority has never changed, this, ironically, inspired me to examine its consequences from a contrasting viewpoint. If diasporic Hmong are similarly positioned as ethnic minorities everywhere, their cultures could have become different, as they are subject to the power structures of the different nation-states in which they reside. And if so, how has this happened?

Diasporas Embedded in Nation-States

Understanding diasporic people's experiences in national contexts is often challenging, because diasporas are primarily understood as denationalized phenomena and associated with migratory displacement and deterritorialization, which produces dispersed, transnational communities (Appadurai 1996; Axel 2000). Although it is well known that diasporized people who have resettled in multiple countries experience the impact of nation-states on their everyday lives, especially those of the second and later generations born and raised in these countries, theorizing diasporic cultures from the perspective of national belonging and identity is not always straightforward.

The diasporic identity and belonging of Hmong in my study are not simply a product of transnational cultural commonalities and connections—namely, kinship relations, familial/clan economies across borders, and shared cultural traditions, such as shamanism. Because Hmong are also subject to national power and pressures, their diasporic cultures are not homogeneous; instead, they are refracted through the nation-state and often selectively "nationalized." Understanding the national presence in diasporic communities reaffirms how diasporic cultures are not simply deterritorialized but are shaped by the continuing influence of various nation-states throughout the process of dispersal and resettlement.

Therefore, instead of a singular and essentialized transnational Hmong culture, a considerable amount of cultural differentiation has occurred among the two diasporic Hmong communities I studied in Laos and the United States because of the influence of the different nation-states where they currently reside. Their diasporic culture has been subject to varying national economic and cultural systems, political policies and regulations, and social pressures from the mainstream host populace. This is an example of how Hmong who are dispersed in various countries have come to modify and practice their cultural traditions in quite different ways because of this selective nationalization. Ultimately, both transnational continuities and national cultural fragmentation simultaneously constitute diasporic identity and have become an important part of "being Hmong" across national borders.

In this context, both this and the next chapters explore how national differences among the two Hmong diasporic communities I studied are manifested in their diasporic cultural practices, and how their partial affiliation to these two nation-states also produces discursive fragmentation because of the contrasting manner in which they perceive each other. This chapter will focus on Hmong funerals as an example of a cultural tradition that has been modified in national contexts because of differing social pressures and economic resources, as well as restrictive state regulations. As a result, notable differences have emerged in how the two Hmong communities conduct funerals, leading to considerable cultural differentiation in the diaspora along with varying discourses about cultural "authenticity."

At the same time, it is important to remember that such cultural differences among diasporic peoples are not simply the product of the nation-states in which they are embedded. Further variations in how diasporic cultures are practiced within a country can be generated by subnational differences within Hmong communities in terms of local socioeconomic factors and religious affiliations. Although there is no doubt that national differences in economic wealth affect how extensive and lavish funerals are in the two countries, they are also affected by local differences in economic means among Hmong families in both countries. In addition, Hmong in Sacramento who have converted to Christianity distanced themselves from funeral traditions and have simplified them considerably, producing further internal cultural and discursive differences within the local community.

In order to demonstrate the ongoing impact of different nation-states on Hmong people's diasporic culture, the chapter also briefly compares funerals with Hmong New Year celebrations in Vang Vieng and California. Unlike the case of Hmong funerals, where the US nation-state (including both the government and the mainstream American public) is more intrusive, for the Hmong New Year, the Lao nation-state seems to be more interventionist. However, there are other national factors and public pressures that have prompted Hmong in California to introduce significant changes to their version of the New Year celebrations. As will also be shown in this chapter, such palpable national differences in cultural customs have become a source of disagreement among Hmong in my study, especially about the "authentic" way to practice their ethnic traditions. In this sense, their discourses of authenticity are incongruous and can be differentiated along national lines, depending on the specific cultural practice.

Hmong Funerals in Different National Contexts

Varying national, social, and economic contexts have produced significant cultural differences in how Hmong practice and perform their cultures, such as funerals and New Year festivals. While there was generally no regulatory control over funerals or burials by the Lao state during my research, the US Hmong community in Sacramento has been under much more nationalizing pressure from both state regulations and the American public.

Cultural practices of ethnic minorities at the margins of the nation-state have long been the subject of governmental policies and national projects (Duncan 2004, 1–3; Eriksen [1993] 2002; Toland [1993] 2009, 1). However, the level of national intervention in minority cultural affairs varies depending on the cultural practice at hand in its relation to national ideologies and agendas. States often produce self-contradicting and selective policies by either glorifying or reducing their cultural differences and diversity (see G. Clarke 2001, 427; Salemink 2007). This is especially the case for multiethnic nation-states that profess multiculturalism as their ideological means to govern society. In Southeast Asia, scholars have demonstrated how the state and governmental policies overtly define "bad" versus "good" minority cultures to promote or regulate (e.g., Jonsson 2010; Petit 2013). For instance, Jean Michaud (2013) illustrates how the "selective cultural preservation policy" of the Vietnamese government promotes "benign and aesthetic" minority cultures but defines Hmong shamanism and funerals as "superstitious" and imposes restrictions on them.

In addition, analyses of the nation-state in general and their relations with ethnic minorities in particular should not be restricted to explicit state power and governmental policies but must also be broadened to encompass pressure from mainstream society and the public (the nation's people). Hmong interviewees in California commonly pointed out that because they do not live in Hmong ethnic villages like in Laos, they feel the influence of American society to a greater extent and face public disapproval of Hmong customs that are perceived to be in violation of American cultural values and sensibilities. This can be part of the impact of the nation-state on Hmong diasporic culture that limits the ability of Hmong communities to perform certain traditional customs such as funerals "properly" as they did in Laos. In contrast to the top-down power of the state, such American public pressure is still part of the governmentality embedded in the ordinary social relations of institutions and communities that discipline immigrants and minority individuals to become proper cultural subjects and citizens (see Foucault 1982; Ong 1996, 2003).

In response to national and public pressures, Hmong in Sacramento have altered their funeral customs to conform not only to state regulations but also to American cultural norms in an act of voluntary self-subjugation. The funeral I attended in a village of Vang Vieng was held at the family's home and in a large, open area outside of the house, and it was attended by both the extended clan community and members from the village. However, for the funeral I observed in Sacramento, only a small gathering was held at the deceased person's home, while the actual funeral rituals and ceremonies were conducted separately in a rented event hall (the Hmong Palace Church). I was repeatedly told that non-Hmong landlords and neighbors are very critical of and clearly object to extensive funeral ceremonies conducted with many people in front driveways or even in the backyards of homes. In response, the Hmong had to conduct the proceedings in a private ethnic community space away from the public's eyes.

In addition, animal sacrifice, which is supposed to connect the souls of the dead to the living, was an integral part of the funeral in Lao Hmong communities. During my fieldwork, there was no government pressure on the Hmong villagers against engaging in animal slaughter, nor was there any official regulation of it.[1] In contrast, because of US state regulations that strictly prohibit the uncertified slaughter of animals by private citizens, this critical component of the ritual was completely missing; instead it was conducted remotely, as will be described below. Finally, the relative access to economic resources among US Hmong in Sacramento compared to their co-ethnics in Laos enabled them to hold much more ornate and luxurious funeral ceremonies. In sum, funerals in these local settings clearly show the interconnected relationship between cultural differentiation and national differences in diasporic Hmong communities.

Funerals as a Communal Event: Hmong Villages in Vang Vieng, Laos

One afternoon during my fieldwork in Laos, Yia, a young father, generously gave me a ride to attend a meeting in one of the Hmong villages located on the other side of Vang Vieng. Despite the loud and rusty noises that his motorcycle engine constantly made, Yia and I talked about how my fieldwork was progressing, and we reviewed the Hmong cultural activities and events I had attended so far. Yia noticed that one major event was missing and asked: "Have you ever seen a Hmong funeral?"

AUTHOR: No, I haven't.

YIA: Oh, that's too bad! I hope you can have a chance to see a Hmong funeral while you are here for your research and before you leave.

AUTHOR: [*laughs*] Oh, well, but in order to do that, somebody has to pass away. I would rather not see that happen.

YIA: Oh, that's true!" [*laughs*]

At that time, I certainly did not imagine that I would really end up attending funerals in both Laos and the United States during my fieldwork. A few months later, in December, Yia's distant relative from his Lee clan, who lived in a different Hmong village, passed away. I followed Yia the next morning to attend the funeral. We departed Dao Tha early, around five o'clock in the morning and arrived at the village in about thirty minutes. We spotted the house, where many people had already gathered in various small groups and were busy with various tasks associated with the funeral.

Yia and I entered the room inside the house, where a simple wooden coffin was placed that contained the body of a deceased elderly woman who was dressed in a black dress suit and a triangular hat with embroidery on her chest. The coffin had already been in the home for four days of visitations from close relatives and clan members, some of whom had traveled a considerable distance. A group of visitors were standing and sitting around the coffin, crying and talking. They repeatedly apologized for being "late" to come see the deceased and were wishing her soul the best for the journey ahead. These visitations would continue for a week and included all-night vigils.

A man was standing in the middle of the room in front of the coffin, dramatically beating a drum in coordination with another man, who was blowing qeej, the bamboo pipe. A big pile of paper money (joss paper) was being burned on the dirt floor inside the house in order to bestow it on the deceased grandmother's soul to be used for its journey into the afterlife. The man who was drumming recognized that I was not "one of them" and asked me, "Are you *that* Korean?" At that very moment, he forgot to beat the drum and missed several beats. Somebody in the room jokingly asked him to pay attention to his drumming and not be distracted by talking to me. Everyone in the room started laughing.

Soon after all the paper money was burned, the coffin was lifted by a large group of people (mainly men), taken outside, and placed on top of a long wooden table set up on one side of the road. A group of women who followed the coffin started to decorate it with a candle, an umbrella made of clean white paper, and tree branches while they chanted songs of consolation and best wishes. The women then placed on the coffin a glass of *lao lao* (the Laotian rice wine), a pair of new slippers, long sheets of pink toilet paper (which symbolizes blankets), a bowl of rice, and, finally, a small shovel.

All of these items were bestowed on the deceased grandmother to prepare her soul to start the journey back to the unknown Hmong homeland and eventually reunite with her parents in heaven. Food, blankets, an umbrella, and an extra pair of slippers are all seen as necessary for the long journey ahead, which supposedly involves lots of walking and harsh weather, such as rain and extreme cold. The branches are to provide shade from the sun's heat when the soul takes a break during the journey. The soul also needs money when she crosses the Chinese border on the way to the homeland. Because of Hmong's diasporic memories of ethnic persecution by the Chinese in the distant past, the soul may have to "bribe" the Chinese in case they find out that the deceased grandmother is Hmong and refuse to let her continue her journey or even try to "steal" her soul.

In fact, earlier in the funeral ritual, when the coffin was taken outside, a group of men circled around the house clenching their fists and making hand gestures that symbolize fighting and pushing away the Chinese "enemy." Once the women decorating the coffin were finished, the group of men who carried the coffin out of the house knelt around it and bowed to the dead soul. The grass still felt very wet because of the grim gray fog and mist, which was typical morning weather in December.

The male clan members were preparing for the cow sacrifice in front of the house, which was the highlight of the funeral ritual. Because it is believed that the cow's soul is connected to the body of the deceased, when the cow is killed, its soul is supposedly transferred to and inhabits the dead person's body, allowing her soul to depart for the ethnic homeland in the afterlife. Many people had already congregated to witness and participate in this part of the funeral ceremony. An older man slowly approached a slender, midsize cow tied with a long white rope to a small piece of thick wood nailed to the ground. Two other men following behind him picked up the rope from the ground and used it to tightly tie the coffin. The rope thus connects the cow to the dead person and enables the transfer of the cow's soul to the deceased body.

I initially did not realize that there was an ax lying on the ground, because it was buried in the middle of the green grass. The ax was not that big and was worn-out, but when an older man picked it up, it looked intimidating enough, especially compared to his short and slender frame. The cow was peacefully eating some grass, unaware about what was going to happen to him. At that moment, a clan representative who was chanting during the ritual looked at the man holding the ax and waved

Cultural Differences in the Diaspora   187

his hand to signal that it was time to kill the cow. The man immediately swung the ax powerfully and hit the right spot on the cow's head. The cow collapsed instantly and fell to the ground surprisingly fast, without much of a wail or even a sharp groan. Because the man was so effective at slaughtering it, the death seemed to be quick and relatively painless.

Those observing the ritual then took the cow's carcass to a large open area behind the house and began skinning it and cutting the meat into big chunks. The participants started to cook the meat in large metal pots with boiling water to make beef soup. A good portion of the meat was also chopped by a group of men into small pieces to make beef *laab* (a well-known Laotian salad cooked with minced meat and fresh mint) to be served with steamed white rice. People started to distribute bowls and spoons gathered from various homes of clan members. They casually sat here and there in small groups on the ground to enjoy the feast.

Later in the day, the actual burial took place. People got on trucks, motorbikes, and tractors to travel to the burial site in the mountain farther away from the village. We parked at the bottom of a hill and began a long, strenuous hike up to the top of the mountain until we finally reached the gravesite. Several young men had already carried the heavy coffin all the way up the mountain and were digging a large hole in the ground to bury the coffin. I was told that the host family did not have much money at that time and had decided to make the grave in the original "traditional" style, with just soil and tree branches covering the coffin. Based on Hmong's explanations about different ways to make graves, I learned that this one was considered relatively "humble" compared to more ornate, wealthier methods, which consist of a pile of rocks with cement slabs at the front embellished with decorative objects.

Indeed, when I was visiting a different Hmong village in Vang Vieng, people showed me three different types of graves that varied in size and shape. The "wealthier" one was not only larger in size but also was made of a mix of cement and big stones. The front bottom of the grave had a small square opening with a fake flower and a toy shaped like a motorbike. In addition, the details of funeral practices can vary depending on the family, especially according to clan and subclan lineages.

Funerals Away from the Public Gaze: Hmong in Sacramento

Soon after I started my fieldwork in California, there was a funeral of a Hmong woman who passed away in her seventies in Sacramento. I attended the funeral with Steve Thao and his wife, Chia, who were the distant relatives of the woman. While driving to the home where the funeral preparations and the feast were to take place, Steve gave me some background information:

> So, Nia Her [the woman who passed away] had five children. They all live in Sacramento, but they know little about the proper way to conduct a funeral. . . . The landlord of the family's current house did not allow them to hold the full funeral service at home. He is a white American and said, "I rented my house to only two to five people, not for tons of your people to continuously come back and forth!"

As a result, I learned that we were actually going to another Hmong family's house, whose members were in the same clan and closely related to Nia's children, and who volunteered to do all the preparation for the funeral service. Because the home was owned by this family, they at least did not have to worry about complaints from a landlord.

Upon our arrival, the street parking around the neighborhood was already completely full of visitors, who were mainly relatives and members of the Her clan. As soon as we entered the house, Steve joined the elderly male members' clan meeting. I went along with Chia, who walked straight to the backyard of the house. There were more than twenty women washing fresh vegetables and cooking in big pots. The cooking was part of a three-day gathering to prepare for the funeral. For just that day, I heard that the family custom-ordered a large amount of beef and pork from a farm to serve to the visitors. They were also making the rice-noodle soup, *pho*, in a big, silver stainless steel pot. There were enough cooking supplies lying around for me to grab a knife and cutting board, and I started chopping cilantro and spring onions from the largest plastic colander I have ever seen.

A group of young men were setting up long tables and placing the cooked food on them. Unlike the funeral I observed in Laos, where only beef larb salad (minced meat with thinly chopped herbs) and soup were served with steamed rice, there was a wider variety of dishes, including pho, fried garlic shrimp, Caesar salad, and desserts, along with lots of soda. Inside the home next to the open backyard screen door, some women were creating a pile of paper money by folding joss paper in preparation for the upcoming funeral service. In fact, everyone was busy, even the young kids and little babies, who were curious about what their parents were doing. When the preparations and cooking were over, the visitors sat down at the long tables and started enjoying the feast. Some of the prepared food would also be taken to the subsequent funeral service.

Although this gathering in Sacramento was vaguely reminiscent of the food preparation and the funeral feast in Vang Vieng, there were notable differences. First of all, there was no coffin and visitations with the body of the deceased at the home where the cooking and preparations were taking place. Instead, the actual funeral services were to take place later at a Hmong community center (Hmong Palace Church). I was told that because there is generally less ethnic segregation of Hmong in the United States compared to Laos and most US Hmong live close to non-Hmong neighbors,[2] they did not feel comfortable taking the casket outside the home into the street or even their front and backyards in order to conduct funeral ceremonies.

Because Hmong were worried that they would be observed by neighbors and subject to public criticism and disapproval, they conducted the funeral in a private community center away from public view and scrutiny. As noted in chapter 2, this is one of the major Hmong cultural practices that have been the target of public criticism in the United States along with their marriage customs, animal sacrifice, and shamanism. Such social pressure from the mainstream society indicates how diasporic people can feel the presence of the "nation-state," broadly defined to include the people of the nation. This type of power embedded in everyday social relations causes Hmong to change their ethnic practices and traditions in national contexts even without overt or explicit control.

Three days later we finally went to the Hmong Palace Church, the communal hall rented by the family to serve as the funeral ceremony site. In the main hall, the body of the deceased grandmother was placed in an open coffin on a large table, and the walls around it were decorated with bright gold and shiny silver paper folded in the shapes of hearts, moons, and stars. The grandmother's full name was displayed in large letters cut out from the same decorative paper and also posted on the wall. Such ornate decorations, which were the product of days of hard work by the young grandchildren from the Her clan of the deceased, simply did not exist in the funeral ceremony in Laos.

There were many people constantly visiting the deceased and paying their respects. As is the case for many other Hmong funerals, these visitations continued for a week. In fact, many direct family members, and even visitors, stayed with the deceased for the entire time and conducted all-night vigils. The bamboo qeej was played throughout the funeral night and day, in coordination with the beats of a drum, along with the constant chanting by the clan leader. In front of the coffin was a large winter blanket, and small envelopes with money were placed on the floor.

On the blanket a large circle of Hmong youth was kneeling down and bowing their heads to the ground. The clan leader gently ensured that everything was "ready" so that when the soul departed, she could leave her belongings behind for her descendants. As a symbol of the soul's benevolence, he took the money out of the envelopes and distributed it to the youth sitting on the floor. Later I learned that this ritual, which was not performed in Laos, has been made possible in Sacramento because Hmong supposedly have more wealth and economic resources there.

In a large communal kitchen next to the hall, a lot of women in aprons were busy cooking a variety of food to serve to a much larger number of visitors than at the gathering previously held at the home. For both lunch and dinner, there were long lines of people waiting to be served their meals. Leftover food was also available throughout the day in the kitchen. In addition, youth constantly circulated with carts to offer snacks, desserts, and beverages to the guests. In general, there was a much greater abundance and diversity of food both at the feast at the home and the funeral hall than at the funeral ceremony in Laos, where villagers had limited economic resources.

After hours of cooking and washing in the big kitchen with other women, I took a break by going out to the main hall, where the singing and chanting continued. Yeng Vue, one of the young women who accompanied me, explained that the chanting at the funeral lasts for a long time because the chanter (*txiv nkauj*) needs to guide the soul's journey back to its final destination. The journey starts from Sacramento to wherever the person originally came from, and the chanter lists the names of every single village, city, town, and province through which the soul must travel before it reaches "heaven," where the ancestors are supposedly waiting. As noted in chapter 5 about shamanism, although souls are deterritorialized and supposed to be present everywhere, spatiality is still encoded in the nonmaterial, spiritual world and invoked by the funeral ritual. In this sense, souls become "reterritorialized" and thus need to "travel" geographically.

This reminded me of the conversations with Hmong in Laos about the journey of the soul of the deceased. I once asked an elderly shaman at the funeral in Laos, "When someone passes away, where does the person's soul eventually return to?" The shaman told me, "In general, you send the soul to go back to wherever you were born. Regardless of where you lived after you left your place of birth, you must go back to that hometown." The qeej player and a clan representative whom I met in Sacramento gave me the same story: that the soul will be sent to its

Cultural Differences in the Diaspora   191

birthplace because the deceased person needs to go back and pick up the "placenta buried under the ground of the house of their birth."[3] The soul then continues its journey back to the "homeland," whose location is ultimately unknown. However, unlike in Laos, I did not see women placing slippers, umbrellas, toilet paper rolls, or branches on the coffin to assist the soul in its journey back home, although I was present during most of the three days of the funeral ceremony at the hall.

Most importantly, there was no sacrificial ritual of a cow at the funeral site before the feast, as was the case in Laos. Hmong in Sacramento could not perform this supposedly important and required ritual at the funeral site, because animal slaughter for community events is strictly prohibited by the state government.[4] In addition to such overt governmental regulations, there has always been ongoing tension between the multicultural rights of ethnic minorities and public criticism of their cultural practices associated with killing and consumption of animals as Claire Jean Kim (2015) discusses in her study of animal-human relations among immigrants and minorities in the US context. In fact, scholars have noted the legal, financial, and public challenges confronted by the US Hmong community in relation to their funerals that involve shamanism (Helsel 2019; C. Vang 2010; Zhang 2020).

Because of such restrictions, the funeral's host family had purchased cows from a remote farm in advance of the ritual slaughter and prearranged the delivery of the chopped cow carcass to the Hmong Palace Church. During one of my visits to the funeral, I followed a group of Hmong men to the farm before the cow sacrifice was to be held. After driving a couple of hours, we arrived at the farm, where an elderly white American farmer with a beard and gray hair welcomed us. An elderly Hmong man and the farmer started to engage in a conversation, translated by one of the youth in the group.

Back at the Hmong Palace Church a couple days later, when the cow sacrifice ritual was about to start, a small group of men gathered, constantly checking their cell phones. One of them was talking on his phone to another Hmong man who had gone back to the farm and was standing by for the order from the funeral site to kill the cow. When the clan representative who was directing the proceedings looked at the group of men, the man on the phone raised his voice and said, "Now!" thus giving an order to those waiting at the farm to initiate the cow slaughter at precisely the right moment. Because the sacrifice had been done remotely at a distance, there was no rope connecting the cow to the coffin to enable the transfer of the cow's soul to the deceased. In fact, more

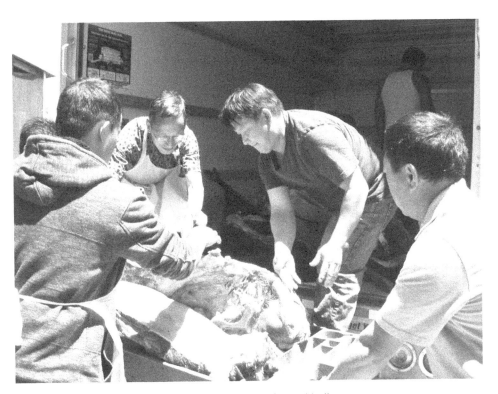
Delivery of additional cow carcasses to the funeral hall.

cows had apparently been slaughtered at the farm later on, because in the afternoon about seven cow carcasses were delivered in a large rental truck to the funeral hall for further butchering and cooking. A variety of food cooked with beef was eventually served to the guests during the funeral ceremony, ensuring that there was an overabundance of food at the funeral. The choicest cuts of meat were given to the people in charge of the funeral and others who played important roles during the ceremony.

Since Hmong in Sacramento could not bury their dead on any plot of public land they might select (such as on a mountain in Vang Vieng), they had to do so at cemeteries in the "American style." On the last day of the funeral ceremony, the attendees first gathered at the communal hall in the morning to complete the final ritual to remove the coffin and let the soul know that it could depart the body. We left the Hmong Palace Church and arrived at the Vietnamese Memorial Garden, which was not far away. An elderly Hmong woman in the group standing next to me noted that other Hmong had been buried at the cemetery in the past, including her own young daughter, who tragically committed suicide. Despite her cheerful voice, I sensed her inner agony. Not knowing how to respond properly, I just looked around the gravestones nearby and realized that almost all the engraved last names were Asian, including Hmong, Korean, and Vietnamese surnames. It occurred to me that maybe that is why the cemetery was attractive for the Sacramento Hmong community, as well as other Asian Americans who lived in the area.

Unlike the funeral I attended in Laos, the burial at the cemetery itself was quite brief and rather mechanical, as the casket was simply lowered into a pre-dug hole in the ground. The attendees were trying to stand near each other because of the lack of space at the burial site, which was surrounded by other graves. I was struck by how ornate the casket was with wood molding, handles, a shiny lacquer finish, and a decorative, colored pattern on the lid. It was quite a contrast to the simple coffin that was made of unfinished trimmed wood that I observed in Laos.

Apparently, there are most likely significant local variations not only in coffin ornateness but also in overall budget for funerals, depending on family wealth within US Hmong communities. As people explained to me, the number of cows sacrificed at a Hmong funeral is often an indicator of the family's wealth and is frequently compared by guests with other funerals they attended (in contrast, in the Vang Vieng village in Laos, only one cow was sacrificed during the funeral). Thus, although national differences in economic development certainly account for the greater lavishness of American Hmong funerals compared to those of co-ethnics in Laos, local differences among Sacramento families in wealth can produce internal variations as well. The exact number of sacrificed cows and the volume of meat served at funerals can therefore vary depending on the family's economic means. Although I thought that seven cows seem to be a lot to be sacrificed for one funeral, Steve (with whom I attend the funeral) mentioned that eleven cows were purchased two years ago for his mother's funeral.

The family of the deceased in the funeral was known to be less wealthy, and the total cost (estimated at over forty thousand dollars) was funded by donations from clan members and visitors as well as the deceased woman's life insurance and Supplemental Security Income. The rest of the expenses were covered by immediate family members. Some families with greater financial means (such as Steve's) can fund the funeral on their own without expecting donations or financial contributions. Despite such localized differences, this can be an indication of the money and economic resources that US Hmong have been able to gather in order to conduct relatively extensive and elaborate funerals (to make the dead soul "happy"), which is far beyond what was possible in Laos. In fact, if the funeral ceremony is seen as too "humble," some visitors may gossip that the family is "stingy and does not truly love the deceased person," as people frequently noted.

Further Fragmentation in Diasporic Cultures: Christian Hmong in Sacramento and Religious Differences in Funeral Practices

As noted above, the social forces that culturally fragment diasporic cultures are not simply the policies of the nation-state and pressures from its host population but also involve localized community differences. In addition to variations in family wealth, local religious differences in the Sacramento Hmong community must be taken into account. The conversion of some US Hmong to Christianity has produced further local differentiation in traditional cultural practices compared to their diasporic co-ethnics in Laos that cannot be simply subsumed under national differences. Although many studies have focused on how religion keeps dispersed diasporic communities cohesive and connected despite geographical separation and national differences (see Bowen 2004; Brodwin 2003; Werbner 2002), internal religious differences can certainly emerge among diasporic peoples living in different nation-states, leading to further cultural differentiation in their shared ethnic traditions.

The Hmong I studied in Sacramento who have converted to Christianity and are members of the Christian and missionary alliance church (part of an evangelical Protestant denomination) have further modified their funeral traditions according to their religious beliefs. Although my primary research focus was not directly about the religious dimensions in the Hmong diaspora, during my fieldwork I connected with the local Hmong church in Sacramento, the second largest in the nation, and diligently attended church services every Sunday. On one Sunday, the pastor and his wife were absent because they had to travel to Fresno to help with a funeral ceremony at the Hmong church there. As a result, the sermon that day was delivered by a substitute speaker, a very devoted deacon, who wanted to actively promote Christianity among Hmong.

The sermon became passionate when he started to talk about Hmong traditions and began questioning specifically the need for extensive and difficult funeral ceremonies in the Hmong community. Although the church members had already truncated their funerals to three days, the guest deacon said to the audience, "A three-day funeral service! Is it really to support the family or is it just another burden?" Someone in the audience answered with confidence, "Another burden!" prompting a few attendees in the back to laugh softly. The well-prepared and ardent deacon continued:

> Funerals are for letting go, saying "good-bye" to the dead and honoring them. It should not be for three days with all-nighters. There is no reason to demand vigils for twenty-four hours. Also, funerals have the meaning of cheering up the reborn and new life of the dead person. Weddings are the same thing. *Mej koob* [a Hmong term that refers to marriage negotiations between the families of the bride and groom] is another unreasonable custom. If the husband really loves and cares for the wife, you should not practice the culture of negotiation over money![5]

After the service, a few younger Hmong church members and I continued the conversation about the sermon. They pointed out that the original weeklong duration of Hmong funerals was a tradition that had been passed down to them from the distant past. They felt that in the past, funerals in Laos and Thailand were held for many days because it took a long time for relatives and visitors to gather from around the country due to the lack of proper transportation.

However, Christian Hmong funerals in Sacramento may not be that different from "traditional" funeral ceremonies in terms of their structure. As church members explained to me, their funerals tend to be shorter and the rituals are abbreviated and simplified. The funeral service usually lasts for only three days, although a large amount of food is still prepared to serve family, relatives, friends, and acquaintances. Services are held at the Christian church, unlike the Hmong Palace Church. Since the church closes around 10 p.m. and is not open for twenty-four hours a day, I was told, the funeral participants must go home at the end of the day and leave the coffin behind instead of having all-night vigils. The ceremony is also administered by the pastor, not clan leaders or shamans, who provides sermons and leads a prayer session, which is followed by a Bible reading and singing that lasts for about three hours. The rest of the time, people gather to eat and catch up with one another. Likewise, in a study about spiritual religions among Southeast Asians in "exile," Jean Langford (2013) examined which funeral practices have been adopted or discarded by Hmong Christians. She found that Hmong Christian communities have synthesized their religious beliefs with traditional Hmong funeral customs instead of completely disregarding the latter.

Hmong American Funerals and Discourses about the Loss of Cultural Authenticity

Regardless of localized variations, the significant national differences in the practice of ethnic traditions in the diaspora ultimately raise issues of cultural authenticity. Hmong interviewees in Laos and the United States engaged in discourses about who is doing a "better" job of apparently preserving their culture in a more "proper" manner. The subjective experience of authenticity as a *social discourse* (see Clifford 1988; Jackson 1991, 1995) is primarily based on temporal continuity, so cultural forms that appear to resemble more closely what was practiced in the distant past are perceived as more "authentic" (Hobsbawm 1983). The more cultural traditions have been modified in response to current circumstances, the more they are liable to be branded as less authentic by their practitioners because they are supposedly not based on the preservation and persistence of past cultural forms.

Because the various constraints of living in America have led US Hmong to substantially alter their funeral ceremonies, Hmong in Dao Tha explicitly claimed that their funerals are closer to more "authentic" Hmong tradition. This is especially the case for Lao Hmong residing in ethnic villages, who have apparently been able to maintain their funeral rituals without substantial modification in the relative absence of state and public intervention. For instance, Kong Her, during our interview in Dao Tha, said:

> Our relatives have been living in the US for a long time, so whatever they do is like what other Americans do. For example, in our funeral tradition, when someone passes away, Hmong Americans can only go to a community center for the funeral that they rented for the ritual. But it is not their real home or village, and they don't own that place. For us Hmong in Laos, this is not allowed. Funerals must be done at home in the village, which is the right way.

Chong Lee, another elderly resident in Dao Tha, also emphasized the proper practice of funeral customs in Laos compared to the United States: "In the US, Hmong cannot practice our culture in the same way as we do in Laos. For instance, like [with] funerals . . . Hmong should go outside the house to sacrifice the cow, but Hmong Americans cannot do it outside but stay inside every day until the end of the funeral. They no longer really know *who the Hmong truly are* [emphasis mine]." Such a strong and critical statement indicates not only Chong's disapproval about how co-ethnics in the United States have strayed from "true" Hmong traditions but also his belief that they are losing their "Hmongness."

Interestingly, Hmong I interviewed in California did not directly challenge or reject such criticism. In fact, some of those who have visited Laos or spoken to relatives there were aware of the negative appraisals of their funeral customs in the United States by their co-ethnics in Laos. They acknowledged that they had to considerably modify their practices in accordance with state regulations and in response to American public disapproval. For example, Sheng Her, one of the older 1.5-generation clan members at the Sacramento funeral, spoke about why US Hmong communities had to change a number of aspects of the ritual. "You can't just take the dead body outside on the street, because people will panic!" Sheng remarked. "Because we live in an environment where you can't do certain things, you just don't do it. We have to follow the laws of this society." In fact, elderly Hmong I met during my fieldwork in California regretted that the actual funeral services with the coffin have to be held in a separate hall instead of at home. They lamented that they cannot properly conduct the cow sacrifice in the United States and have been consoled by 1.5-generation Hmong, who help them understand local regulations and American cultural norms and tend to be more tolerant of the changes that Hmong have made to their funeral practices.

In addition, the apparent loss of cultural authenticity among Hmong in the United States was attributed by interviewees to the overly lavish and materialistic way they conduct funerals. One of the members of the 1.5 generation, Steve Thao, for example, criticized this as follows:

> At our funerals, we do unnecessary things. Too much food, too many snacks, drinks, and fruits. Those are not required and there really doesn't need to be someone carrying around a cart and delivering them to the guests. These were what Hmong Americans invented. It is just that some people started to do it; then others said since you do it, I will do it. It's like that. For example, the decoration on the wall with gold and silver paper [near the coffin] is a totally new thing that only started about seven, eight years ago. I would say it is really not necessary.

Other interviewees throughout California similarly questioned whether funerals have to be so luxurious and whether such elaborate ceremonies are really for pleasing the dead soul or a display of wealth and social status to impress others. Hmong Christians were especially critical about such funeral practices.

The Variable Power of the Nation-State: Hmong Funeral Ceremonies and New Year Festivals Compared

In the case of funeral ceremonies, Hmong in Sacramento have faced more intervention from the nation-state (both the state and the public) compared to their Lao compatriots, resulting in greater alteration to their funeral rituals. In Vang Vieng the state was relatively absent and did not enforce policies or exercise direct regulatory power that interferes with Hmong funeral ceremonies or burials. Apparently, Hmong who live in ethnically segregated villages have the relative freedom to practice their funeral customs without the probing gaze and scrutiny of their non-Hmong neighbors.

However, it is important to note that the relationship between the nation-state and a certain ethnic minority population varies depending on the specific cultural tradition at hand and how they interface with nationalist agendas. Unlike with Hmong funeral rituals, the Lao government has regulated and restricted their New Year festivals. In contrast, Hmong in California experienced the strong presence of the nation-state when conducting their funeral ceremonies, whereas for their New Year festivals, both the state and the American public have been quite laissez-faire. Thus, intervention by the nation-state over diasporic cultures is selective and variable, not permanent or consistent, even for the same ethnic minority group. This also confirms that minority cultures are constantly subject to change through different governmental polices and public pressures at different times.[6] I will illustrate this with a brief comparative discussion of the Hmong New Year.[7]

Like many other Southeast Asian countries, the Lao state's desire to prioritize labor productivity in a supposedly "underdeveloped" national economy has led to a multicultural policy based on *economic equality*. As a result, the local government in Vang Vieng implemented a policy to regulate and restrict the Hmong New Year celebration in specific Hmong communities, because it believed that excessive ethnic festivities among minorities (especially subsistence farmers like Hmong at the margins of the national economy) are detrimental to the country's development goals and detract from their "equal" economic opportunity to become productive citizens. Because systems of wage labor and capitalist productivity have not yet been hegemonically entrenched among farmers in rural Laos, the state was eager to actively enforce economic discipline

Cultural Differences in the Diaspora   199

and make sure they do not "waste" too much time with prolonged rituals and ethnic festivities.

As a result, the Hmong New Year celebration in Dao Tha has been reduced because of newly introduced rules by the local government mandating that Hmong confine their public celebrations to three days (including the weekend) instead of over one week or longer, as was previously the case. During my three visits to Laos over a decade, this cultural control by the government led to significant reductions in the length, size, and scale of public celebrations and outdoor events during the Hmong New Year. Thus, the New Year was mainly celebrated in private among individual families rather than in public with the larger community. In addition, the relative lack of economic resources among Hmong villagers in Laos has also forced them to cut back on the length and scale of their New Year festivities, since they cannot afford the costs of food, supplies, or "fancy" ethnic dress.

Although I expected the New Year celebration in Dao Tha to be a major opportunity to conduct extensive participant observation, the village was strangely quiet during most of the celebration. In fact, if I had not run into a few little girls in their traditional Hmong dresses, I would have had no idea that the celebration had started. After following the girls to an open area between some houses in the middle of the hill, I finally found a small group of male and female teenagers in the corner of the village who had lined up in two rows facing each other and were tossing tennis balls back and forth as part of a traditional Hmong courtship ritual (called *pob pov* in Hmong). There were almost no young adults participating in pob pov.

Indeed, it was an ordinary workday and most Hmong adults had gone to town for their jobs or were working in the rice fields. Only a small group of elderly Hmong, teenagers, and the little girls in Hmong dresses were present and participated in the New Year festivities. During the three-day celebration, there were far fewer activities compared to my previous experience of the event in the past, when the village was filled with people of all ages wearing colorful dresses engaging in various outdoor festivities for the entire week.

In contrast, Hmong in the United States have been able to organize extensive and highly commercialized New Year festivals across the country, as they are consistent with the American ideology of liberal multiculturalism, which emphasizes the right of ethnic minorities to celebrate their traditional practices and ethnic differences in the name of *cultural* equality. Overt state control of ethnic festivities is unnecessary because

Food vendors at the Hmong New Year festival in Sacramento.

the capitalist economic system is pervasive and already hegemonic in the United States, ensuring that minorities remain productive economic subjects, even if they extensively celebrate their cultural differences. In this context, while US multicultural ideology does not necessarily embolden Hmong in California to engage in extensive New Year festivities, it ends up granting them the freedom to do so in the name of cultural diversity without direct governmental scrutiny and control. In addition, in contrast to their co-ethnics in Laos, Hmong communities in California clearly have the economic means to organize much more extensive and elaborate New Year festivals on large city fairgrounds in multiple locations. According to those at an organizational meeting I attended, the largest New Year festival lasts for a week in Fresno and can draw up to twenty-five to thirty thousand Hmong and other visitors from different communities throughout the country as well as abroad.

The New Year festivals I attended in Sacramento, Stockton, and Fresno had very large crowds and a bewildering array of vendors selling ethnic food as well as consumer goods, produce, rice, herbal and pharmaceutical medicines, Hmong traditional dresses, and numerous other ethnic items imported from across the Hmong diaspora. Also on sale were DVDs of popular foreign dramas, Hmong music videos, and books and published materials related to Hmong history, autobiographies, and literature. It is also notable that there were plenty of cultural performances and contests at the festival, such as a Hmong beauty pageant, popular singing, dancing, acting contests, and fashion shows with traditional Hmong outfits, as well as the ball-tossing ritual and other traditional Hmong New Year games.

The Hmong New Year has become quite similar to other ethnic festivals in the United States, such as the Chinese New Year in San Francisco (see Yeh 2008) and Nisei Week among Japanese Americans in Los Angeles (see Kurashige 2002), which are also highly commercialized and feature ethnic food vendors and public cultural activities, including ethnic performances, fashion shows, beauty pageants, and dancing. In short, unlike the funerals held by Hmong in Sacramento, the New Year festival seems to be a culturally accepted and approved venue for them to display, celebrate, and commercialize their ethnicity without much disapproval or criticism by the American public. In fact, an increasing number of non-Hmong Americans also attend Hmong New Year festivals in California to experience the ethnic and cultural diversity that the Hmong offer.

Diasporic discourses about cultural authenticity regarding New Year celebrations differ considerably from those about funerals. Since Hmong in both Vang Vieng and California realize that their New Year practices have been heavily modified in different national contexts, neither of them claimed to have retained the original, "authentic" New Year tradition. Hmong in Vang Vieng felt that they practice a more impoverished and less authentic version of their New Year celebrations when compared to the past because of limited economic resources and the Lao state's cultural restrictions. Meanwhile, many Hmong interviewees in California were also critical of their own New Year festival as "inauthentic" and no longer "traditional" because so much of it has become commercialized and commodified for business and profit, making them feel less culturally "sincere."[8] Indeed, the notion of cultural authenticity cannot be generalized but depends on the specific cultural tradition and the amount of perceived change introduced in the different national circumstances in which it is practiced (for further discussion, see S. Lee 2022).

As demonstrated in this chapter so far, the relationship between the nation-state and the diasporic minorities cannot be understood by focusing only on one type of cultural practice. In Laos, the Hmong New Year celebration in Vang Vieng was more subject to the power of the nation-state than funeral rituals, whereas the opposite was true in California. Even for the same ethnic minority group, the power of the nation-state over its diasporic culture is variable and selective, ranging from intrusive to laissez-faire and constantly changing in response to global forces.

Therefore, discourses of cultural authenticity should also be differentiated by changing and specific local, national, and global contexts. Furthermore, discourses about the loss of "authenticity" in the Hmong New Year celebrations can emerge internally in different local contexts, for there are rural/urban differences that can cause further cultural differentiation in diasporic cultures that are not merely products of national difference. Although Hmong in my study who live in rural villages of Laos have been under considerable governmental pressure from economic development projects, more extensive, large-scale, and public Hmong New Year celebrations with an array of different ethnic vendors can be found in major cities where large Hmong populations reside, such as Xieng Khouang and Luang Prabang in northern Laos and Lak 52 near the capital city of Vientiane.[9] Because some urban Hmong in such cities own local businesses and are already somewhat integrated into the national economy as productive citizens, it is possible that the Lao state does not restrict their New Year festivals, which also generate income for these municipalities (S. Lee 2022).

In addition, as mentioned in chapter 2, some of these urban Hmong New Year celebrations are attended by not only local Hmong but also global tourists who want to experience the Hmong people's distinctive culture (Tappe 2011). This may encourage Hmong to engage in public performances and even alter their ethnic culture to cater to touristic desires. However, although global tourism has also affected rural Vang Vieng, as discussed in previous chapters, it did not affect the New Year holiday in Hmong villages in the region, because it was predominantly celebrated in the privacy of people's homes and villages. Foreign tourists in Vang Vieng were generally not interested in local ethnic groups and had limited interactions with local villagers except for those employed in tourist businesses (see chapter 2; S. Lee 2023).

It should also be noted that during the height of the 2020–2021 coronavirus pandemic, I heard through my ongoing personal communications with Hmong in Dao Tha that any type of group gathering was prohibited by the government in Laos, even home gatherings for dinner, in the name of preventing virus transmission. This further reduced their ability to celebrate the New Year, even in private. Likewise, Hmong communities in California postponed the New Year festival in 2020 and when the festival in Fresno, California, was revived the following year, there were substantially fewer attendees compared to the years before the pandemic (personal communication with a former research participant in Sacramento, March 2022).

Conclusion: Cultural Fragmentation in Practices and Discourses in the Hmong Diaspora

Although Hmong in my study have been living transnational lives and have developed a shared diasporic ethnic identity across borders, their diasporic cultures are simultaneously nationalized, as they are subject to the political, economic, and social forces of the nation-states in which they currently reside. The impact of the national on Hmong diasporic culture in Vang Vieng and California was not simply limited to differing state policies and regulations but also everyday social constraints and pressures from the public—that is, the nation-state's people. In response, Hmong in Sacramento have substantially altered their funeral practices to align with dominant American cultural norms and state regulations in an effort to become disciplined cultural citizens. In contrast, Hmong in the villages of Vang Vieng did not experience such explicit national and public pressures and continued to conduct funerals in a "traditional" manner.

However, the power of the nation-state over different minority cultural practices varies depending on what specific activities are targeted and how much they are seen as conflicting with the nation-state's economic objectives and cultural standards of "acceptable" behavior. For the Hmong New Year event, it was the Lao state that imposed direct controls and reduced the festivities in the name of economic equality and development, whereas the United States has been hands-off in the name of multicultural equality. Ultimately, as shown in this chapter, the inevitable modifications to Hmong ethnic traditions in response to different national pressures produced fragmented discourses about authenticity among Lao and US Hmong interviewees who deemed cultural practices that have been subject to greater change as "less authentic" than those who have not. As a result, considerable variation has emerged in the discourses about diasporic cultural practices among Hmong in these two communities who live in different national contexts.

In this sense, diasporas are not only constituted by transnational connections and continuities across borders but also national differentiation and difference. Such cultural fragmentation I observed during my fieldwork indicates that Hmong diasporic identity is not based on some kind of essentialized and uniform "Hmongness" across borders. In fact, it is impossible for diasporic peoples scattered in various countries to remain homogeneous with an "authentic," unchanged culture from the past, as they are subject to the influence of different national and local contexts.

The significant national differences that have emerged among diasporic Hmong communities produce further discursive fragmentation in the diaspora. As will be discussed in chapter 7, the Hmong in both Vang Vieng and California have come to perceive their counterparts in a critical manner and position themselves hierarchically in relation to each other according to their national contexts. Indeed, their diasporic belonging is based not just on a mutually shared identity as transnational Hmong but also on selective and relative affiliations with the separate nation-states to which they partially belong.

7

Diaspora's National Affiliations

Relative Belonging to the Nation-State and Discursive Fragmentation

After living apart in the diaspora for decades, the two Hmong communities where I conducted research have come to recognize the salient national differences between Laos and the United States. Not only have their diasporic cultures become differentiated along national lines as analyzed in the previous chapter, but they have also developed contrasting and critical perceptions toward each other based on their selective, partial affiliation with the nation-states where they reside. Such nationalized discourses have produced considerable discursive fragmentation and have become another source of national differentiation and division among Hmong in the two countries. This is again an example of how the presence of nation-states affects Hmong living in the diaspora and is an integral part of the simultaneous trans/national affiliations that constitute their diasporic identities.

Almost all Hmong I met and interviewed in Laos and the United States, regardless of their age, gender, religion, or generational status, spoke about the remarkable national disparities between the two countries in terms of economic development, living standards, and political systems. While Hmong I studied in Laos believed that the relative economic wealth of the United States has had negative repercussions on the social well-being and morality of their co-ethnics living in America, the latter believed they have an ability as well as a moral obligation to lead and assist the rest of the Hmong diaspora. The two communities also differ in terms of their opinions about the constraints and opportunities of living in different national economies. Hmong interviewees in Laos claimed that their relatively underdeveloped national economy grants them *freedom from* an "oppressive" capitalist economy, allowing them to pursue a leisurely life compared to Hmong in the United States. In contrast, Hmong in California believed they have the *freedom to* pursue economic opportunities and social mobility in their country, unlike their impoverished counterparts in Laos.

When Hmong in both countries spoke about these national differences, they contrasted "Lao Hmong" with "US Hmong" in a broad, homogeneous manner that often did not recognize internal diversities inherent in each local diasporic community. This was especially the case when they referred to essential aspects of "Hmongness" and discussed how they felt their co-ethnic counterparts no longer upheld "true" Hmong culture, which is another example of the voluntary self-essentializing noted in previous chapters. In addition, the discourses of my interviewees are derived not only from national differences in economic development but also from disparities between urban and rural lifestyles. Hmong in the villages of Vang Vieng felt that their lives are freer and more consistent with traditional Hmong cultural values because many were farmers in a rural area, who are less subject to capitalist constraints. They perceived their co-ethnics in the United States as living in urbanized spaces and working as wage laborers. In contrast, Hmong in California I spoke with cherished their freedom to engage in economic opportunities and socioeconomic success, commonly regarding those in Laos as poor, rural farmers.

However, such simplified characterizations based on separate national affiliations are an apt illustration of the fragmented discourses that can exist among diasporic subjects. The fact that these discourses are fragmented does not imply that they were once "unitary" (for instance, before Hmong dispersed into the diaspora to different countries). Indeed, discourses are *always* fragmented to some extent, because they are embedded in different social positionalities. In this case, we have discourses among diasporic people that are fragmented by national differences; however, such fragmentation can also occur between people in the same country based on differences of ethnicity, gender, social class, or region.

I consider the statements that my interviewees made to be "discourses" because they resemble a conversational exchange or debate in contexts of social power (see Foucault 1972) that goes beyond simply personal, subjective opinions (Taylor 2013, 2–5). Of course, Hmong in the two diasporic communities in Vang Vieng and California are not directly talking to each other, as I interviewed them separately. Instead, my eth-

Diaspora's National Affiliations   207

nographic presentation of their statements is what makes them appear discursive, for I am bringing them into conversation with each other in this chapter. This may be seen as part of the anthropologist's "ethnographic authority" to represent others that is inherent in ethnographic writing, which is embedded in power relations with research participants (see Clifford 1983).

However, the statements made by Hmong interviewees are also discursive because they involve relations of power where the interlocutors from each diasporic Hmong community attempt to position themselves hierarchically in relation to each other by claiming that their own country is "better" in terms of socioeconomic and political status. Such diasporic hierarchies are not simply based on the level of economic development or political power between Laos and the United States in the global order. Even though the United States was unanimously perceived to be in a "higher" geopolitical position than Laos, Hmong interviewees in Laos did not uniformly privilege the United States over their country. Instead, each diasporic community deemed itself as relatively "better" based on specific national qualities and attributes that their co-ethnic counterparts apparently do not have.

Although political difference is often the central source of divisions and conflicts in diasporic communities (e.g., Bernal 2004, 2005), it is important to note that the fragmentary discourses and disagreements among Hmong in my research did not necessarily lead to actual social conflicts or mutual alienation in their transnational relations. Rather, the critical perceptions that Lao and US Hmong interviewees have developed about one another remain at the level of discourse. In fact, they discussed their hierarchical positioning in the diaspora carefully instead of decisively, for instance, by using phrases such as "in my narrow understanding" and "although I might be wrong." It is thus "crucial to make clear distinctions between theoretical and actual conflicts," since there are "many propositions about rival loyalties and competing identifications" expressed by diasporic communities (Naujoks 2010, 14).

It should also be noted that the national identities and affiliations conveyed in the discourses of Hmong in this chapter are different from nationalism based on a strong loyalty toward entire nation-states and their peoples. Instead of being nationalistic per se, diasporic people can selectively adopt a particular feature of the nation-state to make positive generalizations about themselves and comparative judgements about their co-ethnics residing in other countries. Therefore, Hmong's national affiliations should be understood as a "relational nationalism" based on contrasts with selective aspects of the lives of their diasporic counterparts in other countries. For example, Hmong in Vang Vieng believed that their economic lives in Laos are "better and freer" when they compare themselves to the restrictive, capitalistic lives of US Hmong, not because they feel strong nationalistic pride and loyalty to the Lao nation-state.

This type of relational nationalism therefore remains relative to the diaspora, making it an important component of diasporic identity and belonging. Thus, this chapter demonstrates how diasporas and nation-states are not incompatible or antagonistic but can be relational constructs that mutually constitute the trans/national diasporic condition. The simultaneous coexistence of transnational continuity and national fragmentation indicates that Hmong in Vang Vieng and California live in diasporic ethnic communities while also developing cultural and discursive differences in relation to each other as partial members of separate national communities. In this sense, diasporic belonging among Hmong in my study is not simply based on identifications with transnational communities of dispersed co-ethnics across borders but also on different host countries where they have lived for a considerable period of time. Clearly, diasporic communities are not homogeneous and deterritorialized entities removed from specific national contexts.

Relative National Economic Hierarchies between Laos and the United States

The comparative difference in economic status between Laos and the United States was probably the most prominent issue that led to discursive fragmentation along national lines among Hmong in the two diasporic communities. They unanimously agreed that the United States has a higher economic status in the global order, which is perhaps the most salient national difference they emphasized when comparing their lives with each other.

For instance, the following comments of Lena Thao, a professional in her late twenties in Sacramento, were shared by many other Hmong I interviewed in California:

> There are a lot of differences [compared to Laos], like economic growth. After we came to America, we have become assimilated to this wealthy society. But in Laos, it's still a Communist, poor country, so whatever resources or money they have are what their relatives in the US sent. And that's all they have. I have friends who went to Laos

to visit. They said that Hmong there are still living like they were thirty or forty years ago.

Likewise, Malina Xiong, a middle-aged woman in Sacramento who visited Laos recently, noted that she is still "very sad," whenever she thinks about the poverty of Hmong in Laos, which she felt is a striking contrast with her own life in the United States. She shared her impressions from her previous trip to Hmong villages in the northern part of the country:

> It's obvious that poverty is everywhere back in my country [Laos].[1] Some of the major cities may be growing and Hmong people move there, but their national economy is still the same. The population grows but there is no work for them. Also, when people live in the city, they don't have a good school system for kids. If the city kids cannot access good education, it could be even worse in rural areas.

Other first-generation Hmong interviewees who were born in Laos like Malina occasionally and inadvertently continued to refer to the country as their "home" or "my country" while commenting on the Lao national economy, which implies their ongoing emotional attachment to their former homeland (see Loizos 2009, 69).

However, such transnational emotional affiliations among US Hmong interviewees coexist with salient national disparities in economic development that produce differing perceptions about Hmong lives in the two countries. In another interview, a 1.5-generation man in his late forties named Meng Thao, also called Laos his "own country," even though he previously defined the United States as the country where he "belongs." Based on his trip to Laos in early 2000, Meng succinctly compared life in Laos versus the United States in the context of different national economies. "If you are not lazy, you won't die in this country [the United States]," Meng said. "You have choices like going to school or to work, and you can do whatever you can to earn money. But back in our country, because of the Lao economy, you don't have choices to make things work out. It's very different."

Interestingly, Hmong in Vang Vieng supported these views about the greater socioeconomic development and affluence of the United States as an important national difference and seemed to admit that it promotes the intellectual and knowledge capacity of Hmong living in that country. Such discourses were sometimes reiterated by Lao Hmong like Poa Moua, a farmer in Dao Tha, who noted, "America is a very rich country and here [Laos] is still a developing country. I think people living in a rich, developed country also have higher thoughts and better ideas. People in developing countries do not yet develop their knowledge, so they have lower understanding."

Another Dao Tha resident, Lee Yang, made a similar point based on how differences in the national socioeconomic development of the two countries affect the way Hmong make a living:

> Since Hmong have been living in the US, they have higher knowledge, because they have a lot of educational institutions. They can also work in various places. Living style and dietary culture have also become different. In Laos, on a daily basis, if we want to eat, we must do physical labor by using our hands and feet. But for them, if they want to make a living, they use their brains [*samong*] and knowledge.

However, it is equally important to understand that not all Hmong I interviewed in Laos made the same connection between the level of economic development and "ideal" living conditions for Hmong. Even if they generally agree that such disparities in national wealth may advance knowledge and intellectual ability, they also believed that it can lead to negative moral consequences for Hmong in the United States. Those Hmong I studied in California, however, disagreed, demonstrating how their national affiliation to the country leads to discursive fragmentation in the diaspora.

Problems of American Wealth: Discourses of Well-Being and Morality among Hmong in Vang Vieng, Laos

Diverging discourses emerged among Lao and US Hmong in my study about the social consequences of the national differences in wealth and economic systems between the two countries, which reflect their partial sense of belonging to these nation-states. Although there was no dispute about the higher economic status of the United States in the global order of nations, this did not determine how Hmong interviewees in both countries position themselves hierarchically in relation to each other, especially in terms of their subjective understandings. While Hmong in Vang Vieng live in a technically underdeveloped country, when they compared their lives to those of their US counterparts in the diaspora, they did not feel inferior simply because their country is poorer and economically underdeveloped. Instead, they actually claimed to be "better off" in terms of general well-being and moral behavior based on their relative national identification with Laos.

Regardless of the prosperous US economy and the apparent poverty of their country, Hmong I spoke with in Laos differentiated between national economic wealth and general social well-being, claiming that they do not always correspond. In fact, this perceived discrepancy is encapsulated in an expression they used to describe the lives of their co-ethnics in the United States: "rich (comfortable) body [*tua sabai*], poor heart [*tuk nai-jai*]."[2] In contrast, they characterized themselves as people with a "rich (comfortable) heart [*sabai jai*] but poor (tired) body [*tua muai*]."

This comparative discourse is indeed commonly shared among many Hmong in Laos, who primarily live as less wealthy, rural farmers. Consider the following comments from one of Dao Tha's rural villagers:

> The good thing about living in America is the value of money, since the American dollar has a much higher value than Lao Kip. But inside their heart, Hmong in America are poor [*tuk nai-jai*]. Here, we can't make much money, but our heart is comfortable [*sabai jai*]. It's up to you here [in Laos]. If you want to work, you can work, but if you don't, you don't have to. . . . Living a leisurely life is fine.

Interestingly, a small number of Hmong individuals residing in the United States, especially those who migrated from Laos in the 2000s through family-sponsored visas or marriages, shared somewhat similar views. For instance, Chi Her also employed the "rich body, poor heart" discourse to compare his experiences in Laos and the United States:

> The life of Hmong in the US is very different from those in Laos. In Laos, everything is *sabai* (comfortable, carefree). Things are up to you, and you can do anything you want in the mountains, hills, and fields. You can also own your gardens and don't have to waste money paying taxes. The only difficulty is that the national economy is still undeveloped. This country, America, is sabai in terms of food. But things are not easy here and there are many bills to pay. You may earn a lot, but you also have to spend as much as you earn. This gives many people headaches and hardship.

The critical perceptions of Lao Hmong villagers of their urban diasporic counterparts in the United States also extended to what they believed were negative changes in the behavior of Hmong there, which they ascribed to the highly developed, American national economy. From a moral standpoint, they believed that Hmong in the United States are less altruistic and more "selfish" as they have become "Americanized," referring to their predominantly economically oriented lifestyles as workers in a fully urbanized country.

For example, Xou Her, in his forties, spoke critically about how life in the United States had changed the charitable behavior of his relatives, despite having bought a tuk tuk with their remittances:

> In the past, we lived together, so our *nixay* [nature/habit] was the same. But now they moved to America and have lived separately for a while, so they have forgotten about us here in Laos. If I ask my old friends in the US who used to live in the same hometown and hung out together, "We are old friends, can you help me financially?" they would answer, "Oh, I have a lot of debts. Although I have cars and a house, I don't have money to help you." Their nature has changed. They are forgetting us.

Xou also added that he is more concerned about future generations of Hmong in the United States, who might eventually become disconnected and detached from their Hmong relatives in Laos and stop caring about them.

In this sense, Hmong in Laos that I interviewed have received the impression that Hmong in the United States have become *morally* impoverished by living in an economically wealthier country and no longer share the value of "helping, caring, and supporting other Hmong with money." This also has broader implications for the larger Hmong diaspora, because helping each other economically is perceived as an important aspect of the transnational ethnic community and a crucial part of "being Hmong," in their words (see chapter 4). In other interviews, similar critical comments were frequently made in terms of how Hmong in the United States have become "selfish and less caring" in contrast to "the way Hmong are supposed to be." According to Pao Her, a farmer in Dao Tha: "Hmong are supposed to look after each other, in terms of our living condition and to make sure everything is all right with our families, relatives, and friends. I only know a little about America, but they do not seem to know how to live together and take care of each other. They have become Americans and they live like Americans."

Likewise, many Lao Hmong I spoke with attributed other negatively perceived differences of US Hmong to their national economic status. As Cha Lee, a government officer in Vang Vieng, noted, "Hmong in Laos and the US have come to think differently. Hmong in Laos respect people more. In the US, the Hmong community there has changed and does not have much respect anymore since they are economically developed [*pattanaa*]." Kong Her, another Dao Tha villager, also had a poignant reaction to how US Hmong no longer respect elderly Hmong or treat them well:

> Hmong in the US go to study, get educated, and live in a place where they don't see any relatives or family around. All they do is go to school, come back, and study. So even when the grandparents go to visit their grandchildren, they don't take care of their grandparents anymore. They would say, "Oh, why do these old people come to stay with us for this long? Go away!"[3]

In fact, Kong affiliated himself with Laotian national culture by comparing the American lifestyle unfavorably to Laos and said, "In Laos we don't act like that. I would say we still know how to love other Hmong and how to respect our grandparents and great-grandparents. Over there [in the United States], what kids learn is only English and they no longer respect Hmong language and culture."

In another interview, Tou Yang, a farmer in his late forties, similarly explained that social relationships among Hmong in the United States are less emotional and intimate and have become more formal and strictly organized, reflecting a general characteristic of American sociality:

> Oh, everything is different for Hmong between Laos and the United States. Nothing can be similar. For example, here [Laos], if I want to visit somebody to have fun, talk, and be with them, I can of course do that anytime. But there [the United States], it's impossible. If you just visit your friends without giving them a phone call [advanced notice], they will close their door in front of your face. So different!

These Hmong interviewees in Laos positioned themselves above their US counterparts by positively identifying with life in their country. Instead of assuming that the higher level of economic development of the United States produces superior outcomes, they concluded that it can lead to negative changes that are not consistent with Hmong culture, resulting in US Hmong supposedly losing traditional cultural values because of the corrosive effect of American society. Such relational national affiliation based on comparative evaluations of their US co-ethnics allowed Hmong interviewees in Laos to claim a higher cultural status in the diasporic order by indicating that they have maintained "proper" (respectful) behavior and therefore done a "better" job than US Hmong.

Although these discourses are framed by interviewees in strictly national terms between an economically developed United States and an underdeveloped Laos, they also resemble the rural-versus-urban distinction. Hmong villagers in Vang Vieng believe they have better lives that are more leisurely, carefree, and comfortable because they live in Laos as rural farmers, unlike their urbanized co-ethnics in the United States. From their perspective, US Hmong are wage laborers and forced to live disciplined, busy, and less social lives in cities, which supposedly makes them more "selfish" and less "caring" toward others. Although some Hmong in Laos are urbanized and many in the United States are farmers, such internal urban/rural differences were not considered by most interviewees, who subsumed them under broader national differences, which apparently had much greater impact on their fragmented discourses.

The Power of National Wealth: Discourses of Morality among US Hmong

Discourses among Hmong interviewees in Laos about their co-ethnics in the United States directly conflict with how Hmong I studied in California portray themselves, producing considerable discursive fragmentation between the two diasporic communities. Because of their national affiliation with the positive aspects of US society, they strongly emphasized how they can use their superior economic status to financially help and economically develop the impoverished, rural Hmong community in Laos. Many of them perceived their co-ethnics in Laos as subjects who need considerable financial, educational, and charitable assistance from them. Indeed, their discourses about national economic differences emphasize how they have transformed their relative economic wealth into a moral obligation based on sympathy toward their co-ethnics in Laos, thus implicitly positioning themselves above their counterparts in the country.

Although Hmong interviewees in California were often concerned about their own socioeconomic and ethnic marginality in the United States (see chapter 2), their relative positioning became different when asked to reflect on and compare their lives to Hmong in Laos (and elsewhere). Apparently, they felt economically well-off relative to the diaspora as members of a wealthy nation-state, a self-perception found among many other similarly situated resettled refugees and immigrants in Western societies, including members of the Vietnamese diaspora (e.g., Thai 2014). To some extent, they seem to have embraced and internalized American discourses of the country's economic power and the need to assist less fortunate co-ethnics living in underdeveloped countries. For example, Steve Thao, a successful businessman, said:

I believe that all eyes are on the Hmong in the United States. I haven't been to China, but based on the stories that I heard from other people, when Hmong Americans visit Hmong in China, they are very happy about us, and they are waiting for us to support them. I heard they even call us Hmong from "the big land." The United States is not necessarily that geographically big, but it's a prestigious and powerful country. Hmong in Thailand and Laos also want the support, contribution, and leadership from the US. So if I just generalize, I would say Hmong in the US will be the leading group of Hmong [in the diaspora] in the years to come.

Similarly, Lena Thao, a 1.5-generation woman, also confirmed this view of US Hmong's capacity to help not only their co-ethnics in Laos but the Hmong diaspora globally when she said, "We have Hmong [in the United States] serving in higher offices and law agencies, or the United Nations, working for policies for global Hmong people, so I would say Hmong in the US have more economic means and political power to hold leadership and help the whole Hmong community."

Even some young US-born Hmong Americans who have no living experiences in or memories about Laos similarly compared the economic and political conditions of the United States and Laos in a nationalistic manner and were convinced that their country is the most important community among Hmong in the world. Lily Moua, a college student in her twenties, explained why the Hmong in the United States should play a leading role as a representative of the entire Hmong diaspora because of the country's economic development and democratic capabilities:

I would honestly say that America has more economic resources and definitely has more money than Laos. We have perhaps better laws too, and living in a democracy, we have a lot more rights as citizens and are more educated as opposed to people in Laos. They are passive and do what they were told by the government, especially the Hmong women and children, who are in a weaker position.

In fact, many of the US Hmong in my study felt that their superior access to resources should be the basis for assisting and looking after other less developed, rural, and poorer Hmong communities elsewhere in the diaspora. The comments of Peng Xiong, a professional in his forties in Sacramento, is a good example of this widespread sentiment:

I think in terms of education, experiences, and in terms of having more *freedom*, Hmong Americans are in a better position to impact and [influence] policy changes, nongovernmental actions, and even governmental actions in the world. . . . I think we do have those advantages, and I really hope that Hmong Americans take leading roles and reach out to other Hmong folks in the world. [emphasis mine]

In another interview, Ying Thao, a senior former veteran from the Vietnam War, also had such benevolent sentiments toward other diasporic Hmong living in rural areas in developing countries:

I think the leading role [in the diaspora] should be taken by the United States in the future, because there are Hmong here who care and look after Hmong groups everywhere in the world. We [Hmong Americans] have a good idea of how to communicate with many other Hmong in the world. In some rural areas and the countryside in China, we still have Hmong who are very poor and have no education. We feel for them and Hmong here will have a good idea about how to help them.

Yia Lor, a real estate agent in her thirties, seemed to idealize the overall sociopolitical and economic conditions of the United States:

Honestly, I would say America is the most important country in the world, because we have the American tradition of greater kindness and fairness, to teach and learn how we can [financially] help other Hmong in the world. If they were to find people to represent the Hmong community, I think it would be better to have someone from the US.

In fact, Kheng Xiong, a 1.5-generation Sacramento resident who worked at a state enforcement office, directly related the rural poverty in Laos to lack of political freedom by pointing out that Lao Hmong still suffer economically because the Communist government discourages and controls efforts by Hmong Americans to financially assist their co-ethnics and improve their economic situation. As former refugees who fought against the Communist Lao state during the Vietnam War and fled the country, part of the US Hmong community does not feel free to return to help their co-ethnics in Laos, especially for the long term (see chapter 1). Kheng expressed this concern as follows:

I would say, if Laos were free like other countries, we would go over there and help the Hmong financially, making their lives easier. But that country does not allow us to help Hmong or educate and teach them. That's why they are so poor. If we can help them to change, their life in Laos will be better. . . . So Hmong in the US, we have a better life here.

In this sense, such discussions of national economic differences between Laos and the United States not only lead to moral discourses about as-

Diaspora's National Affiliations   217

sisting "less fortunate" peoples but are also related to the apparent lack of political freedom in Laos, as will be discussed in greater detail below.

In addition, some of my interviewees argued that US Hmong should be "the most important and leading community" in the diaspora because America's "modernized and developed" economy provides them with the capacity to maintain and promote Hmong ethnic culture and traditions. One of the most salient examples was from an interview with Mia Vang:

> Here [in America], people can do a lot of research and receive a higher level of education so they can keep our culture alive. Even though the Hmong are spread out within the US, I think we are more equipped to continue the culture because of the better educational system here. Other countries like Thailand and Laos are maybe a little bit under-developed to do so, although I don't know much about China.

These responses contrast with the perceptions of Hmong I interviewed in Laos who critically noted that their American counterparts are "losing touch with traditional Hmong" cultural values precisely because of their developed economy and modernized American lifestyles. As shown here, diasporic communities hierarchically position themselves as culturally better than each other based on partial affiliations to the nation-states in which they live, producing fragmented and often conflicting discourses.

Contested Notions of Economic Freedom in National and Diasporic Contexts

Freedom emerged as a key concept employed by Hmong in their diasporic discourses when they differentiate themselves from each other based on national economic differences. As was the case with well-being, morality, and cultural values, there is again considerable discursive fragmentation, as Hmong I interviewed in both Laos and the United States claimed they enjoy more freedom than their diasporic counterparts because of their different national economic systems. This is another example of a relational nationalism in which these Hmong individuals feel a relative sense of affiliation with their country's social system as they favorably compare their lifestyles compared to those of their diasporic co-ethnics elsewhere.

As Foucault notes, freedom can be seen as an "inherently political" matter, because it inevitably results in individuals negotiating and struggling against dominant power dynamics in order not to be a "slave" (Foucault 2000, 286). However, in the case of the diasporic Hmong in my study, freedom is not always a product of power struggles but can be a form of "self-fashioning" (see Laidlaw 2002, 322) that enables them to understand themselves in a favorable manner in relation to other co-ethnics in the diaspora. This is similar to Foucault's "technologies (techniques) of the self" that allow individuals to "transform themselves in order to attain a certain state of happiness, purity, wisdom, perfection, or immortality" (Foucault 1988, 18).

Although Hmong communities in both Laos and the United States fashioned themselves in diasporic contexts by engaging in discourses about freedom, what they meant by "freedom" differs considerably and is based on contrasting interpretations. In *Escape from Freedom*, Erich Fromm ([1941] 1994) discusses the nature of freedom by distinguishing between positive *freedom to* pursue something and negative *freedom from* something (that is, to "escape" from something). Fromm analyzes the dialectical relation between the two by noting that human beings are reassured through their membership in collective groups, such as "clan, social, or religious" communities ([1941] 1994, 30–35). However, he argues that once individuals pursue *freedom from* group power and influence by seeking *freedom to* become an independent self, they will likely become lonely and isolated as a result. Needless to say, the realization of the self is a valuable state, but it may be achieved at the expense of security, comfort, and social support obtained from conformity to group norms.

Likewise, the two Hmong communities I studied believe in different types of freedom in terms of whether one can be *free from* a dominant economic system or *free to* pursue economic possibilities as an individual. Lao Hmong in Vang Vieng referred to individual social *freedom from* capitalist economic constraints as predominantly rural farmers, whereas Hmong in California valued their economic *freedom to* pursue individual economic opportunities and upward mobility as urban residents in a wealthy country. Their contested definitions and discourses about freedom indicate how diasporic people come to develop different understandings about the same concept based on varied national contexts.

Clearly, the fragmentary discourses of my interviewees are derived from generalized national differences in economic development. However, Hmong villagers I spoke with in Laos felt that their rural lives are much freer and more consistent with traditional Hmong cultural values because they compared themselves with their co-ethnics in the United States, whom they assume live in urbanized spaces as wage laborers without freedom. In contrast, Hmong interviewees in California valued their freedom to pursue socioeconomic opportunities and success (and thus lead the diaspora) and homogeneously perceived that all Hmong in Laos have no such freedom as rural villagers of lower socioeconomic status who live in a "poorer" country.

Diaspora's National Affiliations 219

These discourses resemble some long-lasting academic debates on freedom as well. For Karl Marx, the proletariat under capitalism are unfree because they are alienated from their labor and its products, which are appropriated by the bourgeois for the accumulation of capital. Workers can become free only by overthrowing the oppressive shackles of capitalist domination, which will allow them to become truly self-conscious beings who realize themselves through free, creative, and voluntary life-activity (Marx [1844] 1978, 72–76, 111). On the other hand, for modern economist Milton Friedman, it is precisely economic capital that allows individuals to maximize their freedom. Friedman firmly believes that "competitive capitalism" enables impersonal free markets to promote political freedom for individuals (Friedman [1962] 2002, 9, 21). Therefore, it is not a coincidence that the Hmong in Laos, one of the few remaining one-party socialist countries in the world, and those in the United States, one of the most prominent capitalist-driven countries, would produce similarly contrasting discourses about freedom.

Ultimately, the relative affiliations of my US and Lao interviewees, with their respective nation-states (and urban/rural localities), enabled them to hierarchically position themselves as "better" and "freer" than their counterparts, again producing discursive contestation in the diaspora. Indeed, scholarly analyses of freedom not only range from philosophical, political, or economic discussions but also combines these various disciplinary perspectives. Therefore, it makes sense that freedom can be understood only in specific, comparative national contexts as a discourse instead of assuming that the concept is universally applicable to all cases and events (see Carter 1999). Anthropological interest in freedom focuses on how it is manifested in social relationships and contexts and experienced at both individual and community levels. Freedom is a relational and contextual concept rather than a universal principle and was once understood as the "antithesis to unfreedom" (Leach 1963, 74).[4] As a result, when people evaluate the degree of freedom that they possess, they will likely do so by comparing themselves to what is *not* freedom among other social groups or different societies (see Gourevitch and Corey 2020, 386).

Social Freedom from Capitalist Economic Systems

Discourses about freedom among Hmong interviewees in Laos commonly valued the kind of freedom obtained by escaping from regulations and domination—in particular, hegemonic economic systems. They claimed they have more freedom in their country because of the noncapitalistic, rural subsistence-farming economy under which most of them live, in contrast to what they perceived to be the absence of freedom among their co-ethnics in the United States, who toil in a high-pressure, urban capitalist system that leaves little time for leisure and a relaxing social life.

Like a lot of his compatriots, Nia Her, a young farmer in Dao Tha, believed that rural village life in Laos allowed for more flexible work schedules, unlike the urbanized American capitalist system based on wage labor and control over worker productivity:

> For me, Laos is a better country for living, because I can freely live a natural life and go wherever I want. In America, it is a life constrained by time. Every day at 7:00 a.m., you must go to work. If you miss just one hour, they won't pay you for that hour. Also, if I want to go visit my relatives here in Laos, I can of course go anytime. But for them [in the United States], it is difficult to do that, because they only have one day off from work each week. This means that they will have just one or two weeks to visit their relatives over the entire year. So living in my own rural village here in Laos is better.

Toua Her, another farmer, first compared the two countries in terms of economic disparities. He did acknowledge that Hmong economic lives in Laos are "insufficient" because they are rural villagers who still rely on farming, but he added that even some urban wage workers in Laos are day laborers without a secure and stable income while workers in the United States earn a monthly salary in addition to receiving benefits. However, Toua ultimately claimed that lack of individual freedom (implicitly defined as free time for leisure) is the problem of an American capitalist economy based on wage labor:

> When you live as a rural farmer in Laos, if you just stay home because you don't want to work, no one will complain or scold you. As long as you harvest your crops and keep sufficient rice in storage for the rest of the year, you will have enough *freedom* to do what you want. Hmong over there in America get upset easily, because if you take one day off, your salary will be reduced right away. You have to worry whether you have enough money to pay for many things, all the time. [emphasis mine]

Based on this observation, despite the lack of economic wealth in Laos, Toua concluded that "life in Laos is much better. It is more comfortable here."

The discourses of freedom among Hmong villagers commonly emphasized the negative aspects of the American capitalist system, which restricts freedom to socialize and pursue a leisurely life compared to Lao nationals in a rural farming economy. Although they acknowledged global economic hierarchies between the United States and Laos, they did not perceive themselves to be subordinate or inferior in such a system. Rather, they affiliated with their national economic status as "better" with regard to freedom. Implicit in these perspectives is that one can feel free under what are presumably "unfree" circumstances, such as a country that grants very limited resources to live a sufficient economic existence, especially in rural areas. In Karla Slocum's study, rural banana farmers in St. Lucia similarly felt that even if they are impoverished, the ability to farm on their own land is considered a source of freedom. They were "feeling free," as one farmer put it, to work at their own pace, even though the scheduling of production as well as the marketing and pricing of "their" product were nonnegotiable and determined by a foreign transnational company in concert with the St. Lucian state (Slocum 2006, 94).

The underdeveloped Lao national economy also seemed to provide other economic freedoms for Lao Hmong interviewees as well, since they felt economically and relatively less subject to bureaucratic control in terms of paying bills and taxes, especially in rural areas, where governmental power is not as entrenched. Although local government officers issue utility (electricity) bills for residents, they were not able to effectively collect money from each household in the villages of Vang Vieng during my fieldwork. In fact, I frequently observed bill collectors going around the village on their motorbikes. They shouted to people in the house from outside: "Pay your utility bills for the past month! You haven't paid for several months. Your fees are now 25,000 Lao kip (US$3)!" In response to such requests, Hmong from inside their houses would simply shout back by responding, "I have no money yet. Please come back next time; I'll pay then!" The collectors would then just leave the house and move to the next one (which responded similarly) without imposing a firm deadline for payment or leaving a warning notice.

Paying bills and taxes indeed seemed to still be a very informal and flexible practice for both Hmong residents and government agents in rural Laos, which also shows the lower degree of subjugation to national governmental control compared to the United States because of lax state enforcement. Of course this does not mean that Hmong rural life is free from state control, for it is clear that the Lao state has exercised its power to regulate the economy in ways the US government cannot and effectively imposed cultural control over the Hmong New Year (see chapter 6).

As the Lao state continues to pursue its agenda to promote its economy and national development, the extent to which rural Hmong in Dao Tha and other surrounding villages will continue to enjoy social freedom from capitalist domination and wage labor is uncertain. Perhaps they may no longer feel that free as they face increasing economic pressures to adopt more rigorous work schedules or pay taxes and bills. However, they may continue to feel *relatively* free when they compare their lives to the hegemonic American economic system to which their co-ethnics are subject. Such seemingly simple national differences further indicate that Hmong in Laos partly affiliate themselves with the nation-state (its relatively less developed economic condition), as well as their rural lifestyles, and hierarchically position themselves in the diaspora through comparisons with their counterparts abroad.

Individual Freedom to Pursue Economic Opportunities

The discourses of Hmong interviewees in California generated interesting and fundamentally different, if not opposed, understandings of the concept of economic and social freedom in a different national context. Most of them did not consider their current economic status as wage laborers in a capitalist system to be oppressive or exploitative but, rather, took them for granted. In fact, for them, economic freedom is an essential right that enables them to enjoy a "better" life, materialistic affluence, and financial power as consumers in a capitalist market, even if they are sometimes working in irregular jobs. In contrast, they felt that the Laotian rural economy does not provide the same economic freedom to maintain a decent standard of living and restricts the consumption of goods.

Such perceptions among my interviewees in California again reveal discursive fragmentation with their counterparts in Laos, who perceived them to be less free under the confines of wage labor and the capitalist work ethic. Based on their relative identification with the American nation-state in terms of its economic status, they felt that their lives are "better" because they enjoy greater economic freedom compared to Laos, thus reversing their hierarchical positioning in the diaspora by appropriating the meaning of freedom differently from their co-ethnics in Laos.

Mee Lee, a retired Hmong woman in Sacramento, viewed the wealth of her country as essential for the individual freedom to obtain a good income and standard of living. For her, freedom is what enables everyone to fully participate in a capitalist economy and earn wages, an unquestionable and fundamental right that is not available in Laos. According to Mee, "The difference is that here [United States] it's a free country, so you can do whatever you want to make money as long as you don't do anything bad. But in Laos you have to work really hard, because it's a poor country. Of course, if you work hard, you will feel free too, but their country is just too poor and not the same as here." Interestingly, Mee's statement directly conflicts with the way Hmong interviewees in Vang Vieng characterized their lives as free because they did not have to constantly work as rural subsistence farmers.

Neng Vang, an insurance sales agent, expressed a common opinion among US Hmong by saying, "Nobody can stop people from pursuing and achieving their economic goals in America." He emphasized how education can lead to economic freedom to improve one's standard of living. Noting that educational opportunities are not readily available for those living in rural Laos, he pointed out that Hmong people there lack economic freedom and implied that Laos is in a "lower" position than the United States:

> Most of my family and other Hmong in Laos do not have education. They just go to the farm and work in the fields, so of course they don't have freedom. This country, you have education, and you know how to run a business and make money. That's freedom. You can go to school, and nobody can stop you from making your dream come true.

The tendency of my interviewees to emphasize the connection between national economic development and individual freedom indicates that they do not necessarily find the American economic system oppressive or constraining, unlike the discourses of Hmong in Laos. It is quite evident that some of them were undoubtedly discussing the differences between Hmong in the two countries in a somewhat binary manner based on personal impressions or what they had heard from others. Nor did they fully acknowledge in their discourses that these supposedly national characteristics partly reflect contrasts between urban and rural living that can also exist within the United States or Laos.

In addition, the discursive fragmentation between diasporic Hmong in the two communities is based on a fundamental disagreement about the relationship between capitalist systems and freedom. Hmong in rural villages of Vang Vieng believe capitalism creates a state of "unfreedom," whereas for Hmong in California it is a fundamental source of freedom.

Many Hmong interviewees in Laos, who are still subsistence farmers and not subject to wage labor, had a critical attitude toward the negative consequences of capitalism. In contrast, US Hmong interviewees not only have adopted capitalist ideologies but also consider the accumulation of wealth to be an indispensable precondition for freedom. As Zygmunt Bauman writes, "Modern renderings of freedom and definitions of capitalism are articulated in such a way that they presume the necessity of an unbreakable connection between the two and make the supposition that one can exist without the other logically flawed, if not absurd" (Bauman 1988, 44).

Although Hmong diasporic communities in both Laos and the United States position themselves as having more freedom in their own national economic contexts, there are drawbacks to each type of freedom that are not fully reflected in their discourses. Hmong farmers in Vang Vieng valued their freedom from capitalist constraints, but as Erich Fromm notes, such "negative freedom" may grant individuals independence from external domination at the expense of loneliness and possible isolation (Fromm [1941] 1994, 256–57). This partially explains why they have remained separated and marginalized from the country's national economic development and may continue to suffer from constant poverty as a result (which some of them alluded to in their discourses).

Ironically, US Hmong I spoke with who valued a different type of freedom to pursue economic opportunities and accumulate wealth may also face similar consequences. According to Daniel Fridman, financial success is possible only when individuals can "help themselves" and have "transformed themselves into individuals who *actively* strive for *freedom*" (Fridman 2017, 7; emphasis in original). Self-transformation into an autonomous individual who seeks freedom appears to be not only ideal but also "ethical," the kind of characteristic valued the most in a capitalist economy (see Weber [1958] 2003). As Aihwa Ong notes (1996, 2003), refugees are thus disciplined by institutions to become ideal, neo-liberal subjects who are self-sufficient and economically independent. According to Fromm, even as capitalism freed individuals through the "growth of an active, critical, responsible self" (an ethical standard to be successful in Protestant modern capitalism), "at the same time, it made the individual more alone and isolated and imbued him with a feeling of insignificance and powerlessness" (Fromm [1941] 1994, 108). Undoubtably, this echoes Marx's critique of capitalist domination, which produces alienation of workers from their labor, its products, and ultimately from other social beings and their own self-consciousness.

Contrasting Political Systems and Contested Claims of "Betterment"

In a classic anthropological study on freedom, David Bidney, writing during the Cold War, argues that the world is divided into two conflicting political systems: Communism (which he defines as "Totalitarian Democracy") and Liberalism ("Constitutional Democracy"). According to him, "Both sides profess themselves as the champions of freedom and appeal to the uncommitted peoples of the world for support and allegiance" (Bidney 1963, 20). Although we do not live in such a starkly bipolarized world, because the contemporary Hmong diaspora is the product of Cold War geopolitics, it is not surprising that Hmong communities in Laos and the United States have developed fragmented discourses about the different political systems in the two countries (see also chapter 1).

For those living in American democracy, political freedom is regarded as "unimaginable" in Communist Laos. However, Hmong in Laos rejected such assumptions and highlighted the individual political success story of Hmong in Laotian national history, believing that similar political opportunities and prominence are not possible for Hmong in the United States. This type of political discursive fragmentation is also based on relative national affiliations to different political systems and enabled Hmong in each country to claim higher political positionality over their co-ethnics in the diaspora, which indicates that both communities are highly influenced by and reproduce their nation-state's political ideologies and nationalist discourses.

However, I must note that this national political difference was not the dominant focus of Hmong's comparative discourses in my interviews, compared to national economic differences. Only a small number of Hmong individuals in both countries discussed political systems extensively as a major fragmenting national force in their transnational diasporic community. Indeed, Hmong in Laos I spoke with may not have felt comfortable discussing national politics freely in public or would make only positive political statements to avoid any possible government scrutiny. Those who willingly engaged in comparative political discourse about the Hmong diaspora held positions in local governmental offices were not as politically marginalized as rural Hmong villagers, and wanted to improve the country's national political image about ethnic minorities, in alignment with the state's political ideologies.

National political systems were more frequently raised by Hmong in California as a source of difference between Hmong diasporic communities. However, while the current Laotian political system is an important concern for the Hmong community in California because of their diasporic memories about fleeing the Communist government after the Vietnam War, it seems to have become less prominent in their consciousness over time and has perhaps been superseded by other priorities.

National Political Discourses among Hmong in Vang Vieng

The global political hierarchy between nation-states (that places liberal democracies higher than authoritarian and Communist regimes) is challenged and even inverted by Hmong interviewees in Laos, who place themselves in the better political position among the two diasporic communities. Although the Communist Party system in Laos was regarded negatively by US Hmong interviewees from an American democratic context, some of the Lao Hmong in my study who spoke about politics did not consider it an obstacle that prevents them from obtaining governmental positions and occupations. Vang Lee, a successful governmental administrator in the capital city, spoke about this with national pride and a sense of achievement as an ethnic minority individual:

> Hmong in Laos are entitled to a lot of opportunities and are placed in the highest position in the government. Do you know that in the National Assembly, the first member ranked the highest out of eleven is a female Hmong person? This means that Laos has already achieved gender equality and equal rights for all. This kind of success is very unique for Hmong in Laos and cannot be found anywhere else in the world.

Because of a few Hmong individuals who achieved political prominence in the nation, Vang believed that Hmong people's political success was possible only within the Lao political system and not in the United States, despite its economic wealth and status at the top of the global hierarchy. He continued:

> The US is maybe the most developed and richest country in the world, but its citizens cannot be compared to us here [in Laos] in terms of individual political success. The highest status that Hmong Americans can achieve is still lower, maybe like a city mayor or some local governmental officer. However, if you go to the national museum here [in the capital city of Vientiane], you will learn that the most prominent national hero in Lao history is Hmong. This shows that our country

really values Hmong's contribution to national history. The only problem that Hmong in Laos have is that there are still many households in poverty with a low level of knowledge overall.

Vang emphasized that the statue of this Hmong individual is the biggest one displayed in the museum; therefore, he believes that the political contribution of the Hmong to Lao national history is highly valued and recognized by the Lao government. He strongly recommended that I should visit the museum and find the statue of this Hmong leader.[5]

Political Discourses among Hmong in California

Not surprisingly, the view of Hmong interviewees in California contrasts with such ethnonational sentiments that claim Lao Hmong are better positioned in their country's political system. Instead, they assumed that the current Laotian political system has produced negative cultural and ethnic consequences for Hmong in Laos. Similar to how their co-ethnics in Laos felt that the American economy and lifestyles had led to undesirable cultural characteristics, some of them perceived certain behaviors of their counterparts in Laos quite negatively, as products of the country's Communist political system. Such discursive political difference is also based on a relational nationalism that assumes life is better under a democratic government in accordance with American national ideologies.

According to Mor Her, a retired resident in California, the US Hmong are "[General] Vang Pao Hmong" (the political military leader of the Hmong who initiated the alliance with the CIA during the Vietnam War in Laos). In contrast to this, Mor claimed that Lao Hmong, despite being co-ethnics in the old homeland, are "New Hmong" who were negatively influenced by the rise of the Communist regime after the war and thus became very different from his Hmong community in the United States In a different interview, a 1.5-generation public school teacher, Ker Cha, expressed no interest in going back to Laos and explained the reason for his disillusionment with the country, which he attributed to the negative behaviors of Hmong that result from living in a Communist country: "I know the living environment in Laos and what life is like there. Because there, it is a corrupted Communist country, you never know what to expect. In recent years, Hmong people in Laos have also become corrupted, greedy, and perhaps a little brazen in terms of finding ways to get money." Since Ker had a long personal history of sending remittances to financially support his (distant) relatives in Laos, whom he had never met, he seemed to acutely believe that the Communist political system contributes not only to economic hardship but also to attributes he dislikes among the Hmong living there. Despite his continued financial contributions, Ker believed his Hmong relatives' ongoing economic impoverishment in Laos was caused by the national political system.

Conclusion: National Affiliations and Discursive Fragmentation in Diasporic Communities

While being members of a transnational diasporic community, the Hmong I studied in Vang Vieng and California have also come to nationally affiliate with the countries where they reside to varying degrees, which produces contrasting and divergent discourses that reflect national differences. This indicates that even if diasporic peoples do not feel strong nationalist loyalty toward their host countries because of their sense of partial belonging, they undoubtedly become incorporated into their nation-states over time and adopt their ideologies and hegemonic perspectives, thereby developing comparative, critical discourses about the lives of their diasporic co-ethnics in other countries.[6]

Regardless of the actual position of their countries in the global economic hierarchy, Hmong in both communities positioned themselves above their co-ethnic counterparts in terms of well-being, morality, and freedom based on differing national economic and political systems. Many of the quotes featured in this chapter refer not only to national differences per se but also to localized divisions between rural farmers and urban wage laborers that can also occur within a country. In fact, one of the Hmong interviewees I met from the capital city of Vientiane, who had higher educational, socioeconomic, and occupational status, described the life of Hmong in rural areas of Laos in a somewhat similar manner to the way US Hmong in California understood their co-ethnics in the country. Nonetheless, because the national differences between the Lao and US diasporic Hmong communities in my research overlap with localized ones between the rural (villages in Laos) and the urban (cities in California), the local is understood within the framework of the national in their discourses. Indeed, when localized distinctions are seen as nationalized divisions, they may appear more insurmountable and immutable and become part of self-essentialized discourses about "Lao Hmong" versus "US Hmong."

Therefore, diasporic identity is not simply a product of deterritorialized, transnational continuities in social relations and culture that transcend nation-states. Instead, it also encompasses diasporic people's relative sense of national belonging to the country in which they have resided for extended periods. Such partial affiliations to nation-states are important components of diasporic identities because they develop when diasporic peoples compare certain aspects of their national lives with those of other co-ethnics in the diaspora. In other words, their sense of national belonging becomes salient and meaningful mainly in the context of the broader diasporic community.

In this respect, nation-states and diasporas are not antithetical or opposed but are simultaneous forces that constitute diasporic identity and belonging. The nationalization of diasporic peoples is not based on their adoption of exclusionary, nationalist agendas but instead are constructed in relation to each other transnationally across national borders. Such national comparisons within the diaspora are what enhances their sense of satisfaction about their current lives within nation-states, making them feel "better" (or even superior) in certain aspects than their co-ethnics elsewhere. Therefore, Hmong interviewees' discourses about national differences have become fragmented over time, not because they were previously unified but because of the different social positioning of the interlocutors who are in active debate with one another across national borders and embedded in hierarchical relations of power. Nonetheless, discursive disagreements based on national differences do not necessarily lead to actual ethnic conflicts, divisions, or social fragmentation of the transnational diasporic community of Hmong in Laos and the United States but remain on the discursive level. Kinship relations remain strong between Hmong in the two countries, diasporic cultures are still shared transnationally, financial and emotional remittances continue to flow across borders, and Hmong in the United States continue to visit family and relatives in Laos. In sum, one cannot assume that there is irreconcilable tension or conflict between the national and the transnational when it comes to diasporic belonging.

The Hmong case also illustrates how diasporic people's national affiliations are not always correlated with their level of national assimilation. Scholars no longer assume that assimilation is a coercive project unilaterally imposed by nation-states on immigrants and minorities (Alba and Nee 1997; Faist 2000). In fact, these groups can "voluntarily" desire to meet the norms and expectations of mainstream society and not be marked by difference (Nagel 2002, 263–64).

In this sense, the national sentiments of diasporic Hmong in the two communities are not directly related to their level of assimilation but are a result of selectively and comparatively reflecting on their national lives in diasporic context. Although diasporic peoples do not have a desire to assimilate and be the "same" as the rest of the society in order to develop stronger national identifications, their diasporic communities and transnational engagements can become a compelling reason for them to affiliate more strongly with the nation-state. Regardless of how much Hmong interviewees in Laos and the United States have "assimilated" to mainstream society and culture, they have increased their national sentiments, at least temporarily, by contrasting themselves favorably with co-ethnics in the diaspora. Nation-states therefore, perhaps, should not target the supposedly lower levels of assimilation or be concerned about national loyalty of diasporic minorities with transnational ties to other countries. The case of the Hmong diaspora examined in this chapter indicates that diasporic connections and national sentiments are not in inherent opposition but instead are mutually constitutive.

Conclusion

"We never had a government or country of our own, but we live together as a scattered people," remarked Nou Thao, a Hmong farmer in Dao Tha, at the end of an interview in a calm but robust tone as he stared into the evening light that shone into the dark room through his half-open wooden door. Nou's statement succinctly reflects similar sentiments by many Hmong with whom I spoke during my fieldwork about their diasporic lives. Instead of simply considering themselves "nationals" who are members of particular nation-states, they identified themselves as geographically dispersed diasporic people without a coherent ancestral homeland they can claim as their own.

I suddenly realized that Nou's statement was perhaps the reason why Hmong villagers frequently asked me, "Do you know where Hmong are *really* from?" when I first stayed in Laos as a young foreign volunteer. Although I was a foreigner, they wondered if I had encountered any new written or online sources that mentioned their ancestral origins. The question surprised me for a number of reasons. Is it not Laos where Hmong are from? If Hmong have been living there for generations, why would their ethnic origins still matter, and what made them wonder about it? As an outsider who knew very little about Hmong at that time, I did not feel qualified at all to give an answer to such a question (see S. Lee 2009). This irresoluble question was precisely what got me initially interested in doing research on Hmong and their diasporic condition.

Elusive Homelands and Nation-States

Throughout my research and while writing this book, I have grappled with the issue of belonging in the Hmong diaspora and what made Hmong in my study refer to themselves as a "people without a country." As discussed in this book, they do not have transnational attachments to a commonly recognized country of ancestral origin that they can claim as their ethnic homeland. Because of the decentered nature of their diaspora, I have instead analyzed the diasporic conditions that cause Hmong, in Vang Vieng, Laos, and Sacramento, California, to simultaneously retain transnational continuities across borders while their cultural practices and discourses are also inflected by a sense of partial belonging to the countries where they currently live.

Since the Hmong diaspora was constituted by multiple geographical dispersals and the absence of a definitive ethnic homeland, their diasporic consciousness has been an ongoing historical process. Not only is their diaspora the product of numerous dispersals; there is also a considerable time gap between the initial and subsequent migrations. The history of the Hmong diaspora thus involves complicated relations with multiple nation-states, including China, Laos, Thailand, and the United States, all of which influence the Hmong's diasporic condition and identity formation to varying degrees.

As mentioned in the introduction to this book, although there have been efforts by certain Hmong political groups to envision a united or territorialized homeland, Hmong in my research were not involved in such movements in either Laos or the United States. Nonetheless, they did not passively accept scholarly theories about their diasporic history or their apparent "homelandless-ness" with an attitude of resignation. Instead, they persistently and passionately discussed with me how their historical dispersal and absence of a territorial homeland affect their lives as ethnic minorities in various nation-states (as part of the diasporic condition). They continued to search for not only their ethnic origins (even if they have to imagine various homelands) but also a sense of transnational diasporic belonging. In this context, I reexamined the transnational power of "culture" and its continued impact on diasporic Hmong lives in the two communities where I conducted research. Cultural practices and discourses enable dispersed ethnic peoples to claim diasporic identities by constructing a collective sense of transnational ethnic commonality and belonging across national borders while simultaneously referencing internal differences among co-ethnics who are situated in vastly different national contexts.

As part of their ongoing diasporic consciousness of continued displacement and dispersal over the centuries, Hmong in my study developed ambivalent feelings toward both Laos and the United States. Although Laos became the geographic center and is the natal homeland of much of the contemporary Hmong diaspora after the Vietnam War, Hmong in both countries have developed ambivalent perceptions and relationships to it. Lao Hmong in my study have continued to feel marginalized socioeconomically and ethnically across generations as ethnic minorities in the country. Thus, despite functioning as an ethnic homeland that provides some centripetal unity to the post–Vietnam War Hmong diaspora, Laos is also positioned as one of the lateral transnational communities of dispersal that are connected to the other nation-states where Hmong reside.

US Hmong in my research did not always feel that the United States is "their country" because of their status as socioeconomic and racialized "outsiders" who do not fully belong. As discussed throughout this book, even US-born second-generation Hmong with whom I interacted in California, who may be more culturally and socially integrated in mainstream US society, continued to feel racially and ethnically marginalized in other ways and sometimes did not feel like bona fide Americans. Such experiences are also shared by other Asian Americans, including those of Japanese, Korean, Filipino, and Chinese descent (e.g., Espiritu 2003; N. Kim 2008; Tsuda 2014; Tuan 2001). Even third- and fourth-generation Asian Americans are often racialized as "forever foreigners" and not real Americans because of their Asian racial appearance, despite their greater cultural assimilation and social integration in mainstream American society (Tsuda 2016; Tuan 2001).

The Search for Trans/national Belonging: Continuities and Discontinuities

Diasporas can therefore be characterized by relative alienation from multiple nation-states, which is historically constituted through geopolitics and ethnic frictions that produce forced migrations as well as internal national inequalities that can result in socioeconomic and ethnic marginality from the nation-state. Such a condition of partial national belonging is exacerbated among diasporas with uncertain ethnic homelands, especially in a globalized world where nationalities are no longer an assumed indicator of people's identifications.

Hmong people's ambivalent and partial national affiliations produced an ongoing effort among interviewees in Laos and the United States to promote diasporic affiliations and ethnic solidarity across borders through transnational cultural continuities and socioeconomic connections that transcend national territories. Regardless of whether territory really matters for the identity of geographically dispersed peoples like diasporic Hmong, their sense of ethnic belonging is contextualized transnationally and generates multiple meanings for their everyday lives. This enables them to live beyond the nation-state's territorial boundaries, because they are embedded in transnational networks across national borders and develop ethnic affiliations with diasporic co-ethnic communities located elsewhere. As a result, they can imagine a collective ethnic community in the diaspora that overcomes the limitations of national, territorialized belonging.

As these two Hmong communities are sustained by transnational social systems (e.g., kinship) and economic relationships (remittances), there are modified continuities in cultural practices (e.g., shamanism, funerals, and New Year's celebrations) across national borders despite their geographical separation, and these can serve as a source of diasporic belonging in the absence of a coherent ethnic homeland. This does not mean that some type of essentialized and homogeneous ethnic culture keeps the Hmong diaspora together. Instead, such cultural traditions can be commonly shared among diasporic Hmong in Vang Vieng and California because they are flexible and adaptable to both transnational circumstances and different national contexts.

As Luis Guarnizo (2003) notes, diasporas thus provide a holistic picture of "transnational living" that is subject to constant change because migrants' economic, sociocultural, and political lives are all intertwined in historical contexts. In contrast, he argues that the concept of transnational *life* does not sufficiently capture such conditions but rather emphasizes a more stable state, whereas transnational *livelihood* is limited to economic means of subsistence. While this perspective distinguishes among these three terms and prefers transnational *living* as the most appropriate term to describe diasporic people, I consider all three concepts useful for understanding the Hmong people's diasporic condition.

Transnational influences on local peoples stem from migration and mobility, since migrants are the ones who maintain socioeconomic and cultural connections with their families in the homeland (Smith 2005;

Vertovec 2001). However, it is important to note that individuals do not always have to migrate in order to become transnational and conduct lives that are socially linked to other countries. Those who do not move across national borders and remain in the sending country (like Hmong in Laos) can also develop and maintain transnational relations with co-ethnics who have migrated to the diaspora abroad. They can therefore be equally affected by cross-border social forces as those engaged in transnational mobility.

This does not mean that transnational lives consign diasporic people like Hmong to a permanent stateless or deterritorialized condition without the concrete presence of the nation-state in their daily lives. National differences among members of the two Hmong communities in the diaspora that I studied have also produced contested and quite critical perceptions about their co-ethnics residing in other countries. Such diverging perceptions indicate how diasporas are often culturally and discursively fragmented and result in different diasporic communities positioning themselves hierarchically in relation to each other. Not only do differences in shared diasporic cultural "traditions" emerge as they are practiced under varying national contexts and sociopolitical pressures, but Hmong research participants in Laos and the United States have contrasting and conflicting perceptions about the authenticity of their cultural traditions, economic versus cultural impoverishment, and the meaning of "freedom" in different national contexts. This is one of the many examples of how diasporas continue to produce contested meanings and different interpretations of the same concepts and values among its members dispersed in different countries. In other words, the impacts of national power are not the same for different communities in the diaspora and can lead each community to prioritize their national identity over their diasporic affiliations, producing cultural and discursive discontinuities.

It is possible that hierarchical differentiation and internal disagreements among diasporic Hmong living in different countries can be based on the desire to become and remain "similar" to each other and avoid complete separation or disengagement.[1] The concern among Hmong interviewees in Laos that the funeral traditions of their co-ethnics in the United States have strayed from "tradition" may reflect a sense of regret that their co-ethnics abroad have become different instead of staying the same. Likewise, discursive disagreements, where Hmong in one country claim that those in the other are not as "free" as they are, reveal an underlying wish that their diasporic counterparts could enjoy

Conclusion   237

the same freedom that they cherish in their own country. Indeed, the fine line between diasporic difference and sameness for dispersed ethnic communities is only meaningful when the specific national factors that cause such cultural and discursive differentiation are recognized and considered.

Reclaiming Diasporic Identity

In this manner, diasporic identities are ultimately ambivalent, because they are based on transnationally shared cultural practices and discourses that are reconfigured locally in national contexts, revealing simultaneous affiliations with both nation-states and transnational communities. In general, addressing both the national and the transnational at the same time is a challenge, as the two forces are often seen as contrasting, if not incompatible. The transnational is understood as enabling migrants to supersede national boundaries and even evade state power (Berg 2017, 14; Blanc et al. 1995; Werbner and Modood 2015). In contrast, this book demonstrates that both the cultural differentiation that emerges through each national locality and transnational continuities and mobilities across borders are critical components of diasporic identities and belonging.

My research on the Hmong diaspora therefore argues that we examine how diaspora as a social formation is a result of the mutual interplay of both the national and the transnational. Over time, nation-states can become more salient for a diaspora as its members live in them for extended periods and eventually develop new, nationalized homes. This is especially the case for the second- and later-generation descendants in the diaspora who may develop a sense of belonging and affiliation to their current "home" and feel attached to it. As this book has shown, however, local discontinuities in cultures and practices do not hinder transnational continuities across the diaspora.

Ultimately, this book's framework of diasporic identity overcomes binary analyses that posit the nation-state against the transnational nature of diasporas. By examining both the sociocultural continuities and discontinuities in cultures and ethnic consciousness among two communities of Hmong, my research demonstrates that we should understand diasporic identity through *relations* between the transnational and the national and the simultaneous presence and mutual influences of both. This approach to diaspora can be more productive than debating whether dispersed ethnic communities live in a permanently displaced and deterritorialized condition or must be centered on territorialized nation-states.

The transnational and national identities of diasporas are fundamentally not in conflict but rather complementary, as they are situated in simultaneous and mutual relations, even if localized differences in these communities are understood by diasporic subjects through nationalized discourses about cultural differences (see chapter 7).

A diasporic identity perspective also allows us to examine how diasporic groups selectively and strategically position themselves in a global context. The fact that diasporas are often based on transnational continuities and commonalities of course does not mean their specific communities are characterized by egalitarian relations. Thus, it is necessary to consider how diasporas are constituted and internally differentiated by a global hierarchy of nation-states, which influences the way they transnationally connect to one another and produce fragmented discourses. Indeed, their diasporic positioning in relation to their own national communities reflects global inequalities within the diaspora. This illustrates how diasporic people are also embedded in and affiliate themselves with different global ideologies.

Diasporic people's ethnic ("minority") consciousness, ambivalent and partial belonging to different countries, and their transnational connections with each other all constitute diasporic identity, which therefore defies any simple and homogeneous characterization. The Hmong diasporic communities examined in this book may not be the only ones that exhibit this ambivalent and intertwined complexity of diasporic identity. Therefore, we can revisit many other existing diasporas resettled in different nation-states and reexamine how they simultaneously demonstrate both common and diverging identities as a multifaceted phenomenon.

Conclusion   239

Notes

Introduction

1. This research was conducted with ethics approval from CUREC (Central University Research Ethics Committee) under the Social Sciences and Humanities Interdivisional Research Ethics Committee (SSH IDREC) at the University of Oxford, UK, in 2011. Village names in Laos, as well as all Hmong first names in this book, are pseudonyms.

2. Mai Na Lee (2015) points out that there were some Hmong ancestors who left China seeking agricultural land (see also Hillmer 2010).

3. Estimated in 2009. Luong and Nieke 2013.

4. Lao Statistics Bureau 2015. Hmong residing in Laos are the third-largest ethnic group (9.2 percent of total population) after ethnic Lao (Lao Loum) and Khmu.

5. Lemoine 2005.

6. Pew Research Center 2017. https://www.pewsocialtrends.org/fact-sheet/asian-americans-hmong-in-the-u-s/.

7. Lemoine 2005.

8. "Chinese Ethnic Groups: Overview Statistics," UNC University Libraries (2022) https://guides.lib.unc.edu/china_ethnic/statistics. Chinese census data from 2010 seems to be the most recent source available in English and cited by scholars.

9. For example, such scholars include Gary Y. Lee and Nicholas Tapp (Australia), Ian Baird, Jacob Hickman, and Prasit Leepreecha (Thailand), and Jean Michaud and Tam Ngo (Vietnam).

10. Some examples in popular culture include the Hollywood movie *Gran Torino* (Eastwood 2008). For media representations that invoke similar images, see "International Marriages Come Under Criticism in Hmong Commu-

nity," *StarTribune* (October 2015): https://www.startribune.com/international -marriages-come-under-criticism-in-hmong-community/339129011/.

11. All citations to "S. Lee" throughout this book refer to Sangmi Lee unless spelled out otherwise.

12. The relation between place and identity in general is also relevant to nonmigratory, diasporic contexts. Akhil Gupta and James Ferguson (1992) note that even for non-migrants, the experience of locality and place always consists of various interactions among individuals, which supersede territorialized places that are not subordinated to localized and bounded social groups.

13. Some scholars' historical approaches to migration suggest that migrants' lives can be understood from a "transcultural" perspective, since they used to have much stronger regional or smaller-scale group identities rather than concrete national ones (see Freund 2012).

14. All the fieldwork data including interviews and field notes were transcribed and coded with ATLAS.ti.

15. The Song River is one of the main branches of Mekong River that goes through the villages and town of Vang Vieng.

16. Based on my conversations with the owners of the local tourism industry and estimates from four different guesthouses and hotels in Vang Vieng, the top three largest groups of tourists in the area were from Australia, the United Kingdom, and the United States, followed by Germany, France, and Israel.

17. Although the United Nations High Commissioner for Refugees stipulated that they return "voluntarily," Hmong interviewees generally expressed that they felt they had no choice but to return to Laos since there were no other alternatives.

18. As of 2019 there were twenty-seven thousand Hmong living in Sacramento, making it the second-largest Hmong community in California after Fresno (Pew Research Center 2017).

Chapter 1. Hmong Diasporic History and Multiple Homeland Narratives

1. Depending on the pronunciation, scholars use slightly different spellings when referring to the same groups, including "Hmong," "Hmu," "Kho Hsiong," "Mong," and "Hmao" (Mottin 1980, 5).

2. Also known as the "Hmong-Mien" linguistic family. Sharing a similar history of dispersal with Hmong, Yao are an ethnic group currently understood as "(Iu-)Mien," residing in southwest China as well as dispersed around Southeast Asia and in the United States. Although it is believed that Hmong and Mien share linguistic commonalities, their languages today are no longer mutually intelligible. For more research on contemporary (Iu-) Mien identity formation outside China, see Jonsson (2005).

3. Most ordinary Chinese today have not known or heard about the ethnic

name "Hmong," and even if they have, it was only recently that they have encountered the name through the media, Hmong tourists from the United States, or scholarly sources.

4. In fact, Hmong are conscious of and dislike the word "Miao" because it resembles the pronunciation of the word "cat" (*meo*) in the Lao language, which has a derogatory connotation. Elderly Hmong in both countries often made sure I understood that the term is demeaning and that I should never accept it if I heard someone using it.

5. Some local Hmong in Laos have also occasionally heard about or encountered Miao workers from China who came to Laos as "Chinese labor migrants" and work for development projects.

6. In fact, I also noticed that the production of hand-made traditional clothes and sewing (*paj ntaub* [pronounced *pandau*]) has considerably decreased and is rarely found in Hmong villages in Laos (see S. Lee, 2022).

7. This literally means "52km," referring to a town fifty-two kilometers away from the capital city, Vientiane. It is known as one of the largest urban cities populated by many Hmong people.

8. In the Hmong language, *paj tawj lag* (pronounced *pa tal lang*) means "land of flower," a mythical place that is commonly referred to by Hmong as the possible original location of their ancestors.

9. For more studies on transnational linkages between Hmong Americans and Miao in China, see Schein's work on transnational marriages (2005) and media productions (2004b).

10. The written Hmong language, known as Romanized Popular Alphabet, was allegedly created by a French missionary in the 1950s. However, the accurate pronunciation of "Hmong" is actually *mong*, which makes it similar to the pronunciation of the word "Mongolian."

11. *Txiv xaiv* refers to the last song sung during funeral rituals; *zaj tshoob* are traditional songs for wedding ceremonies.

12. Nong Het is a district located in Xieng Khouang province in northern Laos. It has one of the largest Hmong populations in the country. It was also where much of the fighting connected with the Vietnam War took place in Laos.

13. It is worth noting that from a historical perspective, the Royal Lao Government's prime minister played a role by demanding that the war should be kept secret in hopes that Laos could remain neutral (see Wolfson-Ford 2018).

14. General Vang Pao resided in the United States after the Vietnam War and died in 2011.

15. Wat Tham Krabok is a Buddhist temple that provided shelter for Hmong refugees who needed to be treated for illnesses and could not leave Thailand. This site became the last remaining shelter for Hmong refugees, especially those who prolonged their decision to leave Thailand and return to Laos or resettle in the United States.

16. For an ethnographic study on Hmong's daily lives in Thai refugee camps, see Lynellyn Long's book *Ban Vinai: The Refugee Camp* (1993).

17. There are a number of books that detail and describe Hmong experiences of resettlement in the United States written by both Hmong and non-Hmong writers that convey people's narratives, personal accounts, oral histories, and autobiographies (e.g., see Chan 1994; Donnelly 1994; Faderman and Xiong 1998; Koltyk 1993; Serge Lee 2020, K. Yang 2008).

Chapter 2. Locating the Hmong Diaspora in Ambivalent Local Belongings

1. Lao Statistics Bureau 2015. Hmong residing in Laos are the third-largest ethnic group (9.2 percent of total population) after ethnic Lao (Lao Loum) and Khmu.

2. These are official ethnonyms to refer to the main ethnic groups created by the Lao government based on their residential pattern (altitude). "Lao Loum" reflects the geographical location of their residence in the lowland, while "Lao Theung" refers to Khmu, whose residence is seen as uphill (or "middle" land). The term "Lao Soung" was coined to refer to Hmong, who were understood as "highlanders" (see also Ovesen 2004).

3. When Khmu families resettled in Dao Tha in the 1990s, they were granted land to build their houses but were given no farmland. As a result, the young children stayed in the village to attend school, while their parents had to live separately on their farms located in the mountains and only came down to the village during breaks in the farming. The parents of Khmu students often came to my English class during their short visits to see their children. The Lao government's relocation project with ethnic minorities progressed gradually (see Michaud 2009, 33).

4. Because of colonial influences, the term "farang" initially meant French people, but it has come to refer to all foreigners whose race appears to be white.

5. Although Hmong in Thailand have already been using longer Thai-sounding names, in Laos such naming practices were introduced rather recently.

6. UNDP Lao PDR 2018. https://www.la.undp.org/content/lao_pdr/en/home/presscenter/pressreleases/2018/3/19/lao-pdr_s-eligibility-for-graduation-from-least-developed-countr.html/.

7. "Laos May Not Graduate from Least Developed Country in 2024," *Laotian Times*, November 5, 2020.

8. For more details about global tourism and its impact on Dao Tha and Vang Vieng, see S. Lee 2023.

9. Such ongoing precarious local economic conditions also apply to another ethnic minority group, the Khmu, who were in a similar socioeconomic position with limited opportunities.

10. "The State of the Hmong American Community," Hmong National Development (HND) 2013, 26.

11. Based on her research with the Sacramento Hmong community, Bao Lo notes that female Hmong students received higher GPAs than the male students in their eleventh and twelfth grades (Lo 2018, 117).

12. "Hmong in the U.S. Fact Sheet," Pew Research Center, September 8, 2017, https://www.pewsocialtrends.org/fact-sheet/asian-americans-hmong-in-the-u-s/.

13. For a comparative study of Asian American youth gang involvement, see Kevin Lam's (2015) recent study of the Vietnamese American community.

14. For other scholarly research on the visibility and voices of sexual minorities and queer US-born Hmong, see B. Ngo 2012; B. Ngo and Kwon 2015; B. Thao 2016.

15. Or what Lisa Marie Cacho (2012) analyzes as "disease," a metaphoric term to critique how Southeast Asian gangs are viewed and criminalized.

16. "Key Facts about Asian Origin Groups in the U.S.," May 22, 2019, Pew Research Center, 2019, https://www.pewresearch.org/fact-tank/2019/05/22/key-facts-about-asian-origin-groups-in-the-u-s/. In the US Census, Hmong are counted separately from other Laotians.

17. This can be compared to history education and textbooks in Laos, which actually recognize the existence of ethnic minorities, including Hmong, based on the national agenda to promote ethnic unity.

Chapter 3. An "Imagined" Community of Transnational Kin

1. This is a substantially rewritten and extended version of my article originally published in *Identities: Global Studies in Culture and Power* (S. Lee 2020).

2. Sao's statement spoken in English aptly indicates my double-sided positionality. In reality, I am not Hmong, but in principle, my last name allowed me to be temporarily included in the Hmong clan system.

3. The relations between Hmong's clan and surnames are complex, and some of the origins of their last names may be influenced by Chinese surnames that were passed down and modified from their ancestors.

4. The coincidental similarities of clan names between Hmong and other cultures are quite interesting and can be a subject for future study. Some of the eighteen Hmong clan names are similar to how Korean last names are pronounced, such as Her, Xiong, Yang, Khang, Lee, Vang, and Cha. Some of these names are also found among Han Chinese in China.

5. Although younger Hmong in the United States may no longer be aware of their subclan and lineage membership, the exogamy principle applies at the broader level of the clan (and thus automatically applies to the subclan level). Therefore, knowledge of subclan lineage is not seen as necessary in order to properly marry outside the clan, for it is based on different surnames.

6. As of 2015, the Pew Research Center finds that about 29 percent of newly wedded Asians in the United States are intermarried (to someone of a different race or ethnicity), the highest percentage of any ethnic group. It also reports that 46 percent of those intermarried Asians are US born. See Bialik 2017.

7. Race was a concern among some US interviewees who discussed their view on intermarriage and ethnic endogamy. They emphasized that their ethnic preference is not because of any negative prejudices about other races and ethnicities but is based on their desire to retain cultural heritage (e.g., language, traditional cultures, beliefs). In fact, some of the parents who have children attending college and were not against intermarriages also hoped their children would date "at least Asians," if not Hmong, because they believed their grandchildren might face discrimination against their biracial identity.

8. It should also be noted that there are emerging structural shifts among Hmong families in the United States, and not all of them can be assumed to be heterosexual, "traditional" families. There are also Hmong who pursue homosexual relationships while spouses can separate, divorce, and remarry (e.g., see Leepreecha 2016). Such increasing diversities in sexuality, marriage, and family structure may increase future resistance against the kinship principles that have so far been pervasive and taken for granted.

Chapter 4. Compassionate Money

1. Some transnational communities maintain and value emotional support even without the presence of financial remittances. It is worth noting that in such cases the economic disparities between the homeland and the host country are less. For an example, see Loretta Baldassar's (2007) ethnographic study about the transnational familial relationships between Italian migrants (children) in Australia and their families (parents) in Italy.

2. For a study of remittances in the Filipino diaspora, see Joyce Zapanta Mariano's *Giving Back: Filipino America and the Politics of Diaspora Giving* (2021).

3. The exception is perhaps those involved in marriage migration. US Hmong can send remittances independently and individually to support their partners or potential future spouses in Laos.

4. Many US Hmong mentioned that they would be relatively more willing to help out if their co-ethnics in Laos ask for money for their children's education.

5. The disagreement on the relationship between money and love can cause some other diasporic peoples to perceive familial relationships negatively, get disillusioned, or disconnect from them, as shown in the PBS documentary *Daughter from Danang* (Dolgin and Vicente 2011).

Chapter 5. From Local to Transnational

1. Parts of this chapter are based on an article originally published in *Ethnography* (S. Lee 2021).

2. Jean Mottin (1984, 105–7) provides descriptions of each step of the ua neeb in chronological sequence. For a detailed description of ua neeb and shamanistic practices, see also Tapp (1989b, 75–80), and for specific definitions of Hmong terminology, see Y. Cha (2010, 131–64).

3. Vincent Her (2005) refers to Siv Yig (pronounced *shee yee*), a mythical shaman figure he believes is comparable to Jesus Christ. He coins the term *siv yigism* (with the English suffix "-ism") and defines it as Hmong religion.

4. For example, a local newspaper article profiles a US-born female shaman in Minnesota: Elizabeth Thao, "The Next Wave of Hmong Shamans: Sandy'Ci Moua's Story," *Twin Cities (MN) Daily Planet*, April 2, 2013, https://www.tcdailyplanet.net/next-wave-hmong-shamans-sandyci-mouas-story/.

5. See Seng Alex Vang, "Journey of a Life Coach and Shaman," Hmong American Experience, March 11, 2021, https://hmongamerican.org/journey-of-a-life-coach-and-shaman/.

6. In Laos, when Hmong youth internally migrated from the village to other parts of the country (such as the cities) for work or education, they did not request shamanistic services remotely. Instead, they either returned to their village or asked the shaman to travel to their location.

7. Hmong Palace Church is the name of community hall rented by the Sacramento Hmong community to conduct funerals, but it has no relation to Hmong Christian churches.

8. In addition, some Hmong shamanistic rituals face objections and unwanted scrutiny from the US public (see also chapter 6).

Chapter 6. Cultural Differences in the Diaspora

1. This does not mean the Lao government during other times and in other parts of the country has not pressured ethnic minorities about their animal sacrifice practices. Indeed, governmental policies and regulations on Hmong funeral practices in Laos can also change and vary in different contexts, especially in light of the growing global consciousness about the environment and animal rights.

2. It should not be assumed that all Hmong in Laos live in their own ethnic villages. For those who live in more urbanized areas or the capital city of Vientiane in closer proximity to non-Hmong residents, it may be more difficult for them to practice extensive Hmong-style funerals.

3. For an example of a funeral with detailed sequences, see also Vincent Her 2005.

4. Department of Public Health, County of Fresno 2012.

5. A similar account with strong critical remarks on funerals can also be found in Jacob Hickman's research cited in Faith Nibbs's book (2014) on Hmong in Texas and Germany.

6. For instance, although the US government has been noninterventionist in terms of the Hmong New Year festival, in 2019 I was notified that the US State Department had recently banned herbal medicines and health-related items from being sold at the New Year markets in California in response to the emphasis on public health and growing concerns about unauthorized medical practices. Therefore, the same ethnic culture, once celebrated and encouraged as a marker of ethnic diversity in a multicultural American nation-state, can become a target of criticism and regulation at any time.

7. The following discussion of the New Year festivals is excerpted from S. Lee 2022.

8. Louisa Schein and Chia Y. Vang (2021) note that many Hmong in the United States often imagine that their co-ethnics in Laos still preserve "traditional" cultures.

9. Many video clips that portray major New Year celebrations in Laos can be found on YouTube that were recorded and posted by Hmong individuals from the United States. For a case study of the Hmong New Year in Thailand, see Yangcheepsutjarit 2020.

Chapter 7. Diaspora's National Affiliations

1. Malina constantly referred to Laos as "my country" after clearly stating that she feels the United States is her home country where she belongs (which is not technically the same as homeland). However, she also often referred to both Laos and the United States as her "home country" in an indistinguishable manner.

2. *Sabai* in the Lao language has positive meanings of "happy, comfortable, carefree." It is a key term that Hmong in the two countries repeatedly use to talk about their lives in terms of national differences.

3. Although Kong's statement appears subjective, his negative perception is not completely imagined but is based on the information that he learned from his relatives and acquaintances who visited their families in the United States and shared their experiences.

4. Edmund Leach defines unfreedom as a "state of servitude."

5. This Hmong national hero that Vang Lee refers to is a young Hmong leader who was recognized as a "freedom fighter" by the country during the Japanese invasion of World War II. Later, I visited the Lao National Museum and found the statue that he described.

6. Whereas diasporic subjects cannot always control their incorporation into the countries where they reside, their national affiliations involve a more agentive consciousness, because some of them may not wish to identify

with the nation-states in which they have become (sometimes unwittingly) incorporated.

Conclusion

1. This may also be the case with broader global issues and international relations. In his analysis of the Chinese public's perception of transpacific relations with the United States, Biao Xiang (2014) argues that the interconnectedness of the seemingly conflicting political and economic regimes of the two countries reveals a Chinese desire to become "similar" (rather than different) in order to "compete" with the United States.

Bibliography

Abdelhady, Dalia. 2011. *The Lebanese Diaspora: The Arab Immigrant Experience in Montreal, New York, and Paris*. New York: New York University Press.

Abrego, Leisy J. 2014. *Sacrificing Families: Navigating Laws, Labor, and Love across Borders*. Stanford, CA: Stanford University Press.

Aiyar, Sana. 2015. *Indians in Kenya: The Politics of Diaspora*. Cambridge, MA: Harvard University Press.

Alba, Richard, and Victor Nee. 1997. "Rethinking Assimilation Theory for a New Era of Immigration." *International Migration Review* 31, no. 4: 826–74.

Alonso, Ana M. 1994. "The Politics of Space, Time, and Substance: State Formation, Nationalism, and Ethnicity." *Annual Review of Anthropology* 23:379–405.

Amelina, Anna, and Karolina Barglowski. 2019. "Key Methodological Tools for Diaspora Studies: Combining the Transnational and Intersectional Approaches." In *Routledge Handbook of Diaspora Studies*, edited by Robin Cohen and Carolin Fischer. London: Routledge, 40–46.

Anderson, Benedict. (1983) 2006. *Imagined Communities: Reflections on the Origin and Spread of Nationalism*. London: Verso Books.

Anthias, Floya. 1998. "Evaluating 'Diaspora': Beyond Ethnicity." *Sociology* 32, no. 3: 1–15.

Apiah, Kwame Anthony. 2006. "The Politics of Identity." *Daedalus* 135, no. 4: 15–22.

Appadurai, Arjun. 1996. *Modernity at Large: Cultural Dimensions of Globalization*. Minneapolis: University of Minnesota Press.

Atkinson, Jane M. 1992. "Shamanisms Today." *Annual Review of Anthropology* 21:307–30.

Axel, Brian Keith. 2000. *The Nation's Tortured Body: Violence, Representation, and the Formation of a Sikh "Diaspora."* Durham, NC: Duke University Press.

Baird, Ian G. 2015. "Translocal Assemblages and the Circulation of the Concept of 'Indigenous Peoples' in Laos." *Political Geography* 46:54–64.

Baird, Ian G., and Pao Vue. 2017. "The Ties That Bind: The Role of Hmong Social Networks in Developing Small-Scale Rubber Cultivation in Laos." *Mobilities* 12, no. 1: 136–54.

Baldassar, Loretta. 2007. "Transnational Families and the Provision of Moral and Emotional Support: The Relationship between Truth and Distance." *Identities: Global Studies in Culture and Power* 14:385–409.

Barney, Linwood. 1967. "The Meo of Xieng Khouang Province, Laos." In *Southeast Asian Tribes, Minorities, and Nations*, edited by Peter Kunstadter, 271–94. Princeton, NJ: Princeton University Press.

Barth, Fredrik. 1969. Introduction to *Ethnic Groups and Boundaries: The Social Organization of Culture Difference*, edited by Fredrik Barth, 9–38. Long Grove, IL: Waveland Press.

Bauman, Zygmunt. 1988. *Freedom*. Philadelphia: Open University Press.

Bendix, Regina. 1997. *In Search of Authenticity: The Formation of Folklore Studies*. Madison: University of Wisconsin Press.

Berg, Mette. 2011. *Diasporic Generations: Memory, Politics, and Nation among Cubans in Spain*. Oxford: Berghahn Books.

Berg, Ulla D. 2017. *Mobile Selves: Race, Migration, and Belonging in Peru and the U.S.* New York: New York University Press.

Bernal, Victoria. 2004. "Eritrea Goes Global: Reflections on Nationalism in a Transnational Era." *Cultural Anthropology* 19, no. 1: 3–25.

Bernal, Victoria. 2005. "Eritrea On-Line: Diaspora, Cyberspace, and the Public Sphere." *American Ethnologist* 32, no. 4: 660–75.

Bernatzik, Hugo A. 1970. *Akha and Miao: Problems of Applied Ethnography in Farther India*. New Haven, CT: Human Relations Area Files.

Bhabha, Homi K. 1994. *The Location of Culture*. London: Routledge.

Bialik, Kristen. 2017. "Key Facts about Race and Marriage, 50 Years after *Loving v. Virginia*." June 12. Pew Research Center. https://www.pew research.org/fact-tank/2017/06/12/key-facts-about-race-and-marriage -50-years-after-loving-v-virginia/.

Bidney, David. 1963. *The Concept of Freedom in Anthropology*. The Hague: Mouton.

Bilgrami, Akeel. 2006. "Notes toward the Definition of 'Identity.'" *Daedalus* 135, no. 4: 5–14.

Blanc, Cristina Szanton, Linda Basch, and Nina Glick Schiller. 1995. "Transnationalism, Nation-State, and Culture." *Current Anthropology* 36, no. 4: 683–86.

Blumer, Nadine. 2011. "'Am Yisrael Chai! (The Nation of Israel Lives!)':

Stark Reminders of Home in the Reproduction of Ethno-Diasporic Identity." *Journal of Ethnic and Migration Studies* 37, no. 9: 1331–47.

Boccagni, Paolo. 2016. "From the Multi-Sited to the In-Between: Ethnography as a Way of Delving into Migrants' Transnational Relationships." *International Journal of Social Research Methodology* 19, no. 1: 1–16.

Boccagni, Paolo, and Loretta Baldassar. 2015. "Emotions on the Move: Mapping the Emergent Field of Emotion and Migration." *Emotion, Space, and Society* 18, no. 8: 839–54.

Borja, Melissa May. 2017. "Speaking of Spirits: Oral History, Religious Change, and the Seen and Unseen Worlds of Hmong Americans." *Oral History Review* 44, no. 1: 1–18.

Bourdieu, Pierre. 1977. *Outline of a Theory of Practice.* Vol. 16. Cambridge: Cambridge University Press.

Bowen, John R. 2004. "Does French Islam Have Borders? Dilemmas of Domestication in a Global Religious Field." *American Anthropologist* 106, no. 1: 43–55.

Boyer, Pascal, and Brian Bergstrom. 2008. "Evolutionary Perspective on Religion." *Annual Review of Anthropology* 37:111–30.

Brah, Avtar. 1996. *Cartographies of Diaspora: Contesting Identities.* London: Routledge.

Braziel, Jana Evans, and Anita Mannur, eds. 2003. *Theorizing Diaspora: A Reader.* Malden, MA: Blackwell.

Briggs, Charles. 1996. "The Politics of Discursive Authority in Research on the 'Invention of Tradition.'" *Cultural Anthropology* 11, no. 4: 435–69.

Brodwin, Paul. 2003. "Pentecostalism in Translation: Religion and the Production of Community in the Haitian Diaspora." *American Ethnologist* 30, no. 1: 85–101.

Brow, James. 1988. "In Pursuit of Hegemony: Representation of Authority and Justice in Sri Lankan Village." *American Ethnologist* 15, no. 2: 311–27.

Brown, Richard P. C., and Bernard Poirine. 2005. "A Model of Migrants' Remittances with Human Capital Investment and Intrafamilial Transfers." *International Migration Review* 39, no. 2: 407–38.

Brubaker, Rogers. 1992. *Citizenship and Nationhood.* Cambridge, MA: Harvard University Press.

Brubaker, Rogers. 2005. "The 'Diaspora' Diaspora." *Ethnic and Racial Studies* 28, no. 1: 1–19.

Budgeon, Shelley. 2014. "The Dynamics of Gender Hegemony: Femininities, Masculinities, and Social Change." *Sociology* 48, no. 2: 317–34.

Burawoy, Michael. 2012. "The Roots of Domination: Beyond Bourdieu and Gramsci." *Sociology* 46, no. 2: 187–206.

Butler, Kim D. 2001. "Defining Diaspora, Refining a Discourse." *Diaspora* 10, no. 2: 189–219.

Cacho, Lisa Marie. 2012. *Social Death: Racialized Rightlessness and the Criminalization of the Unprotected*. New York: New York University Press.

Cadge, Wendy, and Elaine H. Ecklund. 2007. "Immigration and Religion." *Annual Review of Sociology* 33:359–79.

Capps, Lisa L. 1994. "Change and Continuity in the Medical Culture of the Hmong in Kansas." *Medical Anthropology Quarterly* 8, no. 2: 161–77.

Carney, Nikita. 2017. "Multi-Sited Ethnography: Opportunities for the Study of Race." *Sociology Compass* 11, no. 9: 1–10.

Carruthers, Bruce G., and Wendy Nelson Espeland. 1998. "Money, Meaning, and Morality." *American Behavioral Scientist* 41, no. 10: 1384–1408.

Carsten, Janet. 2004. *After Kinship*. Cambridge, MA: Cambridge University Press.

Carter, Ian. 1999. Introduction to *A Measure of Freedom*. Oxford: Oxford University Press, 1–7.

Case, William. 2011. "Laos in 2010." *Asian Survey* 51, no. 1: 202–7.

Cha, Dia. 2003. *Hmong American Concepts of Health, Healing, and Conventional Medicine*. New York: Routledge.

Cha, Ya Po. 2010. *An Introduction to Hmong Culture*. Jefferson, NC: McFarland.

Chan, Sucheng. 1994. *Hmong Means Free: Life in Laos and in America*. Philadelphia: Temple University Press.

Cheal, David. 1987. "'Showing Them You Love Them': Gift Giving and the Dialectic of Intimacy." *Sociological Review* 35, no. 1: 150–69.

Cheung, Siu-Woo. 2004. "Miao Identity in Western Guizhou: China during the Republican Period." In *Hmong/Miao in Asia*, edited by Nicholas Tapp, Jean Michaud, Christian Culas, and Gary Yia Lee, 237–72. Chiang Mai, Thailand: Silkworm Books.

Christou, Anastasia, and Elizabeth Mavroudi, eds. 2015. Introduction to *Dismantling Diasporas: Rethinking the Geographies of Diasporic Identity, Connection and Development*, 1–11. London: Routledge.

Clarke, Gerard. 2001. "From Ethnocide to Ethnodevelopment? Ethnic Minorities and Indigenous Peoples in Southeast Asia." *Third World Quarterly* 22, no. 3: 413–36.

Clarke, Morgan. 2008. "New Kinship, Islam, and the Liberal Tradition: Sexual Morality and New Reproductive Technology in Lebanon." *Journal of the Royal Anthropological Institute* 14, no. 1: 153–69.

Clarkin, Patrick F. 2005. "Hmong Resettlement in French Guiana." *Hmong Studies Journal* 6:1–27.

Clifford, James. 1983. "On Ethnographic Authority." *Representations* 1, no. 2: 118–46.

Clifford, James. 1988. *The Predicament of Culture: Twentieth-Century Ethnography, Literature, and Art*. Cambridge, MA: Harvard University Press.

Clifford, James. 1994. "Diasporas." *Cultural Anthropology* 9, no. 3: 302–38.

Clifford, James. 2004. "Traditional Futures." In *Questions of Tradition*, edited by Mark Phillips and Gordon Schochet, 152–68. University of Toronto Press.

Coe, Cati. 2011. "What Is Love? The Materiality of Care in Ghanaian Transnational Families." *International Migration* 49, no. 6: 7–24.

Cohen, Robin. 1997. *Global Diasporas: An Introduction*. London: Routledge.

Collins, Jock. 2002. "Chinese Entrepreneurs: The Chinese Diaspora in Australia." *International Journal of Entrepreneurial Behavior and Research* 8, nos. 1–2: 113–33.

Comaroff, Jean, and John L. Comaroff. 1991. *Of Revelation and Revolution: Christianity, Colonialism, and Consciousness in South Africa*. Chicago: University of Chicago Press.

Conboy, Kenneth. 1995. *Shadow War: The CIA's Secret War in Laos*. Boulder, CO: Paladin Press.

Conquergood, Dwight. 1989. "Establishing the World: Hmong Shamans." *CURA Reporter* 19, no. 2: 5–10.

Conway, Dennis, and Jeffrey H. Cohen. 1998. "Consequences of Migration and Remittances for Mexican Transnational Communities." *Economic Geography* 74, no. 1: 26–44.

Cox, James L. 2003. "Contemporary Shamanism in Global Contexts: 'Religious' Appeals to an Archaic Tradition?" *Studies in World Christianity* 9, no. 1: 69–87.

Culas, Christian. 2004. "Innovation and Tradition in Rituals and Cosmology: Hmong Messianism and Shamanism in Southeast Asia." In *Hmong/Miao in Asia*, edited by Nicholas Tapp, Jean Michaud, Christian Culas, and Gary Yia Lee, 441–56. Chiang Mai, Thailand: Silkworm Books.

Culhane-Pera, Kathleen A., Dorothy E. Vawter, Phua Xiong, et al. 2003. *Healing by Heart: Clinical and Ethical Care Stories of Hmong Families and Western Providers*. Nashville: Vanderbilt University Press.

Deal, David, and Laura Hostetler. 2005. *The Art of Ethnography: A Chinese "Miao Album."* Seattle: University of Washington Press.

de Haas, Hein. 2005. "International Migration, Remittances, and Development: Myths and Facts." *Third World Quarterly* 26, no. 8: 1269–84.

Department of Public Health, County of Fresno. 2012. "Community Event Food Vendor Requirements." https://adminfinance.fresnostate.edu/ehsrm/documents/CommunityEventFoodVendor_18.pdf/.

Dhamoon, Rita. 2010. *Identity/Difference Politics*. Vancouver: University of British Columbia Press.

Diamond, Norma. 1988. "The Miao and Poison: Interactions on China's Frontier." *Ethnology* 27, no. 1: 1–23.

Dolgin, Gail, and Franco Vicente, dirs. 2002. *Daughter from Danang*. PBS.

Donnelly, Nancy D. 1994. *Changing Lives of Refugee Hmong Women.* Seattle: University of Washington Press.

Dossa, Parin, and Cati Coe, eds. 2017. *Transnational Aging and Reconfigurations of Kin Work.* New Brunswick, NJ: Rutgers University Press.

Duncan, Christopher R, ed. 2004. *Civilizing the Margins: Southeast Asian Government Policies for the Development of Minorities.* Ithaca, NY: Cornell University Press.

Dunnigan, Timothy. 1982. "Segmentary Kinship in an Urban Society: The Hmong of St. Paul–Minneapolis." *Anthropological Quarterly* 55, no. 3: 126–34.

Dwyer, Claire. 2000. "Negotiating Diasporic Identities: Young British South Asian Muslim Women." *Women's Studies International Forum* 23, no. 4: 475–86.

Eastwood, Clint, dir. 2008. *Gran Torino.* Warner Bros. Pictures.

Eliassi, Barzoo. 2015. "Making a Kurdistani Identity in Diaspora: Kurdish Migrants in Sweden." In *Diasporas Reimagined: Spaces, Practices, and Belonging*, edited by Nando Sigona, Alan Gamlen, Giulia Liberatore, and Hélène Neveu Kringelbach, 45–49. Oxford: Oxford Diasporas Programme.

Entenmann, Robert. 2005. "The Myth of Sonom, the Hmong King." *Hmong Studies Journal* 6:1–14.

Enwall, Joakim. 1992. "Miao or Hmong?" *Thai-Yunnan Project Newsletter*, No. 17, June.

Eriksen, Thomas H. (1993) 2002. *Ethnicity and Nationalism.* New York: Pluto Press.

Espiritu, Yen Le. 2003. *Home Bound: Filipino American Lives across Cultures, Communities, and Countries.* Berkeley: University of California Press.

Faderman, Lillian, and Ghia Xiong. 1998. *I Begin My Life All Over: The Hmong and the American Immigrant Experience.* New York: Allyn and Bacon.

Fadiman, Ann. 1997. *The Spirit Catches You and You Fall Down: A Hmong Child, Her American Doctors, and the Collision of Two Cultures.* New York: Farrar, Straus and Giroux.

Faist, Thomas. 2000. "Transnationalization in International Migration: Implications for the Study of Citizenship and Culture." *Ethnic and Racial Studies* 23, no. 2: 189–222.

Falola, Toyin. 2013. *The African Diaspora: Slavery, Modernity, and Globalization.* Rochester, NY: University of Rochester Press.

Falzon, Mark-Anthony. 2003. "'Bombay, Our Cultural Heart": Rethinking the Relation between Homeland and Diaspora." *Ethnic and Racial Studies* 26, no. 4: 662–83.

Falzon, Mark-Anthony. 2009. "Introduction: Multi-Sited Ethnography:

Theory, Praxis, and Locality in Contemporary Research." In *Multi-Sited Ethnography: Theory, Praxis, and Locality in Contemporary Research*, edited by Mark-Anthony Falzon, 1–24. New York: Routledge.

Fotiou, Evgenia. 2016. "The Globalization of Ayahuasca Shamanism and the Erasure of Indigenous Shamanism." *Anthropology of Consciousness* 27, no. 2: 151–79.

Foucault, Michel. 1972. *The Archaeology of Knowledge and the Discourse on Language*. Trans. A. M. Sheridan Smith. New York: Pantheon Books.

Foucault, Michel. 1982. "The Subject and Power." In *Michel Foucault: Beyond Structuralism and Hermeneutics*, edited by Hubert Dreyfus and Paul Rabinow, 208–26. Chicago: University of Chicago Press.

Foucault, Michel. 1988. *Technologies of the Self: A Seminar with Michel Foucault*. Ed. Luther H. Martin, Huck Gutman, and Patrick H. Hutton. Amherst: University of Massachusetts Press.

Foucault, Michel. 1995. *Discipline and Punish: The Birth of the Prison*, 2nd ed. New York: Vintage.

Foucault, Michel. 2000. *Essential Works of Foucault 1954–1984*. Vol. 1: *Ethics*. Ed. Paul Rabinow. New York: Penguin Press.

Franzen-Castle, Lisa, and Chery Smith. 2013. "Shifts in Hmong Culture: Competing Medical Frameworks." *Journal of Immigrant and Minority Health* 15:829–35.

Freund, Alexander. 2012. *Beyond the Nation: Immigrants' Local Lives in the Transnational Cultures*. Toronto: University of Toronto Press.

Fridman, Daniel. 2017. *Freedom from Work: Embracing Financial Self-Help in the United States and Argentina*. Stanford, CA: Stanford University Press.

Friedman, Milton. (1962) 2002. *Capitalism and Freedom* (Fortieth Anniversary Edition). Chicago: University of Chicago Press.

Fromm, Erich H. (1941) 1994. *Escape from Freedom*. New York: Henry Holt.

Geddes, William R. 1976. *Migrants of the Mountains: The Cultural Ecology of the Blue Miao (Hmong Njua) of Thailand*. London: Oxford University Press.

Gerdner, Linda A. 2012. "Shamanism: Indications and Use by Older Hmong Americans with Chronic Illness." *Hmong Studies Journal* 12, no. 1: 1–22.

Gerson, Judith M. 2001. "Immigrants in between States: National Identity Practices among German Jewish Immigrants." *Political Psychology* 22, no. 1: 179–98.

Gilroy, Paul. 1987. *There Ain't No Black in the Union Jack*. Chicago: University of Chicago Press.

Gilroy, Paul. 1992. "Cultural Studies and Ethnic Absolutism." In *Cultural Studies*, edited by Lawrence Grossberg, Cary Nelson, and Paula A. Treichler, 187–98. New York: Routledge.

Gilroy, Paul. 1993. *The Black Atlantic*. London: Verso.

Glassman, Jim. 2011. "Cracking Hegemony in Thailand: Gramsci, Bourdieu, and the Dialectics of Rebellion." *Journal of Contemporary Asia* 41, no. 1: 25–46.

Glick Schiller, Nina, Linda Basch, and Cristina Szanton Blanc. 1995. "Transmigrant: Theorizing Transnational Migration." *Anthropological Quarterly* 68, no. 1: 48–63.

Göksel, Nisa. 2022. "A Displaced, Unsettled Political Subject: Kurdish Women's Struggles in Europe." In *Kurds in Dark Times: New Perspectives on Violence and Resistance in Turkey*, edited by Ayça Alemdaroğlu and Fatma Müge Göçek, 356–87. Syracuse, NY: Syracuse University Press.

Gordon, Edmund T., and Mark Anderson. 1999. "The African Diaspora: Toward an Ethnography of Diasporic Identification." *Journal of American Folklore* 112, no. 445: 282–96.

Gourevitch, Alex, and Robin Corey. 2020. "Freedom Now." *Polity* 52, no. 3: 384–98.

Graburn, Nelson H. H. 2001. "What Is Tradition." *Museum Anthropology* 24, nos. 2–3: 6–11.

Gramsci, Antonio. (1971) 1989. *Selections from the Prison Notebooks*. Edited and translated by Quinton Hoare and Geoffrey N. Smith. New York: International Publishers.

Guarnizo, Luis Eduardo. 2003. "The Economics of Transnational Living." *International Migration Review* 37, no. 3: 666–99.

Guarnizo, Luis Eduardo, and Michael Peter Smith. 1998. "The Locations of Transnationalism." In *Transnationalism from Below*, edited by Michael Peter Smith and Luis Eduardo Guarnizo, 3–34. New Brunswick, NJ: Transaction Publishers.

Gupta, Akhil, and James Ferguson. 1992. "Beyond 'Culture': Space, Identity, and the Politics of Difference." *Cultural Anthropology* 7, no. 1: 6–23.

Hajj, Nadya. 2021. *Networked Refugees: Palestinian Reciprocity and Remittances in the Digital Age*. Oakland: University of California Press.

Hall, Stuart. 1986. "Gramsci's Relevance for the Study of Race and Ethnicity." *Journal of Communication Inquiry* 10, no. 2: 5–27.

Hall, Stuart. 1990. "Cultural Identity and Diaspora." In *Identity: Community, Culture, Difference*, edited by Jonathan Rutherford, 222–37. London: Lawrence and Wishart.

Hall, Stuart. 1993. "Culture, Community, Nation." *Cultural Studies* 7, no. 3: 349–63.

Hall, Stuart. 1995. "New Cultures for Old." In *A Place in the World? Places, Cultures, and Globalization*, edited by Doreen Massey and Pat Jess, 175–213. New York: Oxford University Press.

Handler, Richard. 1986. "Authenticity." *Anthropology Today* 2, no. 1: 2–4.

Hannerz, Ulf. 2003. "Being there . . . and there . . . and there! Reflections on Multi-Site Ethnography." *Ethnography* 4, no. 2: 201–16.

Hardt, Michael. 2011. "For Love or Money." *Cultural Anthropology* 26, no. 4: 676–82.

Harrell, Stevan. 1995. *Cultural Encounters on China's Ethnic Frontiers.* Seattle: University of Washington Press.

Hart, Keith. 2007. "Money Is Always Personal and Impersonal." *Anthropology Today* 23, no. 5: 12–16.

Hefner, Robert W. 1998. "Multiple Modernities: Christianity, Islam, and Hinduism in a Globalizing Age." *Annual Review of Anthropology* 27:83–104.

Hein, Jeremy. 1993. "Refugees, Immigrants, and the State." *Annual Review of Sociology* 19:43–59.

Hein, Jeremy. 1995. *From Vietnam, Laos, and Cambodia: A Refugee Experience in the United States.* New York: Twayne Publishers.

Hein, Jeremy. 2013. "The Double Diaspora: China and Laos in the Folklore of Hmong American Refugees." In *Diversity in Diaspora: Hmong Americans in the Twenty-First Century,* edited by Mark E. Pfeifer, Monica Chiu, and Kou Yang, 209–32. Honolulu: University of Hawai'i Press.

Helmreich, Stefan. 1992. "Kinship, Nation, and Paul Gilroy's Concept of Diaspora." *Diaspora: A Journal of Transnational Studies* 2, no. 2: 243–49.

Helsel, Deborah. 2019. "Paper Spirits and Flower Sacrifices: Hmong Shamans in the 21st Century." *Journal of Transcultural Nursing* 30, no. 2: 132–36.

Her, Vincent K. 2005. "Hmong Cosmology: Proposed Model, Preliminary Insights." *Hmong Studies Journal* 6:1–25.

Her, Vincent K. 2018. "Reframing Hmong Religion: A Reflection on Emic Meanings and Etic Labels." *Amerasia Journal* 44, no. 2: 23–41.

Hickman, Jacob R. 2007. "'Is It the Spirit of the Body?' Syncretism of Health Beliefs among Hmong Immigrants to Alaska." *Napa Bulletin* 27, no. 1: 176–95.

Hickman, Jacob R. 2021. "The Art of Being Governed: Apocalypse, Aspirational Statecraft, and the Health of the Hmong Body (Politic)." *Anthropology & Medicine* 28, no. 1: 94–108.

High, Holly. 2009. "Internal Resettlement in Laos—Complicities and Complexities: Provocations from the Study of Resettlement in Laos." *Critical Asian Studies* 41, no. 4: 615–20.

High, Holly. 2021. *Projectland: Life in a Lao Socialist Model Village.* Honolulu: University of Hawai'i Press

Hillmer, Paul. 2010. *A People's History of the Hmong.* St. Paul: Minnesota Historical Society.

Hindess, Barry. 2004. "Citizenship for All." *Citizenship Studies* 8, no. 3: 305–15.

Hmong National Development (HND). 2013. "The State of the Hmong American Community."

Hobsbawm, Eric. 1983. "Introduction: Inventing Tradition." In *The Invention of Tradition*, edited by Eric Hobsbawm and Terence O. Ranger, 1–14. Cambridge: Cambridge University Press.

Hostetler, Laura. 2000. "Qing Connections to the Early Modern World: Ethnography and Cartography in Eighteenth-Century China." *Modern Asian Studies* 34, no. 3: 623–62.

Huennekes, Josee. 2018. "Emotional Remittances in the Transnational Lives of Rohingya Families Living in Malaysia." *Journal of Refugee Studies* 31, no. 3: 353–70.

Hüwelmeier, Gertrud. 2016. "Cell Phones for the Spirits: Ancestor Worship and Ritual Economies in Vietnam and Its Diasporas." *Material Religion* 12, no. 3: 294–321.

Hüwelmeier, Gertrud, and Krause Kristine. 2010. Introduction to *Traveling Spirits: Migrants, Markets and Mobilities*, edited by Gertrud Hüwelmeier and Kristine Krause, 1–16. London: Routledge.

Ireson, Carol J., and Randall W. Ireson. 1991. "Ethnicity and Development in Laos." *Asian Survey* 31, no. 10: 920–37.

Jackson, Jean E. 1991. "Being and Becoming an Indian in the Vaupés." In *Nation-State and Indian in Latin America*, ed. Greg Urban and Joel Sherzer, 131–55. Austin: University of Texas Press

Jackson, Jean E. 1995. "Culture, Genuine and Spurious: The Politics of Indianness in the Vaupés, Colombia." *American Ethnologist* 22, no. 3: 3–27.

Jenks, Robert D. 1994. *Insurgency and Social Disorder in Guizhou: The "Miao" Rebellion 1854–1873*. Honolulu: University of Hawai'i Press.

Jones, Joni. 2002. "Performance Ethnography: The Role of Embodiment in Cultural Authenticity." *Theatre Topics* 12, no. 1: 1–15.

Jonsson, Hjorleifur. 2001. "Serious Fun: Minority Cultural Dynamics and National Integration in Thailand." *American Ethnologist* 28, no. 1: 151–78.

Jonsson, Hjorleifur. 2005. *Mien Relations: Mountain People and State Control in Thailand*. Ithaca, NY: Cornell University Press.

Jonsson, Hjorleifur. 2010. "Mimetic Minorities: National Identity and Desire on Thailand's Fringe." *Identities: Global Studies in Culture and Power* 17, nos. 2–3: 108–30.

Joppke, Christian. 1998. "Immigration Challenges the Nation-State." In *Challenge to the Nation-State: Immigration in Western Europe and the United States*, edited by Christian Joppke, 5–46. Oxford: Oxford University Press.

Julian, Roberta. 2004. "Living Locally, Dreaming Globally: Transnational Cultural Imaginings and Practices in the Hmong Diaspora." In *The Hmong of Australia: Culture and Diaspora*, edited by Nicholas Tapp and Gary Y. Lee, 26–58. Canberra: Pandanus Books.

Kearney, Michael. 1995. "The Local and the Global: The Anthropology of Globalization and Transnationalism." *Annual Review of Anthropology* 24:547–65.

Kim, Claire Jean. 2015. *Dangerous Crossings: Race, Species, and Nature in a Multicultural Age*. Cambridge: Cambridge University Press.

Kim, Nadia. 2008. *Imperial Citizens: Koreans and Race from Seoul to LA*. Stanford, CA: Stanford University Press.

Kleist, Nauja. 2008. "In the Name of Diaspora: Between Struggles for Recognition and Political Aspirations." *Journal of Ethnic and Migration Studies* 34, no. 7: 1127–43.

Koinova, Maria. 2018. "Diaspora Mobilisation for Conflict and Post-Conflict Reconstruction: Contextual and Comparative Dimensions." *Journal of Ethnic and Migration Studies* 44, no. 8: 1251–69.

Koltyk, Jo Ann. 1993. "Telling Narratives through Home Videos: Hmong Refugees and Self-Documentation of Life in the Old and New Country." *Journal of American Folklore* 106, no. 422: 435–49.

Kondo, Dorinne K. 1990. *Crafting Selves: Power, Gender, and Discourses of Identity in a Japanese Workplace*. Chicago: University of Chicago Press.

Kunnath, George. 2013. "Compliance or Defiance? The Case of Dalits and Mahadalits." *Journal of Anthropological Society of Oxford* 5, no. 1: 36–59.

Kuper, Adam. 1982. "Lineage Theory: A Critical Retrospect." *Annual Review of Anthropology* 11:71–95.

Kurashige, Lon. 2002. *Japanese American Celebration and Conflict: A History of Ethnic Identity and Festival, 1934–1990*. Berkeley: University of California Press.

Kymlicka, Will. 1995. *Multicultural Citizenship: A Liberal Theory of Minority Rights*. Cambridge: Cambridge University Press.

Lai, Ming-yan. 2011. "The Present of Forgetting: Diasporic Identity and Migrant Domestic Workers in Hong Kong." *Social Identities* 17, no. 4: 565–85.

Laidlaw, James. 2002. "For an Anthropology of Ethics and Freedom." *Journal of the Royal Anthropological Institute* 8, no. 2: 311–32.

Lam, Kevin D. 2015. *Youth Gangs, Racism, and Schooling: Vietnamese American Youth in a Postcolonial Context*. New York: Palgrave McMillan.

Langdon, Esther Jean. 2013. "New Perspectives of Shamanism in Brazil: Shamanisms and Neo-shamanisms as Dialogical Categories. *Civilisations* 61, no. 2: 19–35.

Langford, Jean M. 2013. *Consoling Ghosts: Stories of Medicine and Mourning from Southeast Asians in Exile*. Minneapolis: University of Minnesota Press.

Lao Statistics Bureau. 2015. "Results of Population and Housing Census."

https://lao.unfpa.org/en/publications/results-population-and-housing-census-2015-english-version

"Laos May Not Graduate from Least Developed Country in 2024." 2020. November 5. *Laotian Times*.

Lavie, Smadar, and Ted Swedenburg, eds. 1996. *Displacement, Diaspora, and Geographies of Identity*. Durham, NC: Duke University Press.

Leach, Edmund. 1963. "Law as a Condition of Freedom." In *The Concept of Freedom in Anthropology*, edited by David Bidney, 74–90. The Hague: Mouton.

Lee, Gary Y. 2004. "Transnational Adaptation: An Overview of the Hmong of Laos." In *Hmong/Miao in Asia,* edited by Nicholas Tapp, Jean Michaud, Christian Culas, and Gary Yia Lee, 441–56. Chiang Mai, Thailand: Silkworm Books.

Lee, Gary Y. 2006. "Dreaming across the Oceans: Media, Globalisation, and Cultural Reinvention in the Hmong Diaspora." *Hmong Studies Journal* 7:1–33.

Lee, Gary Y. 2007. "Diaspora and the Predicament of Origins: Interrogating Hmong Postcolonial History and Identity." *Hmong Studies Journal* 8:1–25.

Lee, Gary Y., and Nicolas Tapp. 2010. *Culture and Customs of the Hmong*. Santa Barbara, CA: Greenwood.

Lee, Mai Na. 2015. *Dreams of the Hmong Kingdom: The Quest for Legitimation in French Indochina, 1850–1960*. Madison: University of Wisconsin Press.

Lee, Sangmi. 2009. "Searching for the Hmong People's Ethnic Homeland and Multiple Dimensions of Transnational Longing: From the Viewpoint of the Hmong in Laos." *Hmong Studies Journal* 10:1–18.

Lee, Sangmi. 2016. "Between the Diaspora and the Nation State: Transnational Ethnic Unity and Fragmentation among the Hmong in Laos and the United States." PhD diss., University of Oxford.

Lee, Sangmi. 2019. "Alternatives to Diasporic Return: Imagining Homelands and Temporary Visits among Hmong Americans." In *Diasporic Returns to the Ethnic Homeland: The Korean Diaspora in Comparative Perspective*, edited by Takeyuki Tsuda and Changzoo Song, 219–38. New York: Palgrave Macmillan.

Lee, Sangmi. 2020. "Diasporic Kinship Hegemonies and Transnational Continuities in the Hmong Diaspora." *Identities: Global Studies in Culture and Power* 27, no. 2: 229–47.

Lee, Sangmi. 2021. "Traditionally Transnational: Cultural Continuity and Change in Hmong Shamanism across the Diaspora." *Ethnography* 22, no. 1: 51–69.

Lee, Sangmi. 2022. "National Differentiation and Imagined Authenticity: The Hmong New Year's Celebration in Multicultural Laos and the

United States." *Ethnography* (Online First). https://doi.org/10.1177/14661381221098605/.

Lee, Sangmi. 2023. "Global Tourists and Local Ethnicity: Reconfiguring Racial and Ethnic Relations in Central Laos." *Critique of Anthropology (Online First)*. https://doi.org/10.1177/0308275X231173567/.

Lee, Serge. 2020. *From Earth to Elite: The Memoir of Dr. Serge Lee.* London: Austin Macauley Publishers.

Lee, Stacey J. 2002. "Learning 'America': Hmong American High School Students." *Education and Urban Society* 34, no. 2: 233–46.

Leepreecha, Prasit. 2008. "The Role of Media Technology in Reproducing Hmong Ethnic Identity." In *Living in a Globalized World: Ethnic Minorities in the Greater Mekong Subregion*, edited by Don McCaskill, Prasit Leepreecha, and He Shaoying, 89–114. Chiang Mai, Thailand: Mekong Press.

Leepreecha, Prasit. 2016. "Divorced Hmong Women in Thailand: Negotiating Cultural Space." In *Claiming Place on the Agency of Hmong Women*, edited by Chia Y. Vang, Faith Nibbs, and Ma Vang, 144–66. Minneapolis: University of Minnesota Press.

Lemoine, Jacques. 2005. "What Is the Actual Number of the (H)mong in the World?" *Hmong Studies Journal* 6:1–8.

Lemoine, Jacques. 2008. "To Tell the Truth." *Hmong Studies Journal* 9:1–29.

Levitt, Peggy. 2001. *The Transnational Villagers.* Berkeley: University of California Press.

Levitt, Peggy. 2003. "You Know, Abraham Was Really the First Immigrant": Religion and Transnational Migration. *International Migration Review* 37, no. 3: 847–73.

Levitt, Peggy, and Deepak Lamba-Nieves. 2011. "Social Remittances Revisited." *Journal of Ethnic and Migration Studies* 37, no. 1: 1–22.

Lindholm Schulz, Helena. 2003. *The Palestinian Diaspora: Formation of Identities and Politics of Homeland.* London: Routledge.

Lindley, Anna. 2009. "The Early-Morning Phonecall: Remittances from a Refugee Diaspora Perspective." *Journal of Ethnic and Migration Studies* 35, no. 8: 1315–34.

Linnekin, Jocelyn S. 1983. "Defining Tradition: Variations on the Hawaiian Identity." *American Ethnologist* 10, no. 2: 241–52.

LiPuma, Edward. 1999. "The Meaning of Money in the Age of Modernity." In *Money and Modernity: State and Local Currencies in Melanesia*, edited by David Akin and Joel Robbins, 192–213. Pittsburgh: University of Pittsburgh Press.

Lo, Bao. 2018. "Criminalization and Second-Generation Hmong American Boys." *Amerasia Journal* 44, no. 2: 113–26.

Loizos, Peter. 2009. "The Loss of Home: From Passion to Pragmatism in Cyprus." In *Struggles for Home: Violence, Hope, and the Movement of People*, edited by Stef Jansen and Staffan Löfving, 65–84. Oxford: Berghahn Books.

Long, Lynellyn D. 1993. *Ban Vinai: The Refugee Camp*. New York: Columbia University Press.

Lopez, Lori. 2021. *Micro Media Industries: Hmong American Media Innovation in the Diaspora*. New Brunswick, NJ: Rutgers University Press.

Luong, Minh Phuong, and Wolfgang Nieke. 2013. "Minority Status and Schooling of the Hmong in Vietnam." *Hmong Studies Journal* 14:1–37.

Malkki, Liisa. 1992. "National Geographic: The Rooting of Peoples and the Territorialization of National Identity among Scholars and Refugees." *Cultural Anthropology* 7, no. 1: 24–44.

Mariano, L. Joyce Zapanta. 2021. *Giving Back: Filipino America and the Politics of Diaspora Giving*. Philadelphia: Temple University Press.

Marcus, George E. 1995. "Ethnography in/of the World System: The Emergence of Multi-Sited Ethnography." *Annual Review of Anthropology* 24:95–117.

Marx, Karl. (1844) 1978. "Economic and Philosophic Manuscripts of 1844. In *The Marx-Engels Reader*, edited by Robert Tucker, 67–125. New York: W. W. Norton.

Mavroudi, Elizabeth. 2010. "Contesting Identities, Differences, and a Unified Palestinian Community." *Environment and Planning D: Society and Space* 28:239–53.

McConnell, Fiona. 2015. "Reconfiguring Diaspora Identities and Homeland Connections: The Tibetan 'Lhakar' Movement." In *Dismantling Diasporas: Rethinking the Geographies of Diasporic Identity, Connection, and Development*, edited by Anastasia Christou and Elizabeth Mavroudi, 99–111. London: Routledge.

McCoy, Alfred W. 1970. "French Colonialism in Laos, 1893–1945." In *Laos: War and Revolution*, edited by Nina S. Adams and Alfred McCoy, 67–99. New York: Harper Colophon Books.

McLoughlin, Seán. 2013. "Religion, Religions, and Diaspora." In *A Companion to Diaspora and Transnationalism*, edited by Ato Quayson and Girish Daswani, 125–38. Oxford: Blackwell.

Michaud, Jean. 1997a. "From Southeast China into Upper Indochina: An Overview of Hmong (Miao) Migrations." *Asia Pacific Viewpoint* 38, no. 2: 119–30.

Michaud, Jean. 1997b. "A Portrait of Cultural Resistance: The Confinement of Tourism in a Hmong Village in Thailand." In *Tourism, Ethnicity, and the State in Asian and Pacific Societies*, edited by Michel Picard and Robert E. Wood, 128–54. Manoa: University of Hawai'i Press.

Michaud, Jean. 2009. "Handling Mountain Minorities in China, Vietnam, and Laos: From History to Current Concerns." *Asian Ethnicity* 10, no. 1: 25–49.

Michaud, Jean. 2013. "Comrades of Minority Policy in China, Vietnam, and Laos." In *Red Stamps and Gold Stars: Fieldwork Dilemmas in Upland Southeast Asia*, edited by Sarah Turner, 22–39. Vancouver: University of British Columbia Press.

Min, Pyong Gap, and Chigon Kim. 2009. "Patterns of Intermarriages and Cross-Generational in Marriages among Native-Born Asian Americans." *International Migration Review* 43, no. 3: 447–70.

Moore, Henrietta. 2007. *The Subject of Anthropology: Gender, Symbolism and Psychoanalysis*. Cambridge: Polity Press.

Mottin, Jean. 1980. *History of the Hmong*. Bangkok: Odeon Store Ltd.

Mottin, Jean. 1984. "A Hmong Shaman's Séance." *Asian Folklore Studies* 43, no. 1: 99–108.

Mulasi-Pokhriyal, Urvashi, and Chery Smith. 2011. "Investigating Health and Diabetes Perceptions among Hmong American Children, 9–18 Years of Age." *Journal of Immigrant and Minority Health* 13:470–77.

Nagel, Caroline. 2002. "Constructing Difference and Sameness: The Politics of Assimilation in London's Arab Communities." *Ethnic and Racial Studies* 25, no. 2: 258–87.

Naujoks, Daniel. 2010. "Diasporic Identities—Reflections on Transnational Belonging." *Diaspora Studies* 3, no. 1: 1–21.

Ngo, Bic. 2012. "The Importance of Family for a Gay Hmong American Man: Complicating Discourses of 'Coming Out.'" *Hmong Studies Journal* 13, no. 1: 1–27.

Ngo, Bic, and Melissa Kwon. 2015. "A Glimpse of Family Acceptance for Queer Hmong Youth." *Journal of LGBT Youth* 12, no. 2: 212–31.

Ngo, Tam. 2016. *The New Way: Hmong Protestantism in Vietnam*. Seattle: University of Washington Press.

Nguyen, Van Huy. 2003. "Tet Holidays: Ancestral Visits and Spring Journeys." In *Vietnam: Journeys of Body, Mind, and Spirit*, edited by Laurel Kendall, Van Huy Nguyen, and Ross E. Gray, 70–91. Berkeley: University of California Press.

Nibbs, Faith G. 2014. *Belonging: The Social Dynamics of Fitting in As Experienced by Hmong Refugees in Germany and Texas*. Durham, NC: Carolina Academic Press.

Ó Brian, Lonán. 2018. *Musical Minorities: The Sounds of Hmong Ethnicity in Northern Vietnam*. Oxford: University of Oxford Press.

Omi, Michael, and Howard Winant. 1986. *Racial Formation in the United States: From the 1960s to the 1980s*. New York: Routledge & Kegan Paul.

Ong, Aihwa. 1996. "Cultural Citizenship as Subject-Making: Immigrants Negotiate Racial and Cultural Boundaries in the United States." *Current Anthropology* 37, no. 5: 737–51.

Ong, Aihwa. 1999. *Flexible Citizenship: The Cultural Logics of Transnationality*. Durham, NC: Duke University Press.

Ong, Aihwa. 2003. *Buddha Is Hiding: Refugees, Citizenship, the New America*. Berkeley: University of California Press.

Ovesen, Jan. 1995. *A Minority Enters the Nation State: A Case Study of a Hmong Community in Vientiane Province, Laos*. Uppsala, Sweden: Uppsala University Press.

Ovesen, Jan. 2004. "All Lao? Minorities in the Lao People's Democratic Republic." In *Civilizing the Margins: Southeast Asian Government Policies for the Development of Minorities*, edited by Christopher R. Duncan, 214–40. Ithaca, NY: Cornell University Press.

Paerregaard, Karsten. 2010. "Interrogating Diaspora: Power and Conflict in Peruvian Migration." In *Diaspora and Transnationalism: Concepts, Theories and Methods*, edited by Rainer Bauböck and Thomas Faist, 91–107. Amsterdam: Amsterdam University Press.

Parkin, Robert. 1997. *Kinship: An Introduction to the Basic Concepts*. Oxford: Blackwell.

Parreñas, Rhacel. 2001. *Servants of Globalization: Migration and Domestic Work*. Stanford, CA: Stanford University Press.

Parreñas, Rhacel, and Lok Siu. 2007. Introduction to *Asian Diasporas: New Formations, New Conceptions*, edited by Rhacel Parreñas and Lok Siu, 1–24. Stanford, CA: Stanford University Press.

Parry, Jonathan, and Maurice Bloch. 1989. "Introduction: Money and the Morality of Exchange." In *Money and the Morality of Exchange*, edited by Jonathan Parry and Maurice Bloch, 1–32. Cambridge: Cambridge University Press.

Pattie, Susan P. 1999. "Longing and Belonging: Issues of Homeland in Armenian Diaspora." *PoLAR: Political and Legal Anthropology Review* 22, no. 2: 80–92.

Peletz, Michael G. 1995. "Kinship Studies in Late Twentieth-Century Anthropology." *Annual Review of Anthropology* 24:343–72.

Petit, Pierre. 2013. "Ethnic Performance and the State in Laos: The Boun Greh Annual Festival of the Khmou." *Asian Studies Review* 37, no. 4: 471–90.

Pew Research Center. 2017. "Hmong in the U.S. Fact Sheet." September 8. https://www.pewsocialtrends.org/fact-sheet/asian-americans-hmong-in -the-u-s/.

Pew Research Center. 2019. "Key Facts about Asian Origin Groups in the U.S." May 22. https://www.pewresearch.org/fact-tank/2019/05/22/key -facts-about-asian-origin-groups-in-the-u-s/.

Pfeifer, Mark E., Monica Chiu, and Kou Yang, eds. 2013. *Diversity in Diaspora: Hmong Americans in the Twenty-First Century*. Honolulu: University of Hawai'i Press.

Pha, Kong Pheng. 2017. "Queer Refugeeism: Constructions of Race, Gender, and Sexuality in the Hmong Diaspora." PhD diss., University of Minnesota.

Pholsena, Vatthana. 2002. "Nation/Representation: Ethnic Classification and Mapping Nationhood in Contemporary Laos." *Asian Ethnicity 3*, no. 2: 175–97.

Pholsena, Vatthana. 2020. Mobility, Familiarity and Prejudice: Living Together in a Multiethnic Town in Southern Laos. *Ethnic and Racial Studies* 43, no. 10: 1872–89.

Portes, Alejandro, and Ruben G. Rumbaut. 1996. *Immigrant America: A Portrait*. 2nd ed. Berkeley: University of California Press.

Portes, Alejandro, and Ruben G. Rumbaut. 2001. "Defining the Situation: The Ethnic Identities of Children Immigrants." In *Legal Legacies: The Stories of the Immigrant Second Generation*. Berkeley: University of California Press, 147–60.

Portes, Alejandro, Luis Eduardo Guarnizo, and Patricia Landolt. 1999. "Introduction: Pitfalls and Promise of an Emergent Research Field." *Ethnic and Racial Studies* 22, no. 2: 217–30.

Robertson, Roland. 1995. "Glocalization: Time-Space and Homogeneity-Heterogeneity." In *Global Modernities, Money, and the Morality of Exchange*, edited by Mike Featherstone, Scott Lash, and Roland Robertson, 25–44. London: Sage.

Rumsby, Seb. 2021. "Hmong Christian Elites as Political and Development Brokers: Competition, Cooperation, and Mimesis in Vietnam's Highlands." *Social Anthropology* 29, no. 3: 701–17.

Safran, William. 1991. "Diasporas in Modern Societies: Myths of Homeland and Return." *Diaspora* 1:83–99.

Salemink, Oscar. 2007. "The Emperor's New Clothes: Re-Fashioning Ritual in the Hue Festival." *Journal of Southeast Asian Studies* 38, no. 3: 559–81.

Schein, Louisa. 1998a. "Forged Transnationality and Oppositional Cosmopolitanism." In *Transnationalism from Below*, edited by Michael P. Smith and Luis Guarnizo, 291–313. New Brunswick, NJ: Transaction Publishers.

Schein, Louisa. 1998b. "Importing Miao Brethren to Hmong America: A Not So Stateless Transnationalism." In *Cosmopolitics: Thinking and Feeling beyond the Nation*, edited by Pheng Cheah and Bruch Robbins, 163–91. Minneapolis: University of Minnesota Press.

Schein, Louisa. 2000. *Minority Rules: The Miao and the Feminine in China's Cultural Politics*. Durham, NC: Duke University Press.

Schein, Louisa. 2004a. "Hmong/Miao Transnationality: Identity beyond Culture." In *Hmong/Miao in Asia*, edited by Nicholas Tapp, Jean Michaud, Christian Culas, and Gary Yia Lee, 273–94. Chiang Mai, Thailand: Silkworm Books.

Schein, Louisa. 2004b. "Homeland Beauty: Transnational Longing and Hmong American Video." *Journal of Asian American Studies* 63, no. 2: 433–63.

Schein, Louisa. 2005. "Marrying Out of Place: Hmong/Miao Women Across and Beyond China." In *Cross-Border Marriages: Gender and Mobility in Transnational Asia*, edited by Nicole Constable, 53–79. Philadelphia: University of Pennsylvania Press.

Schein, Louisa. 2007. "Occult Racism: The Masking of Race in the Hmong Hunter Incident: A Dialogue between Anthropologist Louisa Schein and Filmmaker Va-Megn Thoj." *American Quarterly* 59, no. 4: 1051–95.

Schein, Louisa. 2016. "Thinking Diasporic Sex: Cultures, Erotics, and Media across Hmong Worlds." In *Claiming Place on the Agency of Hmong Women*, edited by Chia Y. Vang, Faith Nibbs, and Ma Vang, 249–79. Minneapolis: University of Minnesota Press.

Schein, Louisa, and Va-Megn Thoj. 2008. "Violence, Hmong American Visibility, and the Precariousness of Asian Race." *PMLA* 123, no. 5: 1752–56.

Schein, Louisa, Va-Megn Thoj, Bee Vang, and Ly Chong Thong Jalao. 2012. "Beyond Grant Torino's Guns: Hmong Cultural Warriors Performing Genders." *positions: asia critique* 20, no. 3: 763–92.

Schein, Louisa, and Chia Y. Vang. 2021. "From Hmong versus Miao to the Making of Transnational Hmong/Miao Solidarity." In *Global East Asia: Into the Twenty-First Century*, edited by Frank N. Pieke and Koichi Iwabuchi, 219–32. Berkeley: University of California Press.

Schneider, David M. 1980. *American Kinship: A Cultural Account*. Chicago: University of Chicago Press.

Schrauwers, Albert. 1999. "Negotiating Parentage: The Political Economy of 'Kinship' in Central Sulawesi, Indonesia." *American Ethnologist* 26, no. 2: 310–23.

Scott, James. 1985. *Weapons of the Weak: Everyday Forms of Peasant Resistance*. New Haven, CT: Yale University Press.

Sheffer, Gabriel. 2003. *Diaspora Politics: At Home Abroad*. Cambridge: Cambridge University Press.

Shi, Tian, Xiao Hua Wu, De Bin Wang, and Yan Lei. 2019. "The Miao in China: A Review of Developments and Achievements over Seventy Years." *Hmong Studies Journal* 20:1–23.

Shukla, Sandhya. 2003. *India Abroad: Diasporic Cultures of Postwar America and England*. Princeton, NJ: Princeton University Press.

Siu, Lok. 2005. *Memories of a Future Home: Diasporic Citizenship of Chinese in Panama*. Stanford, CA: Stanford University Press.

Skrbiš, Zlatko. 1997. "Homeland-Diaspora Relations: From Passive to Active Interactions." *Asian Pacific Migration Journal* 6, nos. 3–4: 439–55.

Slocum, Karla. 2006. *Free Trade and Freedom: Neoliberalism, Place, and Nation in the Caribbean*. Ann Arbor: University of Michigan Press.

Smith-Hefner, Nancy J. 1994. "Ethnicity and the Force of Faith: Christian Conversion among Khmer Refugees." *Anthropological Quarterly* 67, no. 1: 24–37.

Smith, Robert. 2005. *Mexican New York: Transnational Lives of New Immigrants*. Berkeley: University of California Press.

Sparke, Matthew. 2004. "Passports into Credit Cards: On the Borders and

Spaces of Neoliberal Citizenship." In *Boundaries and Belonging: State and Societies in the Struggle to Shape Identities and Local Practices*, edited by Joel S. Migdal, 251–83. Cambridge: Cambridge University Press.

St. John, Ronald B. 2006. "The Political Economy of Laos: Poor State or Poor Policy?" *Asian Affairs* 37, no. 2: 176–91.

Symonds, Patricia V. 2004. *Calling in the Soul: Gender and the Cycle of Life in a Hmong Village*. Seattle: University of Washington Press.

Tapp, Nicholas. 1988. "Geomancy and Development: The Case of the White Hmong of North Thailand." *Ethnos* 53:228–38.

Tapp, Nicholas. 1989a. *Sovereignty and Rebellion: The White Hmong of Northern Thailand*. Singapore: Oxford University Press.

Tapp, Nicholas. 1989b. "Hmong Religion." *Asian Folklore Studies* 48, no. 1: 59–94.

Tapp, Nicholas. 1998. "The Hmong/MIAO in Asia." *Anthropology Today* 14, no. 6: 23.

Tapp, Nicholas. 2002. "Cultural Accommodations in Southwest China: The 'Han Miao' and Problems in the Ethnography of the Hmong." *Asian Folklore Studies* 61, no. 1: 77–104.

Tapp, Nicholas. 2013. "Religion and Mobility in a Globalising Asia." *Asia Pacific Journal of Anthropology* 14, no. 1: 102–12.

Tapp, Nicholas, and Gary Y. Lee. 2004. *The Hmong of Australia: Culture and Diaspora*. Canberra: Pandanus Books.

Tapp, Nicholas, Jean Michaud, Christian Culas, and Gary Y. Lee. 2004. *Hmong/Miao in Asia*. Chiang Mai, Thailand: Silkworm Books.

Tappe, Oliver. 2011. "Memory, Tourism, and Development: Changing Sociocultural Configurations and Upland-Lowland Relations in Houaphan Province, Lao PDR." *SOJOURN: Journal of Social Issues in Southeast Asia* 26, no. 2: 174–95.

Taussig, Michael T. 1987. *Shamanism, Colonialism, and the Wild Man: A Study in Terror and Healing*. Chicago: University of Chicago Press.

Taylor, Stephanie. 2013. Introduction to *What Is Discourse Analysis?* London: Bloomsbury Publishing, 1–6.

Thai, Hung Cam. 2014. *Insufficient Funds: The Culture of Money in Low-Wage Transnational Families*. Stanford, CA: Stanford University Press.

Thao, Bruce. 2016. "Dangerous Questions: Queering Gender in the Hmong Diaspora." In *Claiming Place on the Agency of Hmong Women*, edited by Chia Y. Vang, Faith Nibbs, and Ma Vang, 280–302. Minneapolis: University of Minnesota Press.

Thao, Mai See, and Audrey Bochaton. 2022. "Healing in the Diaspora: Hmong American and Hmong Lao Practices of Care." In *Care Work and Medical Travel: Exploring the Emotional Dimensions of Caring on the Move*, edited by Cecilia Vindrola-Padros, 11–33. London: Lexington Books.

Thao, Thong. 1972. "The Hmoob Had Organized after Kublai Khan Founded the Mongol Dynasty." A paper written by a fourth-year English-language student based upon oral history of his recollection (9 pp.). William W. Sage Collection on Laos. Arizona State University Library, Rare Books and Manuscripts. Tempe, Arizona.

Toland, Judith D. (1993) 2009. *Ethnicity and the State.* New Brunswick, NJ: Transaction Publishers.

Tölölyan, Khachig. 1996. "Rethinking Diaspora(s): Stateless Power in the Transnational Moment." *Diaspora 5*, no. 1: 3–36.

Tsuda, Takeyuki. 2003. *Strangers in the Ethnic Homeland: Japanese Brazilian Return Migration in Transnational Perspective.* New York: Columbia University Press.

Tsuda, Takeyuki. 2009. *Diasporic Homecomings: Ethnic Return Migration in Comparative Perspective.* Stanford, CA: Stanford University Press.

Tsuda, Takeyuki. 2014. "'I'm American, Not Japanese!': The Struggle for Racial Citizenship among Later-Generation Japanese Americans." *Ethnic and Racial Studies 37*, no. 3: 405–24.

Tsuda, Takeyuki. 2016. *Japanese American Ethnicity: In Search of Heritage and Homeland across Generations.* New York: New York University Press.

Tsuda, Takeyuki., Maria Tapias, and Xavier Escandell. 2014. "Locating the Global in Transnational Ethnography." *Journal of Contemporary Ethnography 43*, no. 2: 123–47.

Tuan, Mia. 2001. *Forever Foreigners or Honorary Whites? The Asian Ethnic Experience Today.* New Brunswick, NJ: Rutgers University Press.

Turner, Simon. 2019. "The Social Construction of Diasporas: Conceptual Development and the Rwandan Case." In *Routledge Handbook of Diaspora Studies*, edited by Robin Cohen and Carolin Fischer, 40–46. London: Routledge.

UNDP Lao PDR. 2018. "Lao PDR's Eligibility for Graduation from LDC Status Confirmed." March 18. https://www.undp.org/laopdr/press-releases/lao-pdr%E2%80%99s-eligibility-graduation-ldc-status-confirmed/.

Vang, Chia Y. 2010. *Hmong America: Reconstructing Community in Diaspora.* Urbana: University of Illinois Press.

Vang, Chia Y. 2018. "Thinking Refugee: The Politics of Hmong Place-Making in Argentina and French Guiana." *Amerasia 44*, no. 2: 1–21.

Vang, Ma. 2021. *History on the Run: Secrecy, Fugitivity, and Hmong Refugee Epistemologies.* Durham, NC: Duke University Press.

Vertovec, Steven. 1997. "Three Meanings of 'Diaspora,' Exemplified among South Asian Religions." *Diaspora 6*, no. 3: 277–99.

Vertovec, Steven. 1999. "Conceiving and Researching Transnationalism." *Ethnic and Racial Studies 22*, no. 2: 447–56.

Vertovec, Steven. 2001. "Transnationalism and Identity." *Journal of Ethnic and Migration Studies 27*, no. 4: 573–82.

Vertovec, Steven. 2011. "The Cultural Politics of Nation and Migration." *Annual Review of Anthropology* 40:241–56.

Vitebsky, Piers. 2003. "From Cosmology to Environmentalism: Shamanism as Local Knowledge in a Global Setting." In *Shamanism: A Reader*, edited by Harvey Graham, 276–98. London: Routledge.

Vue, Pao L., Louisa Schein, and Bee Vang. 2016. "Comparative Racialization and Unequal Justice in the Era of Black Lives Matter: The Dylan Yang Case." *Hmong Studies Journal* 17:1–21.

Wahlbeck, Östen. 2002. "The Concept of Diaspora as an Analytical Tool in the Study of Refugee Communities." *Journal of Ethnic and Migration Studies* 28, no. 2: 221–38.

Waldinger, Roger. 2013. "Immigrant Transnationalism." *Current Sociology Review* 61, nos. 5–6: 756–77.

Warner, Stephen R., and Judith G. Wittner. 1998. *Gatherings in Diaspora: Religious Communities and the New Immigration*. Philadelphia: Temple University Press.

Weber, Max. (1958) 2003. *The Protestant Ethic and the Spirit of Capitalism*. New York: Courier Corporation.

Werbner, Pnina. 2000. "Introduction: The Materiality of Diaspora—Between Aesthetic and 'Real' Politics." *Diaspora* 9, no. 1: 5–20.

Werbner, Pnina. 2002. *Imagined Diasporas among Manchester Muslims: The Public Performance of Pakistani Transnational Identity Politics*. Oxford: James Currey.

Werbner, Pnina. 2015a. "The Boundaries of Diaspora: A Critical Response to Brubaker." In *Diasporic Constructions of Home and Belonging*, edited by Florian Kläger and Klaus Stierstorfer, 35–52. Berlin: De Gruyter.

Werbner, Pnina. 2015b. "Introduction: The Dialectics of Cultural Hybridity." In *Debating Cultural Hybridity: Multicultural Identities and the Politics of Anti-Racism*, edited by Pnina Werbner and Tariq Modood, 1–26. London: Zed Books.

Werbner, Pnina, and Tariq Modood, eds. 2015. *Debating Cultural Hybridity: Multicultural Identities and the Politics of Anti-Racism*. London: Zed Books.

Williams, Raymond. 1977. *Marxism and Literature*. Oxford: Oxford University Press.

Wimmer, Andreas, and Nina Glick Schiller. 2002. "Methodological Nationalism and Beyond: Nation-State Building, Migration, and the Social Sciences." *Global Networks* 2, no. 4: 301–34.

Winland, Daphne. 1994. "Christianity and Community: Conversion and Adaptation among Hmong Refugee Women." *Canadian Journal of Sociology* 19, no. 1: 21–45.

Winland, Daphne. 2002. "The Politics of Desire and Disdain: Croatian Identity between 'Home' and 'Homeland.'" *American Ethnologist* 29, no. 3: 693–718.

Wolfson-Ford, Ryan. 2018. "Ideology in the Royal Lao Government-Era (1945–1975): A Thematic Approach." PhD diss., University of Wisconsin–Madison.

Wong, Carolyn. 2017. *Voting Together: Intergenerational Politics and Civic Engagement among Hmong Americans.* Stanford, CA: Stanford University Press.

Xiang, Biao. 2014. "The Pacific Paradox: The Chinese State in Transpacific Interactions." In *Transpacific Studies: Framing an Emerging Field*, edited by Janet Hoskins and Viet T. Nguyen, 85–105. Honolulu University of Hawai'i Press.

Xiong, Yang Sao. 2013. "An Analysis of Poverty in Hmong American Communities." In *Diversity in Diaspora: Hmong Americans in the Twenty-First Century*, edited by Mark E Pfeifer, Monica Chiu, and Kou Yang, 66–105. Honolulu: University of Hawai'i Press.

Xiong, Yang Sao. 2022. *Immigrant Agency: Hmong American Movements and the Politics of Racialized Incorporation.* New Brunswick, NJ: Rutgers University Press.

Yang, Kao K. 2008. *The Late Homecoming: A Hmong Family Memoir.* Minneapolis: Coffee House Press.

Yang, Zhiqiang. 2009. "From *Miao* to *Miaozu*: Alterity in the Formation of Modern Ethnic Groups." *Hmong Studies Journal* 10:1–28.

Yangcheepsutjarit, Urai. 2020. "Celebrating Hmong New Year Not for the New Year Celebration: A Case Study in Urban Community in Chiang Mai City, Thailand." *Hmong Studies Journal* 21:1–25.

Yeh, Chiou-ling. 2008. *Making an American Festival: Chinese New Year in San Francisco's Chinatown.* Berkeley: University of California Press.

Zelizer, Viviana A. 1996. "Payments and Social Ties." *Sociological Forum* 11:489–95.

Zelizer, Viviana A. 1998. "Introduction: How People Talk about Money." *American Behavioral Scientist* 41, no. 10: 1373–83.

Zhang, Weidong. 2020. "Revamping Beliefs, Reforming Rituals, and Performing Hmongness? A Case Study of Temple of Hmongism." *Hmong Studies Journal* 21:1–28.

Zucker, Norman L. 1983. "Refugee Resettlement in the United States: Policy and Problems." *Annals of the American Academy of Political and Social Science* 467:172–86.

Zuntz, Ann-Christin. 2021. "Refugees' Transnational Livelihoods and Remittances: Syrian Mobilities in the Middle East Before and After 2011." *Journal of Refugee Studies* 34, no. 2: 1400–1422.

Index

1.5-generation (Hmong) immigrants, 30, 62, 66, 72, 86–88, 90, 94–97, 115, 119, 163, 173–74, 198. *See also* Hmong in US, youth

African Americans, 85, 97
Afro-Caribbean pop culture, 6
ancestral homeland. *See* homeland
ancestral spirits and souls. *See* rituals; spirit/soul
Anderson, Mark, 8
animal sacrifice, 160, 165, 167, 169–70, 185, 187–88, 190, 192, 194, 197–98. *See also* spirit/soul
Anthias, Floya, 8
Asian Americans, 85–86, 94–95, 97, 118, 126, 194, 235, 245n13, 245n15. *See also* Hmong in the US
authenticity, 19, 67, 165, 183, 197–98, 202–5, 237

Barth, Fredrik, 7
Bauman, Zygmunt, 225
Bidney, David, 226
belonging (to nation-state), partial, 15–16, 19, 69–72, 83–84, 86, 94, 97–98, 182, 205, 211, 229–30, 234–35, 239. *See also* diasporic identity; nation-states, multiple/partial affiliations with
Brubaker, Rogers, 8, 13
Buddhism, 154, 175

Cha, Dia, 150, 151, 152, 156
China, 39, 40, 81, 110; ethnic homeland and, 3, 15, 16–17, 41, 44–48, 50, 51–52, 54, 58, 62, 67, 160; Hmong history and, 41–44, 53, 55–56, 234; Hmong visits to, 48–51, 216. *See also* Miao/Hmong in China
Chinese, 17, 41, 42, 44, 46, 49, 75, 94–95, 117, 160, 187, 202; Chinese Americans, 235; diaspora, 8; Han, 3, 112, 245n4. *See also* Miao/Hmong in China
Christianity, 49, 60, 154, 164–65, 170–75, 176, 195–96; Hmong and, 10, 19, 31, 48, 49–50, 106, 152–52, 158, 162, 163–65, 183, 195–96, 198
Christou, Anastasia, 9
clans, 47, 104–5, 108–9, 119–21, 128, 130, 132–36, 139–42, 144, 146–47, 152–52, 164–65, 177, 188–89, 245nn2–5; exogamy, 18, 106–7, 109, 113–16, 117, 122–24, 125–27, 164; hospitality, 18, 47, 104–7, 109–12, 116, 121, 124–25. *See also* kinship
Coe, Cati, 132
Cold War, 57, 226
commodification, 166, 169–70, 177
commodity fetishism, 141
Communist Pathet Lao, 3, 57–58

criminality/criminalization, 91, 92–94, 245n15
cultural authenticity. *See* authenticity
cultural differences and discontinuities. *See* diaspora, cultural differences and discontinuities
cultural continuities. *See* diaspora, cultural continuities

Dao Tha, Laos, 73–74, 150–51, 175, 212; fieldwork in, 20–28; global tourism in, 23–24; Hmong marginality in, 73–77; multiethnic residents in, 21–22, 24–25, 73–74, 78
deterritorialization, 5, 12, 20, 83, 127, 153–62, 166–67, 176–77, 182, 191, 209, 229, 237; spatial, 155–56, 158–62; spirit/soul and, 158–62; transborder, 155–58. *See also* reterritorialization
diaspora: African/Black, 6, 8, 120; Chinese, 8; conceptualization of, 4–6; cultural continuities, 5–6, 9–12, 18–19, 41, 58, 70, 99, 106, 130, 146–47, 153–55, 170, 176–77, 236; cultural differences and discontinuities, 6, 8, 12–14, 19–20, 153, 162, 164, 182–85, 195–96, 204–5, 207, 209, 215, 224, 229–30, 237–38; Filipino, 246n2; hegemony and, 11, 105–8, 119–21, 124–25, 127–28; history of, 39–44, 55–66; homeland and, 3, 5–6, 13, 15–17, 39–41, 51, 55, 58, 66–70, 121–24, 128, 165, 233–35; kinship and; 11, 106, 111, 115, 122, 133; Kurdish, 12; migratory dispersal and, 4, 12, 16, 39, 40–42, 55–58, 62, 67, 70, 152, 164, 234–35; Muslim, 12; nation-state and, 5–6, 13, 19–20, 34–35, 48, 64, 71, 83, 107, 170, 181–85, 190, 199, 202–5, 206–9, 218–20, 229–31, 233–35, 237; Vietnamese, 155, 215
diasporic condition, 4, 14, 16, 55, 71, 84, 93, 99, 209, 233–34, 236
diasporic consciousness, 4, 5, 11, 14–17, 39–40, 51, 55, 62, 64, 69, 71, 234–35

diasporic identity, 5–14, 18–20, 35, 73, 83–84, 97, 99, 106, 121–22, 130, 134, 139–40, 147, 153, 178, 182, 204–5, 206, 209, 230, 234, 238–39; conceptualization of, 5–9; discursive fragmentation and, 12–14; hybridity and, 6–8, 12–13, 15; national differences and, 12–14; transnational continuity and, 9–10
diasporization, 16, 41, 58, 69, 123
discrimination, 71, 74–77, 86, 94–97, 246n7
discontinuities. *See* diaspora, cultural differences and discontinuities
discourse, 7, 20, 51, 52, 119–24, 127–28, 197, 204, 207, 211–18, 226–29; conceptualization of, 207–8
discursive fragmentation, 12–14, 20, 182, 205, 206–8, 211, 215, 218–19, 224, 226, 229–30, 239. *See also* diaspora, cultural differences and discontinuities
Dunnigan, Timothy, 108–9

economic development, 77, 98, 216; level of, 208, 211, 214, 218; national, 224, 225; national difference in, 194, 206, 207, 210, 219
economy: capitalist, 206, 221, 224–25; clan/familial, 128, 131, 146; local-global, 79–82; national, 67, 72, 77, 79, 136, 145–46, 199, 203, 206, 210, 212, 222; tourism and, 72, 81, 98; transnationalism and, 133–34, 136–37
ecotourism, 23. *See also* tourism
emotional remittances, 18, 130–34, 136, 138–42, 147. *See also* remittances
English language, 21–23, 26, 28, 30, 66, 82, 104, 112, 130, 150, 214, 244n3, 245n2, 247n3
ethnic endogamy, 18, 107, 109, 116–18, 125–26
ethnic homeland. *See* homeland
ethnic identities, 6, 12, 15, 19, 47, 83–84, 95, 121, 153, 178, 204, 239
ethnic marginality, 11, 15, 22, 64, 72–84, 93–98, 105, 235
ethnic minorities, 6, 11, 15–16, 17, 22, 41–44, 48, 55–57, 70–71, 73–

274   Index

79, 84, 95–78, 181, 184, 199, 203, 226, 234–35, 239
ethnographic authority, 208
ethnography, 9, 32, 34–35, 109

Ferguson, James, 242n12
fieldwork, 20–35; multi-sited, 20, 31–35, 131
flexible citizenship, 8
Foucault, Michel, 114, 184, 207, 218–19
fragmentation. *See* diaspora, cultural differences and discontinuities
freedom, 20, 90, 206–7, 218–20, 226, 237, 248n4; from capitalist economic constraints, 219–23; to pursue economic opportunities, 219–20, 223–25
Fresno, CA, 31, 195, 201, 204, 242n18
Fridman, Daniel, 225
Friedman, Milton, 220
Fromm, Erich, 219
funeral ceremonies, 9, 19, 41, 44, 54, 106, 137, 139, 159–60, 162, 183–95, 236–37; animal sacrifice and, 185, 187–88, 190, 192, 194, 197–98; burial/gravesite, 184, 188, 194, 199; Christian Hmong and, 106, 195–96; compared with New Year festivals, 199–204; cultural authenticity and, 197–98, 204–5; homeland and, 187, 192; national cultural differences in, 183–85, 204–5; nation-state and, 183–85, 190, 195, 199. 204, 247n1. *See also* Hmong in Laos, funerals and; Hmong in the US, funerals and

gender, 28, 32–33, 49, 107, 121, 127, 157–58, 206–7, 227
Gilroy, Paul, 8
globalization, 7, 23–4, 79–82, 177, 203, 236, 239
Gordon, Edmund, 8
Gramsci, Antonio, 106, 114
Guarnizo, Luis, 155, 236
Gupta, Akhil, 242n12

Hall, Stuart, 6–8, 13
hegemony, 18, 199, 201; clan exogamy and, 18, 106–7, 109,
113–16, 125–26; clan hospitality and, 18, 106–7, 109–13, 120–21; conceptualization of, 107–8, 114, 127; diasporas and, 11, 105–8, 119–21, 124–25, 127–28; ethnic endogamy and, 18, 106–7, 109, 116–18, 125–26; kinship and, 18, 105–10, 113–16, 119–21, 123, 124–28; resistance against, 107, 115, 124–28
Helmreich, Stefan, 120
Hickman, Jacob, 177, 241n9, 248n5
hierarchies, 20, 77, 92, 205, 208–9, 211, 218, 220, 222–23, 230, 237
Hmong in China. *See* Miao/Hmong in China
Hmong in Laos (Dao Tha/Vang Vieng), 3; diasporic history of, 55–58; discrimination against, 74–77; fieldwork with, 20–28; funerals and, 183–88, 197, 199; homeland and, 45–46, 51–55, 66–69; kinship system and, 103–24; national belonging of, 83–84, 98–99; New Year celebration among, 183, 199–200, 203; perceptions of Hmong in US, 197–98, 206–7, 209–15, 218–22, 224–28; perceptions of Miao in China, 41, 45–48; racialization and stereotyping of, 74–77; shamanism and, 148–53, 156–62, 166–69, 172–73, 175–76; socioeconomic status and marginalization of, 71–74, 77–83; transnational familial economy of, 130–31, 133–41; youth, 21–22, 33, 72, 75–76, 79–83, 109, 111, 115–18, 124, 128, 247n6
Hmong in the US (Sacramento, CA), 3; American public perceptions of, 92–93, 185, 189, 190; criminalization of, 92–93; diasporic history of, 56–66; ethnic community among, 84–86; ethnic marginality and discrimination against, 94–97; fieldwork with, 23, 28–31; funerals and, 183–85, 188–96, 198–99; homeland and, 45, 51, 53–55, 89; kinship system and, 104–9, 111–27; national belonging of, 98–99; New Year celebration among, 183, 199–202, 204; perceptions of Hmong

Index   275

Hmong in the US (*continued*)
in Laos, 136, 146, 206–7, 209–11,
215–19, 223–24, 226, 228–29;
perceptions of Miao in China, 41,
45, 48–51, 112; refugee migration
and resettlement of, 29, 56–66;
shamanism and, 150–54, 156–71,
173–75; social problems among,
88–92; socioeconomic status and
marginalization, 72–73, 86–89,
94; transnational familial economy
of, 130–31, 133–36, 141–46;
youth, 33, 72, 87, 90–97, 109,
115, 118, 124–28, 162–63, 191.
See also 1.5-generation (Hmong)
immigrants; second-generation
(Hmong Americans)
Hmongness, 11, 90, 198, 205, 207
Hmong Palace Church, 159, 185,
190, 192, 193, 196, 247n7
homeland: absence of/uncertainty
about, 9, 11, 15–18, 39–41, 51–55,
58, 84, 95, 106–7, 119, 121, 130,
233–34, 236; China as, 3, 15,
16–17, 41, 44–48, 50, 51–52, 54,
58, 62, 67, 160; diaspora and, 3,
5–6, 13, 15–17, 39–41, 51, 55, 58,
66–70, 121–24, 128, 165, 233–35;
funerals and, 187, 192; kinship
and, 121–22; Laos as, 17, 18, 58,
66–69, 84, 89, 93, 165, 210, 235;
messianic/millenarian movements
and, 15–16; multiple affiliations to,
14, 17; natal, 2, 66, 92, 95, 142,
235; nation-state and, 4, 14, 17, 51,
234–35; Thailand as, 62; refugee,
62; transnationalism and, 45, 70,
167, 234, 246n1. *See also* Hmong
in Laos, homeland and; Hmong in
the US, homeland and
homelandless-ness, 55, 234
hybridity: cultural, 6–8, 11, 12;
diasporic identity and, 6–8, 12–13,
15; hybridized, 6–7, 13, 15; identity
and, 110, 113, 120, 182, 237

ideology, 18, 106–7, 109, 119, 124,
127–28, 184, 201, 224–28
interethnic/racial marriages, 96, 107,
116–17, 126

Jonsson, Hjorleifur, 96, 184, 242n2

Khmu ethnic group, 21–22, 24, 73–
74, 78, 81, 117, 244n1, 2, 3, 9
Kim, Claire Jean, 192
kinship, 109; diaspora and, 11,
106, 111, 115, 122, 133; ethnic
endogamy and, 18, 106–7, 109,
116–18, 125–26; hegemony and,
18, 105–10, 113–16, 119–21,
123–28; homeland and, 121–22;
ideology and, 124–25, 127–28;
transnational, 9, 18–19, 41, 99,
106, 128, 130, 133–36, 147, 155,
164–65, 177, 236. *See also* clans;
Hmong in Laos, kinship system
and; Hmong in the US, kinship
system and
Korean ethnicity/nationality 22, 32,
94, 104, 112, 117, 121–22, 186,
194, 235, 245n4; popular culture,
33

Langdon, Esther Jean, 175
Lao Loum ethnic group, 21–25, 73–
75, 78, 81–82, 98, 175, 244nn1–2
Lee, Gary Yia, 3, 4, 35, 42, 44, 55,
90, 152
Lee, Mai Na, 15, 55, 241n2
love, 130–31, 133; money/remittances
and, 18, 131, 137–47

marginalization/marginality, 22, 40,
69, 71, 105–6, 215, 235. *See also*
Hmong in Laos, socioeconomic
status and marginalization; Hmong
in the US, socioeconomic status and
marginalization
Marx, Karl, 141, 220, 225
Mavroudi, Elizabeth, 9, 11
Miao/Hmong in China, 3, 10, 17,
41–44, 55, 110–12, 243nn4–5,
243n9. *See also* Hmong in Laos,
perceptions of Miao in China;
Hmong in the US, perceptions of
Miao in China
Michaud, Jean, 39, 41, 42, 152, 184,
241n9
migration, 7–8, 10, 13, 29, 55, 71, 81,
95–96, 124, 132–33, 145, 154–58,
167, 184, 230, 235–36, 238,
242n13, 246n3; diasporic dispersal
and, 4, 12, 16, 39, 40–42, 55–58,
62, 67, 70, 152, 164, 234–35.

See also 1.5-generation (Hmong) immigrants; refugees

minorities. *See* ethnic minorities

modernity, shamanism and, 158, 164, 170–72, 176–77

Moore, Henrietta, 7

Mottin, Jean, 247n2

multiculturalism (and the nation-state), 76, 192, 199, 201, 204, 248n6

nation-states: belonging to, 15–16, 19, 69–72, 83–84, 86, 94, 97–99, 182, 205, 211, 229–30, 234–35, 239; diasporas and, 5–6, 19–20, 34–35, 48, 64, 71, 83, 107, 170, 181–85, 190, 199, 202–5, 206–9, 218–20, 229–31, 233–35, 237; funeral ceremonies and, 183–85, 190, 195, 199, 204, 247n1; homeland and, 4, 14, 17, 51, 234–35; multiculturalism and, 76, 192, 199, 201, 204, 248n6; multiple/partial affiliations with, 5, 8, 13–16, 40, 59, 69, 83–84, 97, 178, 182, 205–6, 211, 214, 218, 220, 230, 236, 248n6; nationalism and, 208–9, 218, 228. *See also* diaspora, cultural differences and discontinuities; diasporic identity

nationalism, relational, 208–9, 218, 228. *See also* nation-states, belonging to

New Year celebration, 9–10, 14, 19, 31, 46, 77, 104–5, 183, 199–204, 248n6, 248n9

nostalgic longing, 5, 59, 66–68, 89

Ong, Aihwa, 8, 154, 184

Ovesen, Jan, 76, 77, 244

pandemic, coronavirus (COVID-19), 77, 82, 203, 204

Parreñas, Rhacel, 14, 35, 71, 132

qeej (mouth organ pipe), 49, 104, 186, 190, 191

race/racialization, 8, 31–33, 72, 74–77, 86, 92–97, 175, 235. *See also* interethnic/racial marriages

refugees, 4, 24–25, 30, 70, 72, 145, 225; resettlement of, 29, 56–58, 62–66, 154, 158; in Thailand camps, 3, 24, 30, 56, 58–62, 70, 73, 174, 243n15

religion. *See* Christianity; shamanism; shamans; spirit/soul

remittances, 18, 72, 87, 109, 130–38, 141, 145, 147, 170, 246n1, 246n3. *See also* emotional remittances

reterritorialization, 157, 159, 191. *See also* deterritorialization

rituals: animal sacrifice and, 160, 165, 167, 169–70, 185, 187–88, 190, 192, 194, 197–98; funeral, 185–96; healing, 148, 150, 153, 171–72, 174; shamanistic spirit calling (ua neeb), 1, 139, 148–53, 155, 160, 162, 163, 166–69; 177, 247n2, 247n8; spiritual, 160–66, 169–70. *See also* shamanism; shamans

Royal Lao Government (RLG), 3, 57, 58, 243n13

sacrifice. *See* animal sacrifice

Schein, Louisa, 10, 42, 43, 49, 89, 92, 93, 104, 243n9, 248n8

second-generation (Hmong Americans), 10, 72, 90–91, 94–97, 115, 118, 136, 163, 235. *See also* Hmong in the US, youth

shamanism, 19, 41, 106, 148–54, 154–56, 166, 171, 177, 182, 184, 190–91, 236; Christianity and, 19, 152–54, 162–64, 170, 173–75, 176; commodification of, 153, 166–67, 169–70, 169–70, 177; deterritorialization and, 153, 155–62; ethnic differences and, 154, 175–76, 177; healing rituals, 148, 150, 153, 171, 172, 174; individualization of, 153, 166–69, 177; modernity and, 158, 164, 170–72, 176–77; spirit calling (ua neeb) rituals and, 1, 139, 148–53, 155, 160, 162–63, 166–69, 177, 247n2, 247n8; spiritual rituals and, 160–66, 169–70; transnational cultural continuity/persistence of, 18, 99, 147, 152–58, 162–70, 177; Western biomedicine and, 154, 170–73, 177. *See also* Hmong in Laos, shamanism and; Hmong in

Index   277

shamanism (*continued*)
the US, shamanism and; shamans;
spirit/soul
shamans, 148–52, 156, 159–60, 167–
76, 181, 191, 247nn3–4; birth of,
155–57, 176; gender and 157–58;
transnational power/services of, 89,
149–50, 155, 158–62, 166–69, 177.
See also shamanism; spirit/soul
Slocum, Karla, 222
social activism, 73, 97
socialization, 108, 114, 123, 127
socioeconomic status. *See* Hmong
in Laos, socioeconomic status
and marginalization; Hmong in
the US, socioeconomic status and
marginalization
spirit/soul, 1, 19, 44, 148–50, 151–52,
156–60, 164, 167–68, 171–72,
175, 188, 195, 198; animal sacrifice
and, 160, 165, 167, 169–70,
185, 187–88, 190, 192, 194,
197–98; conceptualization of, 150;
deterritorialization and, 158–62;
mobile nature of, 19, 153, 158–62,
170, 176–77, 191–92. *See also*
rituals; shamans

Tapp, Nicholas, 4, 35, 39, 41, 43, 55,
56, 109, 150, 151, 152, 154, 203,
241n9, 247n2
Tappe, Oliver, 98, 203
Thai, Hung Cam, 132, 214
Thailand, 3, 57, 59, 68, 89, 114, 135,
152; refugee camps in, 3, 24, 30,
56, 58–62, 70, 73, 174, 243n15
tourism, 23–24, 48, 51, 72, 78, 79,
81–82, 98, 137, 203, 242n16,
244n8
traditions, cultural/ethnic, 12, 18–19,
46, 67, 76, 113, 115, 121, 153,
164–65, 167, 170, 172–73, 177,
195, 197, 202, 204, 237
transnationalism: cultural continuities

in diasporas and, 5–6, 9–12,
18–19, 41, 58, 70, 99, 106, 130,
146–47, 153–55, 170, 176–77,
236; diasporas and, 2–6, 8–10, 14,
20, 70, 83, 106–7, 130, 155, 158,
167, 182, 209, 230–31, 234–36,
238–39; economy and, 133–34,
136–37; ethnography and, 34–35;
familial economy, 130–31, 133–46;
homeland and, 45, 70, 167, 234,
246n1; kinship and, 9, 18–19, 41,
99, 106, 128, 130, 133–36, 147,
155, 164–65, 177, 236; national/
nation–state and, 5–6, 9, 13, 41,
56, 83, 107, 182, 209–10, 229–31,
234–35, 237–39; shamanism and,
18, 89, 99, 147, 149–50, 152–70,
177
Tsuda, Takeyuki, 6, 15, 34, 66, 165,
167, 171, 235

ua neeb. *See* shamanism, spirit calling
(ua neeb) rituals and

Vang, Chia, 4, 23, 56–57, 192,
248n84
Vang Pao, 15, 57–59, 228, 243n14
Vietnam War, 3–4, 15, 24–18, 39–40,
56–58, 67, 72, 74, 95, 156 164,
217, 228, 235
Vertovec, Steven, 6, 11, 15, 154, 155,
237

weddings, 54, 85, 136, 139, 156, 163,
196, 243
Werbner, Pnina, 11, 13

Xiong, Yang Sao, 97

youth. *See* Hmong in Laos, youth;
Hmong in the US, youth

Zelizer, Viviana, 132
Zlatko, Skrbiš, 69

SANGMI LEE is an assistant professor of anthropology at Arizona State University.

The University of Illinois Press
is a founding member of the
Association of University Presses.

University of Illinois Press
1325 South Oak Street
Champaign, IL 61820-6903
www.press.uillinois.edu